Jonathan Edwards on Nature and Destiny
A Systematic Analysis

Paula M. Cooey

Studies in American Religion
Volume 16

The Edwin Mellen Press
Lewiston/Queenston

Library of Congress Cataloging-in-Publication Data

Cooey, Paula M., 1945-
    Jonathan Edwards on nature and destiny.

    (Studies in American religion ; v. 16)
    Revision of thesis (Ph. D.)--Trinity University.
    Bibliography: p.
    Includes index.
    1. Edwards, Jonathan, 1703-1758. I. Title.
II. Series.
BX7260.E3C65   1985   230'.58'0924 [B]   85-21499
ISBN 0-88946-660-2

This is volume 16 in the continuing series
Studies in American Religion
Volume 16 ISBN 0-88946-660-2
SAR Series ISBN 0-88946-992-X

The Edwin Mellen Press   The Edwin Mellen Press
Box 450   Box 67
Lewiston, New York   Queenston, Ontario
14092   USA   L0S 1L0   Canada

Printed in the United States of America

For Polly

TABLE OF CONTENTS

PART II: THE HUMAN CONDITION

PART III: IMAGES OF DIVINE THINGS

ACKNOWLEDGEMENTS

Grace is the only word I know that captures both the commonness and the specialness of reality. It takes human misery and sorrow seriously and transforms them. It is the gift of humor, wonder, and joy in the face of calamity. Grace breaks through in totally unexpected moments and yet is somehow present throughout all time and space. To articulate as concretely as possible the meaning of grace as it intervenes in human life and as it permeates all existence is a task well worth the dedication of one's life.

Jonathan Edwards found the words to articulate grace, and it is important that we hear them both for their meaning in his time and for their aid in the search for a vocabulary to articulate grace today. This book, begun originally as dissertation research, is my effort to share Edwards' vision of grace with the reader in hopes that she or he will go directly to Edwards himself. It represents years of work and the help of many friends and lovers, some of whom have died since I first began my research. I want now to commemorate the dead and thank the living.

My grandparents, Mary Isabelle and Ora Irl Miller, helped me to see grace at work in the Bible and nature. Mary taught me my prayers and many a hymn and helped me memorize countless verses from scripture. Together with Ora, she taught me to garden, milk cows, feed chickens, and candle eggs. With them I touched soil, held up earthworms for scrutiny, looked for rainbows on the Georgia horizon and watched tornadoes cross the Oklahoma plains. These experiences not only made grace real to me, they made

Edwards' biblical and agrarian language accessible to me.
I am grateful to have had grandparents who had the patience
and took the time to cultivate my love for this earth and
its heavens with the same care with which they cultivated
the soil.

My father Edward Wilton Cooey was a manifestation of the
power of grace to transform human pain and suffering in the
face of death. His life, his very long illness, and his
death made the meaning of reconciliation real to me. My
relationship with him taught me firsthand that evil and sin
must never be trivialized, and good, never underestimated.

Except for "Sinners in the Hands of an Angry God", I had
never read Edwards' works until Richard Niebuhr required
the *Treatise concerning Religious Affections* and *The
Nature of True Virtue* as reading in a course on the subject
of religious epistemology years ago. I am grateful to Dick
for many things. He introduced me not only to Edwards but
to theology as an academic discipline. He made a host of
religious and theological figures and their thought come
alive in my imagination. He spent countless hours outside
the classroom when I was a graduate student, discussing an
idea, an image, or an historical figure with me; he has
spent many hours since graduation supporting my sometimes
flagging spirits as I revised and extended the original
research. In particular we share a deep and abiding love
for Edwards. It is unlikely that I would have ever discovered Edwards had it not been for Dick.

Had it not been for Philip Nichols, my husband, my work
would simply never have gotten done. He spent days and
nights Xeroxing, proofreading, helping with bibliographical
research, and making corrections. This whole process has
been a continuous series of gestures of love he has made on
my behalf.

Benjamin Cooey-Nichols, our son, has lived his entire
life taking it for granted that mothers write into the wee
hours of the morning and keep their written copy in the
refrigerator next to the cream cheese and the carrot sticks.
His astonishing assumption that my behavior is simply part
of what it means for mothers to be mothers has amazed me and
inspired my confidence when I have faced the prospect of
defeat.

My mother-in-law and father-in-law Mitzi and Phil
Nichols have encouraged me throughout graduate school. They
have always treated me as their daughter rather than their
daughter-in-law. If they thought it a little strange that I
might work for a Ph.D. in theology, they nevertheless felt
that my wanting to do this work made it worth my doing it.
I only wish Phil had lived to see me finish this project.

So many friends and co-workers supported me in this
effort that I cannot possibly thank them individually; they
know who they are. Four, however, deserve special appreciation. I am deeply grateful to Char Miller, my friend and
colleague in the History Department of Trinity University,
for having read revisions of the manuscript and made extensive, valuable suggestions for presenting it in its final
form. Lois Boyd, editor of Trinity University Press, was
immeasurably helpful in giving advice concerning how to make
the transition from dissertation to book. Marigen Lohla
spent countless hours putting the manuscript and its suc-
cessive revisions on the word processor. Judith Lipsett
proofread the final copy.

Last but not least, two institutions played major roles
in the execution and completion of this project by giving
their generous financial support. The Danforth Foundation
funded not only much of my doctoral studies, but the typing
and preparation of this research in its dissertation form.
Trinity University subsequently contributed the additional

financial support necessary to extend my research beyond the
dissertation by granting me hefty summer support and travel
funds to the Beinecke Library in New Haven so that I could
work with Edwards' unedited manuscripts.

I dedicate this book to Polly Miller Cooey, my mother.
She has stood by me every step of the way and insisted that
I *must* do what is important to me. When necessary, she
has stood against the mores of a whole society, not only for
me as her daughter, but also on issues of class, race and
gender. She is one tough and gentle woman. She is the
first and most abiding manifestation of the interaction of
common and special grace in my life.

INTRODUCTION

"I can only say that were I at the beginning, I should want to follow in Edwards' footsteps more," spoke H. Richard Niebuhr in the late fifties, "and undertake an exploration of the land of emotions with a certain hypothesis amounting to conviction . . . the hypothesis that contrary to prevalent opinion about the emotions -- they put us into touch with what is reliable, firm, real, enduring in ways that are inaccessible to conceptual or spectator reason."[1] Following in Edwards' footsteps, which Niebuhr identified with exploring the land of emotions, presupposes a comprehension of Edwards' vision, for the land of emotions and that with which it puts us into touch, from Edwards' perspective, stand in complicated relation to one another. This book is a critical analysis and interpretation of Edwards' vision.

It would be easy in this age of psychological narcissism and political individualism to misconstrue Niebuhr's "bequest to the young theologian"[2] as a mandate to get in touch with oneself. Not only would this misconstrual be an injustice to Niebuhr, it would entail heading in the opposite direction from Edwards himself. For Edwards human emotions, which he calls "affections" and by which he means enduring rather than transitory feelings, themselves reflect the extent to which saving grace governs human knowing and willing. He stands in opposition to those who see virtue in terms of strictly human sentiment, particularly, self-love. In short, Edwards' criterion by which he distinguishes the significance of emotions and consequent human happiness or misery is whether emotions expand the self and relate it

beyond itself to a universal community of being. "Universal
community of being" may sound extremely abstract as a way of
describing what is reliable, firm, real, and enduring for
Edwards. Nevertheless, this community is incarnate in the
present partial manifestations and future fulfillment of the
kingdom of God. Both access to individual participation in
it and exclusion from it are mediated through history
concretely by images taken from nature. In short, nature
historicized serves as a primary means to relate human emotions to what is reliable, firm, real, and enduring. Stated
in a more theological language, it serves, in light of
scripture, as a medium of divine communication and, therefore, a further source of divine revelation.

An examination of the status, role, and destiny of
nature in Jonathan Edwards' works provides a means by which
to grasp the dynamic unity of his thought as a whole, his
vision. Nature, minimally defined as sensible and sentient
reality, is in fact for Edwards an eschatologically conditioned medium of divine communication by which God, or
being in general, communicates the divine destiny.

It is this destiny that is Edwards' central concern.
This concern not only manifests itself in the apocalyptic
writings, but permeates at least implicitly all of his writings. It gives his technical concepts such as *being* and
consent an added dimension of meaning. In addition concern with divine destiny as exemplified or communicated
through nature and history (for Edwards the two are not
nearly so easily separable as they are for twentieth-century
minds) distinguishes Edwards' epistemology from either
Locke's or Malebranche's and his christology and his trinitarian thought from Calvin's.

A major methodological difficulty involved in this kind
of analysis and interpretation arises from the history and

ambiguity of the meaning of the concept "nature" itself.
Nature can refer to a principle by which some thing or some
person or class of things or persons are what they are and
not something else. Nature can also refer to a single principle by which all material reality is organized and
interrelated, for example, the time/space continuum. There
are a variety of other meanings as well.[3]

None of these meanings, strictly speaking, are
appropriate in terms of any systematic application to
Edwards' thought. He is neither a dualist nor a pantheist.
Thus, nature neither exists apart from God, nor is God
totally immersed in the natural order. Edwards
distinguishes the created order from its creator, subor-
dinates the former to the latter, but does not detach one
from the other in some absolute sense. That which makes
some thing or person or class of things or persons be what
they are, that by which *all* reality, including the material
order, is organized and interrelated is ultimately God for
Edwards.

Edwards distinguishes spiritual truth from the sensible
media that communicate it. He further distinguishes among
sentient, specifically human beings, those who by virtue of
regeneration can sense this truth, from those whose senses,
by virtue of the Fall, are spiritually numbed. I have,
therefore, minimally defined "nature" for purposes of this
examination as sensible and sentient reality. While nature,
thus defined, can be contrasted with spirit in Edwards'
thought, nature never exists apart from spirit and, indeed,
can overlap in meaning with spirit as well.

My approach to Edwards' written work involves both
philosophical-theological and literary-critical analysis.
My task has been to analyze and relate to one another philosophical and theological ideas and arguments, on the one

hand, and scriptural exegesis and poetic images, on the
other hand. The relationship between Edwards' images and
ideas, in other words, his vision in its own right, is my
chief concern. Close textual analysis is the primary means
by which I seek to determine this relationship.[4] I am a
philosophical theologian, and strictly speaking not an
historian. Nevertheless, this interpretation is heavily
indebted to the work of historians as well as theologians,
and I hope it may contribute to the history of Christian
thought as well as stimulate continued interest in Edwards'
work.

Several significant works on Edwards have been published
in the last few years. Those most directly pertinent to my
own work include Stephen J. Stein's edition of Edwards'
apocalyptic writings, Conrad Cherry's *Nature and Religious
Imagination from Edwards to Bushnell,* Mason I. Lowance
Jr.'s *The Language of Canaan,* and Norman Fiering's *Jonathan
Edwards' Moral Thought and Its British Context.*

Without Stein's edition of Edwards' apocalyptic writings, this book would have been altogether different. Both
the notebooks devoted to exegesis of the book of Revelation
and the argument for prayer in concert for an outpouring of
the Holy Spirit demonstrate the inseparability of Edwards'
concern for the realization of the kingdom of God from the
rest of his thought. These writings add new dimensions of
meaning to Edwards' metaphysics, theology, and ethics.
Edwards' focus upon the realization of a fullness of being
not subject to corruption underlies all his writings. The
process by which this realization takes place I call the
divine destiny.

Stein's introduction to this volume is extremely
valuable. In addition to placing Edwards' apocalypticism in
its historical context, Stein interprets the significance of

the writings themselves. He emphasizes the importance of
Edwards' apocalypticism to his thought as a whole. He
stresses the gradualness of the process by which the kingdom
of God is realized, first on earth and later in the new
heaven and earth. He furthermore points out Edwards' own
emphasis upon divine involvement in the historical process
as a means to achieving the kingdom. He does not, however,
address two issues raised in the writings and relevant to
this particular study of Edwards' works as a whole: the specific character of nature's role in the process and the
significance of violence in relation to divine judgment.

The most recently published work relevant to a study of
Edwards' view of nature is Conrad Cherry's *Nature and
Religious Imagination from Bushnell to Edwards*. Cherry's
project is to show the relation between Edwards' view of
nature and his religious epistemology for the further purpose of tracing the role of nature and religious imagination
in American preaching and theology up to the middle of the
nineteenth century. His project both overlaps with my own
and differs significantly from it. We share a concern for
Edwards' view of nature and the role played by nature in
religious life, and, not surprisingly, we often come to
similar conclusions.

I agree in large part, though not entirely, with
Cherry's distinction between typology and allegory, most
particularly with his formulation of the aim of the type to
represent for the regenerate soul the opportunity to participate in spiritual meaning and truth. In other words, we
agree that types as Edwards develops them are symbols,
(rather than signs or emblems) primarily for purposes of
experiential participation rather than cognitive edification. We further agree on the significance of Edwards' use
of contrast in the types, and the centrality of scripture to

Edwards' concept of revelation.

Cherry's view of the role played by nature in pre-conversion experience differs from mine, however. Whereas Cherry sees nature as the provider of types, understood as symbols, to the convert, he argues that nature provides only signs to the unregenerate. If he means by "sign" what Edwards meant by "sign" in miscellany 782, then Cherry's distinction is an oversimplification. Nature's role in the intensification of the conviction of sin is precisely to aid in intensifying the conviction by providing clear and lively images of divine judgment and wrath. While such images in themselves do not provide a saving knowledge of God, a positive sense or taste for divine things, they are hardly just signs, for they provide for the convicted sinner an experiential sense of the potential for damnation.

This difference in interpretation reflects in large part a general tendency of Edwards himself to be ambiguous regarding continuities and discontinuities. Whether the issue is the relationship between pre-conversion experience and conversion, this world and the world to come, or history and nature, where Cherry is more likely to emphasize discontinuity, I am more likely to stress continuity as well as discontinuity. These differences tend to be minor, however.

Cherry does not discuss nature as eschatologically conditioned, and herein lies the major difference between his treatment of Edwards' view of nature and mine. This lack of attention to the eschatological character of Edwards' types drawn from nature and of nature's role in the realization of the kingdom of God reinforces an allegorical interpretation of the types in spite of Cherry's rejection of allegory. He fails, as a consequence, to see both the eschatological character and the cosmological dimension of redemption. In other words, unlike Cherry I argue that understanding

Edwards' apocalypticism is essential to understanding his
view of nature and its relation to saving knowledge of God.

Mason Lowance's treatment of Edwards in *The Language of
Canaan*, like Cherry's, includes a study of Edwards' use of
typology and its relation to Edwards' epistemology. Unlike
Cherry, Lowance places Edwards' use of typology into the
context of eschatology. And unlike Cherry, whose field is
Religious Studies and whose background includes theological
training, Lowance's field is English and American
Literature. These differences lead to an interesting set of
differences in conclusions.

Lowance argues that Edwards transforms traditional
Puritan typology by allegorizing it to effect a reconciliation between natural revelation and scriptural
authority. Edwards' notebook of types drawn from nature
serves as Lowance's chief source of examples of allegorization to the extent that according to Lowance nature becomes
an alternative source of revelation. He contrasts this use
of typology as allegory with what he considers to be
Edwards' more traditional use of typological interpretation
in the *History of the Works of Redemption*. He argues that
Edwards' transformation of typology is a consequence of
Edwards' liberal epistemology.

In fact, throughout his treatment of Edwards he continually categorizes Edwards' theology as "liberal" when it
supports what he considers to be the allegorization of types
and "conservative" or "traditional" when it does not.

The strength of Lowance's treatment of Edwards in *The
Language of Canaan* lies in his insistence on placing
Edwards' typology, and by implication his epistemology, into
an eschatological context. He accurately perceives the
prophetic character of the types that makes them at once
historical *and* symbolic. To name the process by which

this occurs "allegorization" is fundamentally misleading, however, and leads to a false use of distinctions such as "conservative" and "liberal" with reference to Edwards' theological writings. It also leads to a false elevation of nature as equally authoritative to scripture as revelation in Edwards' thought.

Whereas Cherry fails to give enough weight to the prophetic character of Edwards' use of types drawn from nature, Lowance misnames the process by which the natural order becomes prophetic and, thereby, sees Edwards' theology as more at odds with itself than it actually is. Like Cherry, I argue that Edwards extends typological interpretation from scripture to nature. This extension makes nature in light of scripture an additional, though not alternative, source of revelation for Edwards. If *allegory* refers to a correspondence between perceivable objects and spiritual truths and if the purpose of allegory is exclusively edification, then the process by which nature becomes a source for prophetic types is not allegorization. For nature to become prophetic presupposes the historicization of nature and the more appropriate term for types of this kind is *anagogy* rather than *allegory*. Edwards' types drawn from nature are anagogic. This becomes clear if one examines these types in light of Edwards' explicitly apocalyptic writings and his *Types of the Messiah*. Once the anagogic character of Edwards' interpretation of nature is recognized, his theology no longer divides easily into the categories of liberal and conservative.

Norman Fiering's recently published *Jonathan Edwards' Moral Thought and Its British Context*, while perhaps the most different from this book in the execution of its project, is also the most valuable in some respects to my own work. Fiering focuses primarily upon Edwards' critical

ethics and the philosophical milieu to which it is a
response, and secondarily upon Edwards' own constructive
ethics.   One might contrast our respective projects by
describing his as a treatment of Edwards' natural ethics and
theology in light of the range of his thought and mine as a
treatment of Edwards' thought as a whole in relation to his
theology of nature.   ("Natural ethics and theology" refers
to one's view of the human condition apart from considerations of redemption; "theology of nature" refers to
the origin, status, and role of nature in the divine economy
and, therefore, in light of redemption.) Though we disagree
at certain points regarding Edwards' constructive ethics, I
am in overall agreement with his analysis of Edwards' critical ethics.

Fiering's work is valuable in part because it confirms a
major argument resulting from my analysis of Edwards'
thought. I have argued throughout this book that Edwards is
a systematic thinker with a coherent vision. Edwards' works
reflect a variety of different concerns expressed in different genres. They are indeed responses to specific philosophical and theological movements. Furthermore, Edwards'
thought in its own right evolves or matures over time.
Nevertheless, Fiering's work stresses the overall coherence
of Edwards' thought by examining his ethics, critical and
constructive, in light of Edwards' own theological categories of sin and redemption. Fiering's attention to
Edwards' eschatology, however brief, and his lengthy analysis of the relationship between Edwards' view of sin, damnation, and hell, on the one hand, and secondary virtue, on
the other hand, disallows segregating Edwards' doctrinal
theology from his philosophical theology and ethics, and
classifying the former as "conservative" in contrast to the
"liberal" character of the latter.

Fiering's exploration of the intellectual influences upon Edwards' thought further confirms its unity. Fiering dispels the previously held view of Edwards, fostered by Perry Miller, that Edwards was a brilliant, but relatively ignorant and isolated, thinker trapped by Calvinist dogma, with only Newton and Locke for intellectual companionship. Fiering's treatment of Edwards' intellectual context demonstrates persuasively that Edwards was anything but isolated or trapped by Calvinist dogma. Fiering's emphasis on the Puritan heritage shared by Edwards and the Cambridge Platonists and his discussion of Malebranche's influence upon Edwards' idealism suggest that Edwards understood fully the implications of his philosophical as well as his theological differences with his opponents. Indeed, he was perfectly capable of appropriating their language and using it to refute them.

It is perhaps this appropriation and use that beguiles commentators into the misleading distinctions of "liberal" and "conservative" with reference to Edwards' theology. Rather than being caught in a conflict between his own genius and Calvinist dogma, Edwards chose at different times, due to different concerns, to express his vision, as it developed over time, in different ways.

Each of these recent treatments of Edwards' thought, regardless of differences in aim and differences in interpretation, has furthered directly my own understanding of Edwards. All of them reflect a longstanding tradition of Edwards scholarship that tolerates a wide variety of approaches to Edwards, as well as vastly differing conclusions. There are scholars, the most notable example being Perry Miller, who have seen Edwards as primarily at odds with himself, and those, for a recent example, Patricia Tracey, who have seen him as first and foremost at odds with

his Northampton   congregation and his times. Others, like
Douglas Elwood, have focused on one aspect of Edwards'
thought, or, like Roland Delattre, have sought to understand
Edwards' thought as a whole in light of a particular concept.

This   analysis   and   interpretation   bears   a   formal
resemblance to Delattre's *Beauty and Sensibility in the
Thought of Jonathan Edwards* in that, like Delattre, I seek
to demonstrate the coherence of Edwards' thought.   Like
Delattre's treatment of Edwards, this treatment depends on
philosophical, theological analysis and is not historical in
the narrowest sense of the word.

On a substantive level, however, this work differs from
all previous attempts to demonstrate the dynamic unity of
Edwards' vision in a variety of ways.   It is, as far as I
know, the first work of its kind to relate in depth Edwards'
apocalyptic writings to the rest of his thought.   In addition, it is the first of its kind to show the   relations between Edwards' doctrine of creation and his doctrine of
redemption, his religious anthropology and his eschatology,
and his morphology of individual religious experience and
his vision of the redemption of the cosmos.   It is furthermore a comprehensive treatment of the range of Edwards'
thought, for it includes attention to the formal theological
writings, the Blank Bible, the sermons, and the various
notebooks of philosophical miscellanies, scriptural exegesis, and observations of nature.

The substantive differences accrue in part because of
the methodological starting point -- namely, nature as the
initial, primary category of analysis.   Though Edwards'
thought is not reducible to a single category, an examination of the status, role, and destiny of nature yields new
dimensions to Edwards' view of the divine destiny and human

participation therein. It most importantly provides access
to the coherence of Edwards' wide-ranging concerns. In
short, it gives access to the overall unity of his thought.
Though it would be misleading to argue that Edwards' thought
is reducible to a single category, regardless of the category, one can say, regarding the single quality that most
dominates Edwards' vision, that his vision is theocentric.
Neglect of Edwards' cosmology and the role it plays in the
divine drama of creation, redemption, and the realization of
the kingdom of God diminishes the richness of Edwards'
theocentricity.

Edwards' theocentricity arose out of his own spiritual
struggles. Edwards' account of his experience of saving
grace contains and relates the major religious themes that
concerned Edwards throughout his life. As a consequence,
the account serves as a paradigm for understanding Edwards'
thought as a whole. Therefore, my analysis begins by
focusing on the account.

The absolute sovereignty of God is of primary concern to
Edwards in his interpretation of his own experience. It is
also the theme which most directly relates his conversion
account to his philosophical and theological doctrine of
God. The meanings of *absolute* and *sovereign* to Edwards find
their fullest expression in his conception of God as self-
communicating being, creating and redeeming for the further
purpose of self-glorification. This process of divine communication is the realization of the divine destiny. Nature
provides the grammar, and history the syntax, for this process. The first part of this book, then, addresses
primarily Edwards' concept of God.

Whereas Part I examines Edwards' ontology and metaphysics in relation to his doctrine of God as creator and
redeemer, Part II focuses upon Edwards' religious anthropol-

ogy. Examination of nature's role in conversion and sanctification, nature's status as type, and the type as a
prophecy of the coming kingdom of God reveals how human
beings become participants in a positive way in the divine
destiny and elucidates Edwards' vision of the fulfillment of
this destiny. This examination requires an understanding of
Edwards' doctrine of the Incarnation of Christ, the role
played by the Holy Spirit in human redemption, and the
significance which Edwards attaches to the realization of
the kingdom of God. In other words, the second part of this
book relates Edwards' christology, his soteriology, his
understanding of typology and his eschatology to his religious epistemology. This study yields his religious anthropology, or his vision of what it means to be human in light
of spiritual regeneration.

Specifically *what* nature, as divine communication,
reveals concerning the divine destiny and human participation therein forms the central theme of the concluding
part of this book. An analysis of the types Edwards
collected from nature reveals much more concretely than his
more doctrinal writings Edwards' concepts of sin and redemption, divine wrath and divine grace. The types further
express most vividly the dynamic quality of being as it
struggles toward fullness by resisting non-being. In short,
an analysis of these types augments and thereby enriches an
understanding of both Edwards' philosophical theology and
his doctrinal theology as they are expressed throughout his
sermons, formal treatises, and personal notebooks.

The overall movement of the book from Edwards' account
of his experience, to his doctrine of God, to his religious
anthropology, to his cosmology reflects what I understand
to be the pattern or organic movement of Edwards' thought as
a whole. It further reflects my assessment of Edwards' own

priorities. God's grace, experienced personally, centers
Edwards' vision of reality, his personal identity, and his
mode of valuing. Human being first and the natural order
second derive their existence, significance, and value from
divine being and glory. The subordination of human being to
God and the subordination of nature to both, do not reflect
a denigration of either. Rather subordination reflects, on
the one hand, the ambivalence of the human creature as it
seeks happiness, or what is firm, reliable, real and
enduring, in all the wrong places and, on the other hand,
the ambiguity of sensible reality as a source for objects of
this happiness. Stated more positively, Edwards' vision is
theocentric rather than anthropocentric or naturalistic, and
both human beings and nature play positive and vital roles,
however subordinate, in this vision.

PART I

THE ABSOLUTE SOVEREIGNTY OF GOD

CHAPTER ONE

NATURE AND THE DIVINE DESTINY
IN EDWARDS' EXPERIENCE

In Edwards' work nature is a medium of divine communication. The natural order communicates the divine
destiny throughout human existence. Nature, both non-human
and human, actively bears the image of its creator,
sustainer, and redeemer. For example, the sun bears an
image of the trinity, the fountain an image of divine
creativity, and the rainbow an image of the Holy Spirit
incarnate in the communion of saints. That the connection
between image and divine meaning is of the utmost significance for human existence is nowhere more apparent in
Edwards' works than in his account of his own experience of
spiritual transformation.

Edwards recorded his experience of saving grace in the
aftermath of the revivalism of the mid-1730's and prior to
the period that was later to become known as the Great
Awakening of the 1740's. It appears to have been written
when he was in his mid-thirties; the last specific date he
mentions is January, 1739. The original manuscript is not
extant and, therefore, the precise occasion for the account
is not known. Patricia Tracey suggests that Edwards wrote
the account to encourage Aaron Burr in his own spiritual
struggles.[1]

The narrative has received attention in a variety of
different contexts, and scholarly interpretations of its
significance vary greatly. Ola Winslow saw the narrative as
a record of mystical experience, forced into the framework

of Calvinist dogma.[2]   Richard Bushman has analyzed it as a
record of the resolution of Edwards' Oedipal complex.[3]
Conrad Cherry has most recently addressed, in passing, the
significance of the account in relation to Edwards' view of
nature and his religious epistemology. He has not, however,
analyzed it in its own right but has been primarily concerned with citing it briefly in support for his argument
that nature does not provide an independent source of divine
revelation in Edwards' thought.[4]

Regardless of the occasion or the motive, what has come
to be known as the "Personal Narrative" reflects Edwards'
powers of observation turned inward upon his own life.   He
selected what he felt to be relevant from his own spiritual
experience, and what he chose to record is a paradigm of his
thought as a whole.   The interaction of human nature with
sensible reality plays a dramatic role in the account, for
his responses to natural phenomena provide a measure of his
transformation from an ego-centered identity to a theo-
centered identity.   The major theme of the narrative is the
absolute sovereignty of God.

The Sovereignty of God

The "Personal Narrative" is brief, a mere thirty-three
paragraphs in comparison to Augustine's *Confessions*.
Although the account is filled with details concerning
dates, places, friends, and events having to do with his
responses to natural phenomena in a religious context,
description as an embellishment is noticeably lacking.   No
reference is made to his immediate family, the wife whom he
adored and their eleven children.   Scant mention is made of
his father.   He omits altogether the fact that his mother
nursed him back to health when he was taken ill in New
Haven.   His references to his friendships with Madame Smith

NATURE AND THE DIVINE DESTINY IN EDWARDS' EXPERIENCE   17

and her son John in New York, while dwelt upon at some length, when compared with other events, include no physical description of them whatsoever and precious little description in terms of character. He alludes to being distracted in his spiritual life by "temporal concerns," the nature of which remain unspecified, and the many references to his sense of his own wickedness give few concrete details concerning its character. In short, the account is elliptical.

Ellipsis is precisely the point, however. Edwards' intention was to examine his own experience of sin and grace rather than to study the inner complexities and social interactions of his person for their own sake. The detail included draws its particular significance from the quality of the experience. For Edwards, experience is wider than the human ego involved. Although he himself was the subject of this experience, the full meaning of the experience far transcended Edwards' person.

The "Personal Narrative" is Edwards' documentation of a type of human conversion and sanctification. It is an account of human nature particularized in the experience of Jonathan Edwards. Edwards intended the account to focus on regeneration rather than biography. Hence, the account presupposes an elusive background, the elusiveness of which lends qualities of urgency and suspense to the work that recall biblical narrative, for example, the Marcan account of Jesus' ministry.

In order to understand the significance of the "Personal Narrative" as a type of religious experience we must first understand what "type" meant for Edwards. For Edwards a type is a particular event that has universal implications and a future-orientation. A type is the image or shadow of an event or instance to be fulfilled in the future. We are accustomed to thinking of types as composites, events, or instances which, shed of their particularity, reflect the general. Typology as we understand it does bear some resemblance to Edwards' usage because for Edwards types did carry universal meaning. Nevertheless, Edwards' appreciation of individuality as itself representative of universal meaning and his focus on future fulfillment stands in contrast to what we usually mean by *type*. The type functioned for Edwards in a theocentric context as a divine communication; hence, any given particular sensible reality could serve as a type. We, by contrast, are more likely to restrict types, by and large, to characterization of the human realm. This restriction would have been antithetical to Edwards' conception of typology.

Applied to the religious experience of particular people, Edwards' typology worked in some respects like the case study method as Freud used it. The context for Edwards' studies, however, was radically different from that of Freud . Whereas Freud sought to exemplify structures and dynamics of the human psyche common to all humans and judge human behavior according to standards of normal human growth and development, Edwards' chief interests lay elsewhere. His study of human religious experience focused on the fulfillment of the divine will itself, on human redemption through attunement with the divine will, and on developing the criteria by which to distinguish genuine from counterfeit piety.

The context for those experiences that served as types was social in the sense that the experiences themselves were part of a network of divine communication not only to the person who served as the subject of the experience, but to others with whom the experience was shared. This sharing of experience required criteria by which to determine to some degree its genuineness. Since what was at stake was nothing

less than human redemption from sin, typology, as Edwards
employed it, served the double purpose of eliciting the
clear and lively images that could awaken a new sense of the
heart in the parishioner and at the same time evoke humility
rather than pride in the transformation that might occur.

A comparison of the experiences Edwards chose to represent as images of genuine spirituality indicates that
Edwards, like William James, recognized that there was a
variety of types of genuine religious experience. Nowhere
are the differences more striking than in a comparison of
Edwards' own experience with that of his wife Sarah
Pierrepont Edwards. Though a strong conviction of sin permeates both accounts, the sustained serenity and saintliness
that characterize Sarah's experience, as depicted by
Edwards, stand in striking contrast to the inner struggle
that continues as a major theme throughout the "Personal
Narrative."[5] Edwards concludes his description of Sarah's
sanctification by saying, "Now if such things are enthu-
siasm, and the fruits of a distempered brain, let my brain
be ever more possessed of that happy distemper."[6]   By
contrast Edwards' increased awareness of and struggle with
his own wickedness marks the "Personal Narrative." Near the
conclusion of the account he states:

> I have a much greater sense of my universal,
> exceeding dependence on God's grace and strength,
> then I used formerly to have; and have experienced
> more of an abhorrence of my own righteousness. The
> very thought of any joy arising in me, on any con-
> sideration of my own amiableness, performances, or
> experiences, or any goodness of heart or life, is
> nauseous or detestable to me. And yet I am greatly
> afflicted with a proud and self-righteous spirit,
> much more sensibly than I used to be formerly. I
> see that serpent rising and putting forth its head
> continually, everywhere, all around me.[7]

Whereas personal assurance is a mark of Sarah's sanctification, one of the chief characteristics of Edwards'

account of his own experience is the account's ambiguity and
lack of resolution regarding the status of his soul. He
begins the account by describing "two more remarkable
seasons of awakening, before I met with that change by which
I was brought to those new dispositions, and that new sense
of things, that I have since had."[8] He continues throughout
the account to focus on "those new dispositions and that new
sense of things" in such a way as to make it clear that they
intensified his displeasure with his concern with himself
rather than alleviated it. Although his assurance and trust
in the sovereignty of God is not only sustained but
increases over time, his inner struggles with his own will
provide him little relief or peace. As he puts it in the
conclusion, immediately following his despair, "I would not,
but as it were, cry out, 'How happy are they which do that
which is right in the sight of God! They are blessed
indeed, they are the happy ones!' I had, at the same time,
a very affecting sense, how meet and suitable it was that
God should govern the world, and order all things to his own
pleasure; and I rejoiced in it, that God reigned and that
his will was done."[9] Edwards' use of the third person
plural rather than the first person plural in reference to
"the happy ones" indicates an ambivalence regarding his own
trustworthiness "to do that which is right in the eyes of
God." This outpouring reflects his humility. His own
rejoicing lay in the trustworthiness of God's will, rather
than a self-assurance that he, left to his own devices,
would do his duty.

     The absolute sovereignty of God and the correlative
absolute dependence of human beings dominate the narrative.
The divine will is the source of worth and confidence for
the human soul. Edwards' earlier awakening floundered in
his exertions to attain righteousness or holiness. An

affirmation of God's sovereignty is the chief characteristic of his change in disposition and his new sense of
all reality. Before his conversion the absolute sovereignty
of God, that is, God's governance of the world including the
salvation of some and the damnation of others, had appeared
like "a horrible doctrine"[10] to Edwards, no doubt in part
due to his fear that he would not be numbered among the
saved. His conversion was marked by experiences in which
the doctrine itself "appeared exceeding pleasant, bright,
and sweet."[11] His post-conversion experiences continued to
reinforce his delight in God's sovereignty, and he concludes
by referring to two particular occasions during which he
rejoiced in God's sovereignty.

Edwards' transformation from horror at the doctrine of
God's absolute sovereignty to affirmation reflects a re-
centering of his identity. His disposition underwent a
radical transformation that altered his reception of sensory
data. In some respects the change can be measured by a
shift from his exertions to escape his own sinfulness
through self-determination to his newly found ability to be
attuned to the divine will. Of his prior condition he
wrote:

> I had great and violent inward struggles, till
> after many conflicts with wicked inclinations,
> repeated resolutions and bonds that I laid myself
> under by a kind of vow to God, I was brought wholly
> to break off all former wicked ways, and all ways
> known of outward sin; and to apply myself to seek
> salvation, and practise many religious duties
> . . . . My concern now wrought more by inward
> struggles and conflicts, and self reflections. I
> made seeking salvation the main business of my
> life. But yet, it seems to me, I sought after a
> miserable manner; which made me sometimes since to
> question, whether ever it issued unto that which
> was saving; being ready to doubt, whether such
> miserable seeking ever succeeded.[12]

He contrasts this prior condition with his discovery of a

"sort of inward sweet delight in God and divine things."[13] He goes on to describe this "inward sweet delight" by saying, "there came into my soul, and was as it were diffused through it, a sense of the glory of the Divine Being; a new sense, quite different from anything I ever experienced before."[14]

The alteration is a measure of a newly found affection. Whereas before Edwards could not through his own power sustain his delight in things religious nor his engagement in his religious duties, convictions, and affections, he subsequently "prayed in a manner quite different . . . with a new sort of affection."[15] Edwards' focus shifted from his own "good estate" to "the glory of God."

Edwards records his first experience of his sense of the glory of God as "quite different from anything I had ever experienced before."[16] He recalls that the first instance of "that sort of inward, sweet delight in God and divine things" occurred when he was reading I Tim. 1:17. "Now unto the King eternal, immortal, invisible, the only wise God, be honor and glory for ever and ever, Amen." Yet he concludes the description of that event by saying, "But it never came into my thought, that there was anything spiritual, or of a saving nature in this."[17] In contrast to Augustine's dramatic moment in which he heard the children cry "Take and read!" Edwards recalls an event that did not appear at the time as efficacious and moves on to speak of subsequent such events that included a discussion of the experiences with his father Timothy. It is possible that it was Edwards' father who pointed out their full significance to his son. (One is tempted to speculate concerning the coincidence of the scriptural source with Edwards' father's name.) At any rate, Edwards left his father and "walked abroad alone, in a solitary place in [his] father's pasture, for

contemplation."[18]   He goes on to describe what then hap-
pened to him:

> And as I was walking there, and looking up on the
> sky and clouds, there came into my mind so sweet a
> sense of the glorious *majesty* and *grace* of God,
> that I know not how to express. I seemed to see
> them both in a sweet conjunction; majesty and
> meekness joined together, it was a sweet and gentle
> and holy majesty; and also a majestic meekness; an
> awful sweetness; a high, and great, and holy
> gentleness.[19]

For Edwards the absoluteness of God's rule lay in the conjunction of what had originally appeared to him to be oppo-
sites.   Now, rather than opposite qualities, majesty and
grace conjoined in God as expressions of one another. God's
majesty derived from God's superlative meekness or gentle-
ness -- God's grace. Without this newly experienced sense
of the conjunction of majesty and grace Edwards experienced
only the wrath of God. It was in the soul of the beholder
or recipient, in this case Edwards, that the disjunction of
wrath and grace occurred, and it was redemption that healed
the breach. In the conjunction of majesty and grace lay the
beauty or excellency of the divine will. Edwards' sense of
this excellency marked the turning point from fear to hope,
from his alienation from the divine will to his attunement
with it.

Edwards' Transformation

Natural phenomena commanded Edwards' attention through
direct observation and intellectual study throughout much of
his lifetime, as his essays on insects and the rainbow, his
scientific notes, and his notebook of types drawn from
nature so strikingly reveal. Nature exerts no less an
influence in the "Personal Narrative." While scholars have
recognized this influence in Edwards' explicit writings on
nature, they have generally regarded the "Personal

Narrative" exclusively as a record of the development of
Edwards' faith. The whole account can, for instance, be interpreted as a description of a transformation of his senses
and his dispositions that redirected his attention and
altered his responses to his environment by making him more
acutely aware of what he understood to be nature's true
significance. Body metaphors and references to the human
senses pervade the account as do other natural phenomena and
his metaphorical use of them.

Edwards' description of his second awakening includes a
reference to a time during his college years when he suffered an attack of pleurisy which he interprets as an act of
God "in which he brought me nigh to the grave, and shook me
over the pit of hell."[20] After his conversion he speaks of
being taken ill again, this time in New Haven, for a period
of three months. Of this illness he says, "In this
sickness, God was pleased to visit me again, with the sweet
influence of his Spirit,"[21] a vivid contrast to God's previous shaking him over the pit of hell. References to his
solitary walks in pasture, fields and wilderness and to his
outpourings of weeping and singing to the extent on some
occasions that he "was forced to shut [himself] up and lock
the doors" occur throughout the text.[22] Illnesses, walks,
outpourings, and the new sense itself (not to mention his
fathering of eleven children and actively participating in
their lives and in some cases their deaths) indicate spiritual and sensible wholeness in Edwards that was sensitive to
and affirming of the human body in all its ambiguity of
sickness and health.

This sensitivity and affirmation spilled over into his
choice of metaphors for characterizing the human/divine
relationship as he experienced it. He speaks of "walking"
in the way of duty, of "visions" of the divine, of a

recurring desire to be "swallowed up" in God or in Christ. He compares the naturalness of prayer to the naturalness of breath. In one passage he says, "I felt God, so to speak."[23]

This appreciation of the sensible extended to include not only his body but all sensible reality. Just as he interpreted his body movements and the use of his senses as instruments of divine communication both before and after his conversion, so he interpreted the world in which he moved about throughout his life. His conversion marked a change in the quality of his relationship to God, not a change from unbelief to belief. It marked a change from his being at odds with the divine will to his sense of being positively included in the divine plan. Because the divine plan included God's direct and continual preservation of the universe, Edwards' conversion marked the beginning of a new attunement with nature as the visible manifestation and communication of God's glory.

His conversion was only the beginning for Edwards. Following his discussion with his father and his subsequent experience of the conjunction of God's majesty and grace, Edwards states, "After this my sense of divine things gradually increased and became more and more lively . . . . The appearance of everything was altered."[24] His transformation precipitated a growing, heightened awareness of natural phenomena as manifestations of God's glory. Sun, moon, stars, grass, and trees took on the status of "words of nature" that communicate divine excellency, purity, wisdom, and love.[25]

This altering of appearances reflects an alteration in Edwards' disposition as witnessed by the change in his response to thunder and lightning. He records the contrast:

And scarce any thing, among all the words of nature, was so sweet to me as thunder and light-

> ning; formerly, nothing had been so terrible to me.
> I used to be uncommonly terrified with thunder, and
> to be struck with terror when I saw a thunder storm
> rising; but now, on the contrary, it rejoiced me.
> I felt God, so to speak, at the first appearance of
> a thunder storm; and used to take the opportunity,
> at such times, to fix myself in order to view the
> clouds, and see the lightnings play, and hear the
> majestic and awful voice of God's thunder, which
> oftentimes was exceedingly entertaining, leading me
> to sweet contemplations of my great and glorious
> God. While thus engaged, it seemed natural to me
> to sing, or chant for my meditations; or, to speak
> my thoughts in soliloquies with a singing voice.[26]

Whereas thunder had elicited an uncommon terror in Edwards
before, it now "rejoiced" him; indeed he sought out the
occasion to witness what once had terrorized him.   It
allowed him the opportunity to see God through the lightning
and to hear God's voice -- to feel God. "I felt God, so to
speak" reverberates with a tactile intimacy that recalls
Calvin.   Edwards' exuberant cry "I felt God" communicates
both how he was affected and what affected him. His account
indicates that he was aware that the reality he was encountering is not some sensible entity in the usual terms in
which we encounter one another's bodies through sight,
sound, and touch, hence the qualification "so to speak."
Nevertheless, he was equally aware of encountering the
divine presence in and through the sensible order in a way
that both affected him deeply and related him intimately to
that presence. He is touched, and he touches the majestic
and the awful, the great and the glorious. The presence he
experienced provides the full significance and worth of the
phenomena, thunder and lightning, as divine communication.
Both he and the significance of appearances are altered.

Edwards' responses were to burst into song, and to pray.
These responses were as "natural" to him as breathing. His
own sensibility to divine communication increased, gradually

becoming more and more lively; in short he became more and more positively related to the divine will operating in his life. The "sight" or the excellency of the things of God and the "taste" of their good regenerated him. Insofar as the "things" include natural phenomena, Edwards was quite literally seeing their excellency and tasting their good. That these things are "of God" implies that his sensory awareness included a wider range of possibilities than our usual, more restricted understanding of the senses allows.[27]

He goes on to compare his previous spiritual condition with his transformation. The images he uses to mark the change are again sensory. Whereas he was previously insensitive to color, he has now received his sight.[28] Color and the transformation from blindness to sight are recurring themes throughout Edwards' writings. For Edwards the "new sense" and the sensible reality it perceives are inseparable. The interaction of human nature with natural phenomena is inseparable from God's ever-present rule and therefore God's grace.

Edwards' account is hopeful, rather than optimistic. Edwards' trust in the divine good pleasure contrasts starkly with his own displeasure with himself and his lack of resolution concerning his own character. His desire is for humility before God, rather than self-certainty, and his conflicts emerge from the opposition of his desire with his actual character. Edwards is no once-born optimist of the Emersonian variety portrayed so vividly by William James in his *Varieties of Religious Experience*. One of the major points throughout the narrative is that concern for whether one is saved or damned is not one of the signs of genuine spirituality and pales in comparison to a focus on the glory of God. Edwards' personal hopes were that he might be

"conformed to the image of Christ,"[29] and it was the attractive power of the image itself, not the proprietary acquisition of it, on which Edwards focused first.

The image of Christ included a future orientation for
Edwards. At stake was nothing less than the fulfillment of
Christ's kingdom on earth. Edwards wrote:

> I had great longings, for the advancement of
> Christ's kingdom in the world; and my secret prayer
> used to be, in great part, taken up in prayer for
> it. If I heard the least hint, of any thing that
> happened, in any part of the world, that appeared,
> in some respect or other, to have a favourable
> aspect, on the interests of Christ's kingdom, my
> soul eagerly catched at it; and it would much ani-
> mate and refresh me. I used to be eager to read
> public news-letters, mainly for that end; to see if
> I could not find some news, favourable to the
> interest of religion in the world.

He went on to add that he spent many an hour conversing with
his friend John Smith "on the things of God: and our conver-
sations used to turn much on the advancement of Christ's
kingdom in the world, and to the glorious things that God
would accomplish for his church in the latter days."[30]

These passages are laden with Edwards' apocalypticism.
We know from his other writings that he was a millennialist
throughout his life, and that his millennialism included the
restoration of nature along with the final judgment of humanity. He believed that the kingdom was to come first on
earth. The lure of the future provided past and present
with much of their immediate significance.

Because the kingdom lured the believer toward it with
the promise of things to come, the anticipated future lent a
quality of enigma and mystery to the past and the present.
Edwards' eschatology gave him every reason to trust in God's
aim toward a future fulfillment in which all reality would
be judged or clarified. The divine destiny was in the process of fulfilling itself. The full significance of the

past and the present, as well as the specific events of the
future, nevertheless, remained in part unknown.
Furthermore, because past and present contributed to the
future, past and present bore the image or shadow of the
future at any given time. Past, present, and future conjoined to form a pattern of divine operations.

From the "Personal Narrative" we know that this pattern
had to do with a very realistic and honest assessment of
wickedness, sin, and damnation as well as holiness, good,
and salvation. The unknowable quality of all events due to
their future orientation made true judgment of one's own
good estate, not to mention others', uncertain at best for
any given human being. It is no wonder that Edwards'
account of his experience or anyone else's is elliptical.

Jonathan Edwards' conversion freed him from his terror
of sensible reality symbolized by thunder and lightning, and
freed him for a sensitivity to the beauty of all reality in
a way that did not trivialize the magnitude of evil and
human sin. He sensed the presence of God's grace operating
through all reality toward its end -- an end not fully
known, but trustworthy because it was determined by the
glory of God. From Edwards' perspective this freedom from
fear and attunement to divine grace was true human liberty.
Rather than self-determination aimed toward self-
fulfillment, human freedom meant an encounter with the
divine will that allowed a human being to become a participant in the process of fulfilling the divine plan. As
such, human beings became positive symbols of divine activity.

Edwards' own part in this divinely known and ordained
operation was to preach and to write in as vivid and com-
pelling a way as possible in the hope that others might
begin to recognize the pattern of regeneration at work in

their own experience. He knew well enough that he could not
force salvation upon others, but he hoped that he might
awaken them to the human/divine encounter. For all his
insistence on the absolute sovereignty of God, correlative
human dependence was not a passive state. Rather, human
dependence referred to an attitude that recognized that God
communicated through human activity, responses, and events
as well as natural phenomena. In the concluding paragraph
of the "Personal Narrative" Edwards states:

> Though it seems to me, that, in some respects, I
> was a far better Christian, for two or three years
> after my first conversion, than I am now; and lived
> in a more constant delight and pleasure; yet of
> late years, I have had a more full and constant
> sense of the absolute sovereignty of God, and a
> delight in that sovereignty; and have had more of a
> sense of the glory of Christ, as a Mediator
> revealed in the gospel. On one Saturday night, in
> particular, I had such a discovery of the
> excellency of the gospel above all other doctrines,
> that I could not but say to myself, "This is my
> chosen light, my chosen doctrine;" and of Christ,
> "This is my chosen Prophet." It appeared sweet,
> beyond all expression, to follow Christ, and to be
> taught, and enlightened, and instructed by him; to
> learn of him and to live him. [31]

The words, ". . . my chosen light; my chosen doctrine
. . . my chosen Prophet," occurring as Edwards' response to
his sense of the absolute sovereignty of God summarize the
paradox of Reformed Protestantism that has baffled adherents
and non-adherents alike. Edwards was freed to embrace the
rule of God and to participate in that rule by the grace of
God itself. The rule was, thus, absolute. Past, present,
and future, unknown to Edwards in their full significance
and not without pain and sin as well as joy, conjoined to
form a dynamic pattern that was above all else the trustworthy operation of divine wisdom and love.

Edwards, The Human Being

Edwards was a man of great inward struggles and passions. The narrative presents an overall rhythm of exuberance, wonder and expectation, on the one hand, and self-displeasure and an acute awareness of his own arrogance, on the other hand. The tension between his horrible fear for his own "good estate" and his joyful fear, or awe, of God is sustained throughout the account. His eye for essential detail, the detail of his own moods and the detail of those events both natural and social that communicated to him divine glory, is ever present. His eye for detail exhibits rare sensibility and sensitivity.

His honesty and realism concerning the fluctuations of his piety are consistent throughout the account. Although he includes his "two more remarkable seasonings of awakening" with his genuine awakening in order to present a contrast, there is an overall integrity to the account. Never does he totally discount his pre-conversion experience. However negatively he views it, it is part of his overall experience. The implicit assumption seems to be that he accepted his prior awakenings as part and parcel of his total experience, as events that prepared him to distinguish what was genuine from what was not. Furthermore, his record of his post-conversion upheaval and struggle with himself present the reader with a picture that seriously calls into question any notion that would make redemption a once-for-all event that transforms the redeemed instantaneously into a perfect person who thenceforward lives without struggle. Instead, it is clear from Edwards' account that conversion marks only the beginning of a process of sanctification, best characterized by an increasing attunement to the divine will through a sensitivity to the world as divine communication. This very attunement worked at times for Edwards to intensify his inner struggles.

That Edwards could present his passionate account as a subordination of his ego to his experience presupposes an enormous self-detachment. The detachment was available to him precisely because his transformation entailed a shift in focus from concern with himself (his own "good estate") to the divine pattern at work throughout reality. His focus became the divine plan itself, and within that context, his part in the plan. We know from the passion exhibited within the account and from his biographers that Edwards was actively involved in his family life and the lives of his parishioners and colleagues. The "Personal Narrative" tells us that he formed lasting friendships; other historical records tell us that he was immersed in conflicts with his enemies. He was, in short, a very social being. Yet his detachment pervades not only the account but his observations of natural and social phenomena alike. It presupposes a solitariness, itself recorded in the account. The great lengths of time that he spent alone in prayer, meditation, and contemplation in his room and in the wilderness provided him the opportunity to discipline his focus on divine sovereignty. His focus on divine sovereignty allowed him a certain distance from particular worldly events. His trust in the divine will protected him much of the time from taking too personally either the social and political upheaval that characterized his active ministry or his own inner torments and struggles. It allowed him enough distance to put his own experiences into a broader context.

His own attunement to divine being as recorded in the narrative and the detachment the narrative itself presupposes indicate a conjunction of involvement and distance that characterize his person. He was always listening for, watching for, reaching out toward, anticipating, and otherwise sensing through events a "something more" that qualified events and communicated more fully their true significance. This extended awareness made him more open to events, whether natural or social, whether personally joyful or painful.

Nature and History in Edwards' Thought

Edwards' experience of transformation allowed him to consent to divine being as a willing participant in the divine destiny. His experience further helped provide him with a morphology of spiritual regeneration. His own regeneration involved a transformation of his awareness of nature as an eschatologically conditioned language of God.

Nature's role as medium of divine communication arises from its status as God's work and, as such, comprehended in God. Because all existence shares in the same fundamental structure, whether it is matter, spirit, or some combination of both, nature is an extension of the divine will. It has the potential for revealing divine being and, under the proper conditions, plays a crucial role in the drama of redemption. Had there been no human fall from grace, this epistemological function would have always been actual rather than potential. Human sin requires that divine being become incarnate as human being, through Christ and the Holy Spirit, in part in order that human beings may come to know that all flesh, all matter, is spirit made flesh -- a communication of spirit.

The character of nature as divine communication is anagogic. The book of nature, read in light of scripture, communicates the destiny of divine being. Edwards' "philosophy of history" is redemption history extended to include the redemption of the cosmos. Sensible reality not only plays a role in human redemption, it is itself finally

to be redeemed from the effects of human sin.   In this
sense, nature is historicized.

    Edwards   suffered   no   diremption   between   nature   and
history.   His own experience and his observations of the
experience of others, shaped by his apocalyptic interpretation of scripture, taught him otherwise.   Nature, as sensible reality and sentient being, and history, as time
measured in terms of human events, were for him the unified
playing out of divine being communicating its destiny as it
reached fulfillment.

CHAPTER TWO

BEING

According to the "Personal Narrative" Edwards' conversion occurred in 1723. During this same year he began work on his essay "Of Being." His miscellanies, begun a year earlier, the essay on being, and another essay "The Mind," also begun in 1723, demonstrate an amazing burst of philosophical productivity. They also give expression to Edwards' philosophical idealism, itself a creative way of coming to grips with the absolute sovereignty of God.[1] Edwards' concern with developing his concept of God as being was to continue throughout his life. His later writings, particularly *The Nature Of True Virtue* and the *Dissertation Concerning the End for Which God Created the World*, intended as companion pieces, demonstrate Edwards' genius in combining philosophical with theological skills to express his concept of God as being in general.

The richness of Edwards' concept of God as being has attracted scholars since Edwards' death. Wallace Anderson's introduction to his edition of Edwards' scientific and philosophical writings and Conrad Cherry's *Nature and Religious Imagination from Edwards To Bushnell* include in two different contexts the most recent examinations of the significance of being in Edwards' thought. Anderson's introduction provides an excellent philosophical analysis of being and its relationship to matter, philosophically considered. It was not, however, Anderson's purpose to analyze the relationship between being as a philosophical concept

and Edwards' more explicitly theological concerns. As a
consequence, Anderson does not address the significance of
being as communicative in Edwards' thought, nor does he
discuss Edwards' theology of nature as such. Cherry, whose
concern is to relate theologically being and nature in
Edwards' thought, nevertheless does not go far enough.
Cherry's failure to address the relationship between
Edwards' concept of God as being and his trinitarian writings precipitates in his drawing too hard and fast the
distinctions between divine being and divine glory, on the
one hand, and nature and history, on the other hand.

In order to understand nature's role as divine communication, one must first understand Edwards' concept of
divine being as communicative. This requires a thorough
examination of Edwards' doctrine of God. Consideration of
his doctrine of God indicates that divine being communicates
truth symbolically through nature, and that these symbols
bear the structure of divine consciousness. In short, an
analysis of Edwards' doctrine of God reveals the extent to
which creation bears the image of its creator.

For Edwards, whatever is, is a communication of divine
being. In miscellany 697 he wrote:

> God, as He is infinite and the being whence all are
> derived and from whom everything is given, does
> comprehend the entity of all his creatures; and
> their entity is not to be added to His, as not
> comprehended in it, for they are but communications
> from Him. Communications of being ben't additions
> of being. The reflections of the sun's light don't
> add at all to the sum total of the light.[2]

One may distinguish one kind of being or communication from
another, as in created and uncreated being or material communication and spiritual communication. One may distinguish
one mode of communication from another, for example, divine
knowledge from divine love. One may also look at the same

communication from more than one perspective. For example, divine self-love is a self-communication not only by and to divine being, but includes as well a communication of love (also divine) to the creature. In addition one may speak of divine being as generally communicative, as all-inclusive, complete and comprehending all being and therefore as always present, or one may speak of divine being in terms of particular communications and, therefore, particularly present in one place as distinguished from another.[3]

God is all in all, and God is specifically where God is seen, heard, felt, or otherwise received. In this way God is both being in general and distinguishable by way of communication as a being. To say that God is both being in general and a being can be confusing unless one understands the different ways Edwards distinguishes divine communication in more detail. Avoiding possible confusion requires an examination of Edwards' different ways of discussing being, namely: the idea of being in general as a presupposition of divine communication, and divine being as self-communicative.

The General Character of Being

For Edwards *nothing* is a relative term; it derives its logical status only in comparison to existence or being. That nothing can be, in an absolute sense, is a contradiction. By contrast, *being* is absolute. There always is that from which we derive our relative sense of nothing by way of comparison. Edwards identifies this absoluteness of being with God. God's absoluteness means that God is all there is, that God always is, and that God is always God.

Edwards further identifies God or absolute being with space. This identification makes space simultaneously a set of relations and a process of relating. It follows that

both space and relations are real in the philosophical
sense.

For Edwards, *being*, defined as absolute and as the dynamic establishment of relationships, is necessarily
conscious. Because being is conscious, being is communicative. Because being is all there is, being is
reflexively communicative. It communicates itself to
itself. This self-communication is what makes whatever is
be what it is. Hence, being in general is God. Edwards
states, "The first Being, the eternal and infinite Being, is
in effect, BEING IN GENERAL: and comprehends universal
existence,"[4] and again, God is "the Being of beings."[5] The
general character of being is, for Edwards, self-
communication. Self-communication involves *a communication
by being, a communication to being, and a communication of
being* simultaneously. Being in general is this threefold
process of communication, and, properly speaking, there is
nothing else.[6]

Edwards began his essay "Of Being" by writing, "That
there should absolutely be nothing at all is utterly
impossible . . . . So that we see it is necessary that some
being should eternally be."[7] He goes on to conclude his
first paragraph that this necessary, eternal being must also
be infinite and omnipresent since it is a contradiction to
say that eternal being is located in some one place and not
in some other place. His point is that we think the notion
of nothing always relative to a particular something. Only
being can be absolute since for nothing to be absolute is
for nothing to be, and that is a contradiction. Nothing
presupposes and implies something. Being always and
everywhere is.

Edwards' next move is to identify necessary, eternal,
infinite, and omnipresent being with space -- and space with

God.[8] By identifying being with space Edwards gives space positive existence. Instead of a vacuum or "nothingness" to be filled up with particular things that come into existence individually, space is a necessary condition for the very existence of bodies. Space is a pattern or a set of relations. It follows that to be a body is minimally to be a body in relation to space as well as in relation to other bodies. Not only is space real in the technical sense of having existence apart from human perception, but relation itself is real. Edwards states, "For being, if we examine narrowly, is nothing else but proportion."[9] In other words, for there to be entity, it must be in relation or proportion to other being or entity. The highest expression of proportion or relation is consent.

In the essay "Of Being" Edwards goes on to define being as consciousness: "How is it possible there should something be from all eternity and there be no consciousness of it? It will appear very plain to everyone that intensely considers of it that consciousness and being are the same thing exactly."[10] After working through several thought experiments in which he explores the significance of depriving bodies of light and movement, Edwards concludes that "those beings which have knowledge and consciousness are the only proper and real and substantial beings inasmuch as the being of other things is only by these. From hence we may see the gross mistake of those who think material things the most substantial beings and spirits more like a shadow; whereas spirits only are properly substance."[11]

To be is to be conscious. Extension, light, movement, relation, and all other ingredients characteristic of bodies are ultimately ideas of consciousness. Divine being generates these ideas and thereby guarantees the reality of the existence of matter. This reality shadows forth or com-

municates that which makes matter be what it is, namely,
divine consciousness itself.

The qualities that being, understood as a philosophical
concept, presupposes are thus: that being is absolute in
relation to nothing, that being is space or that which
comprehends and provides the condition for the existence of
all else, and that being is conscious. From Edwards' positive view of space it follows that the category of relation
has the status of being real. Therefore, the identification
of being with consciousness implies that being is
necessarily reflexive and communicative. This implication
is made explicit as one of the major themes in Edwards'
doctrines of the trinity and creation.

Divine Being as Self-Communicative

Edwards' trinitarian thought is the theological
corollary to his philosophical reflections on being. It
gives us an idea of the theological dimension of divine
self-communication. In his trinitarian works Edwards wrote
that the three persons of the trinity "have as it were
formed themselves into a society, for carrying on the great
design of glorifying the deity and communicating its
fulness."[12] Both the Son and the Spirit are divine self-
communications in some sense, but the primary role of divine
self-communication regarding the creature belongs to the
Holy Spirit. In addition, in Edwards' thought the Holy
Spirit as the content of divine self-communication is
directly related to the world; indeed, the world can be said
to be part of the flowing forth of the divine self-love or
Holy Spirit: "the creation of the world is to gratify Divine
love as that is exercised by Divine wisdom."[13] For Edwards,
self-communicating being is necessarily pluralistic; for
Edwards, all creation is grace.

While he uses distinctions such as nature and spirit,
creature and creator, nature and supernature, they are
distinctions, not dichotomies. The primary distinction
regarding nature that he uses is *common* as opposed to
saving grace, both of which are the special operation of the
Holy Spirit working in and through creation or nature.
Common grace refers to the general operations of the Holy
Spirit in providing for and upholding creation as well as
assisting ordinary human conscience. Saving grace refers to
the specific infusion of grace bestowed by the Spirit upon
the redeemed and its consequent virtue.   Since nature as
the realm of common grace is the operation of the Holy
Spirit, it represents, reveals, or communicates divine being
in a trustworthy manner to the creature who has eyes to see
and ears to hear.

Edwards distinguishes the economic ordering of the persons of the trinity in terms of their specific roles in the
covenant of redemption. He is addressing the theological
issue of what redemption presupposes concerning the
character of God, and he is using scripture as his
authority. In addressing this issue he distinguishes "God's
natural inclination to glorify and communicate Himself in
general" from "the particular method that [God's] wisdom
pitches upon as tending best to affect this."[14]   The
method, the covenant of redemption, is added to God's
general inclination. Edwards' aim is to argue that the trinitarian character of God is a prior condition for redemption.   The position he is refuting is that Christ's
mediatorial office as redeemer merited his becoming the
second person of the trinity.

While the point at issue may appear trivial, it is not.
First of all, this inclination to communication refers to
the "order or economy of the persons of the Trinity with

respect to their actions *ad extra* ."[15] Since this inclination is a condition for the covenant of redemption, creativity is, by implication, a condition for redemption.
Edwards states that the covenant of redemption "is a thing
diverse from God's natural inclination to glorify and communicate Himself in general, and superadded to it or subser-
vient to it."[16] Nevertheless, the covenant of redemption is
an eternal covenant and, therefore, logically prior to God's
actual creation of the world. As Edwards puts it, the world
was made so that the elect might be the spouse of Christ.[17]
Edwards has built redemption into the logic of creation
itself. The covenant of redemption as the particular method
pitched upon represents the limits set by God's wisdom in
determining how and for what end God's natural inclination
to self-communication and self-glorification through
creation will take place.

The initial act of creation introduces a notion of time
that gives space a destiny. The logic of this particular
exertion of the divine inclination to create assumes a need
for redemption that involves an eschatologically conditioned
end. The divine inclination to create as qualified by the
covenant of redemption sets the divine destiny into motion.
History as the fulfillment of the divine destiny, communicated through nature, begins.

Divine wisdom and divine love are the modes by which
divine being communicates itself. Edwards stresses
throughout his trinitarian writings the equality of the
three persons of the trinity in the honor due them, their
glory and their excellency. Nevertheless, he also maintains
the logical subordination of the Spirit to the Son; he does
so whether discussing the economic ordering of the persons,
the covenant of redemption, or the three persons viewed as
the unified structure of divine consciousness.

By examining how the three persons interact to exhibit
the unity of divine consciousness we can better understand
the differences in how divine wisdom and divine love are
communications of divine being. Divine consciousness is
distinguishable as direct existence or being (the first
person), as wisdom or understanding (the second person), and
as love or will (the third person). The second person,
divine wisdom, is God's perfect idea of Godself. The third
person, divine love, is the interaction between the first
and second persons. When Edwards considers the trinity
simply in itself, he underscores the fact that the third
person is the communication that occurs between the first
and second persons. Divine love is divine self-love,
generated by the first person in response to the second,
which in turn takes on a reality or what Edwards calls a
subsistence of its own. Though a response that is itself a
person, having equal glory and excellency with the other two
persons, divine love is, logically speaking, subordinated to
both other persons. God acts according to God's wisdom.
Thus the covenant of redemption is a particular method
"pitched upon" by God's wisdom as an exercise of God's
"natural inclination" or will. Creation itself, though it
gratifies divine love, gratifies it as it is exercised by
divine wisdom. When we consider the trinity in itself, the
second person, divine wisdom, is a communication of divine
being by way of repeating perfectly divine being. The Holy
Spirit, divine love, is the communication between the first
and second persons.

When we consider the trinity in relation to the human
creature, both the second and third persons communicate
divine being. As Edwards himself puts it, "[As] it is the
office of the person that is God's idea and understanding,
so 'tis the office of the person that is God's love to com-

municate Divine love to the creature."[18]   While God's acts
are in accordance with God's knowledge, the creature's
knowledge depends upon divine action.   Human reception of
saving grace or divine love is the necessary condition for
human knowledge of God.   The regenerate receive the Holy
Spirit as a gift offered by Christ in order to recognize
Christ as Redeemer.   In this way God's self-communication
is the communication of God to the saints; and, therefore,
as Edwards would say, God dwells in their hearts.[19]

The distinction between the ways in which the second and
third persons communicate divine being to human being and
the way in which divine being communicates with itself have
to do with the structure of the human creature.   Human
access to understanding or knowledge as divine self-
communication is indwelling divine love as divine self-
communication.   The primary role of divine communication to
the human creature belongs to the Holy Spirit.

Edwards characteristically stresses the connection of
creation or nature to God through divine communication by
the Holy Spirit.   The human/divine connection is only one of
several ways in which God communicates, although it is
central to all other connections as their epistemological
presupposition.   Edwards states: "The world was made for
the Son of God especially.   For God made the world for
Himself from love to Himself; but God loves Himself only in
a reflex act.   He views Himself and so loves Himself, so He
makes the world for Himself viewed and reflected on, and
that is the same with Himself repeated or begotten in His
own idea, and that is His Son."[20]   The act of creation is an
act of love;   it is a divine communication in response to
the Son.   Everything that exists is a communication of God.
Creation is related to the Godhead by sharing the structure
of divine consciousness, or the trinity.   As a particular

act of love the act of creation is identified particularly
with the Holy Spirit. In addition creation is related to
the Godhead by being distinguishable from it as an object of
the divine love itself.

Communication extends beyond the human arena to include
non-human nature. Edwards is equally at ease with "family,"
"society," and "soul," on the one hand, and "fountain" and
"sun," on the other hand, as images for the trinity. The
fact that he inevitably connects each of these images with
some form of communication indicates that communication to
human being involves all the human senses. It is a sharing,
an imparting, and a connection that is manifested as visible
movement, gesture, taste, and sound. The images "fountain"
and "sun" yield meaning just as "soul" and "family" or
"society" because non-human nature, as well as human society
and psychology, reflects in its structure the structure of
divine consciousness. There is a symbolic connection between creation and creator that not only allows but requires
metaphorical expression. Anything, by virtue of its
createdness, has the potential for becoming a more or less
adequate metaphor for divine being simply because there is
no bifurcation between existence and meaning.

That the sun can be put to the same imagistic service as
the soul is not simply a matter of anthropomorphic personification for Edwards. Rather, interpreted properly as part
of divine communication, the sun as an image of the trinity
serves to de-anthropocentrize:

> There are two more eminent and remarkable images of
> the Trinity among the creatures. The one is the
> spiritual creation, the soul of man. There is the
> mind, and the understanding or idea and the spirit
> of the mind as it is called in Scripture, i.e., the
> disposition, the will, or affection. The other is
> the visible creation viz. the sun. The Father is
> as the substance of the sun. (By substance I don't
> mean in the philosophical sense, but the sun as to

its internal constitution.)   The Son is as the
brightness and glory of the disk of the sun or that
bright and glorious form under which it appears to
our eyes.   The Holy Ghost is the action of the sun
which is within the sun in its intestine heat, and
being diffusive, enlightens, warms, enlivens, and
comforts the world.   The Spirit, as it is God's
infinite love to Himself and happiness in Himself,
is as the internal heat of the sun, but, as it is
that by which God communicates Himself, it is the
emanation of the sun's action, or the emitted beams
of the sun.
    The various sorts of rays of the sun and their
beautiful colours do well represent the Spirit.
They well represent the love and grace of God and
were made use of for this purpose in the rainbow
after the flood and I suppose also in that rainbow
seen round about the throne by Ezekiel: Ezek 1.28,
Rev. iv.3 and round the head of Christ by John,
Rev. x.1, or the amiable excellency of God and the
various beautiful graces and virtues of the Spirit
. . . . and I believe the variety there is in the
rays of the sun and their beautiful colours was
designed by the Creator for this very purpose, and
indeed the whole visible creation which is but the
shadow of being is so made and ordered by God as to
typify and represent spiritual things for which I
could give many reasons.[21]

In this passage Edwards gives both the human soul and
the sun equal weight as "two more eminent and remarkable
images of the trinity among the creatures." Though he
distinguishes them as spiritual and visible creations, both
operate equally as metaphors in terms of their creatureliness.   Meaning is metaphorical in regard to both images
because it is clear from the juxtaposition of the "soul" and
"sun" that the soul is no more an exhaustive representation
of the trinity than the sun is.   That both "soul" and "sun"
share the same role as metaphors for the trinity emphasizes
the divine relationship to *all* nature, non-human as well as
human.

    The juxtaposition of the two "creatures" further serves
to reinforce the connection between human being and the rest

of the created order. "Soul" and "sun" as images of the
trinity bear a structural resemblance to one another. They
also resemble one another in terms of origin, both being
created by the same creator.

Both "soul" and "sun" are given. Nevertheless, the continued existence of the human soul, so long as it is
embodied, is dependent upon the continued existence of the
sun. As recipients of the light and warmth of the sun whose
existence is not dependent on ours and upon whose existence
our very lives depend, we are reminded not only that we are
part of the natural order but that the rest of the created
order sustains us every moment that we live.

Edwards' juxtaposition of "soul" and "sun" is theocentric. Though Edwards stresses the special relationship
between divine being and human being as distinguished from
the rest of the visible creation in most of his written
work, he does not confuse human specialness with centrality.
In addition, the specialness of the divine/human relationship produces a human sensitivity to the rest of nature,
rather than a breach between the human creature and the rest
of the created order.

Although Edwards uses simile ("The Son is *as* the brightness and glory "), he also reduces distance between image
and its interpretation to a minimum by making the metaphorical connection more direct. The Father "is" the substance.
Similarly the Holy Ghost "is" the action. The Spirit "is"
the emanation. This reduction of distance in the first
paragraph has the effect of giving "represent," as it occurs
in the second paragraph, the same closeness. The rainbow
"presents again" the Spirit rather than standing in its
place as a substitute. The sun and the soul are fit images
of the trinity not because they can stand in its place,
therefore placing the trinity at one remove, but because

they repeat or present again the dynamic structure of the
trinity and therefore bring it closer. Edwards concludes by
saying that he believes that the whole visible creation was
made for the express purpose of typifying and representing
spiritual things and that he considers this belief to be a
divine truth based on scriptural revelation.

"Represent" as he uses it here means "present again."
The relationship between the visible creation and its
creator is direct because the structure of the visible
creation as a whole shadows forth the structure of divine
consciousness. The process of representing distinguished as
activity, is the operation of the Holy Spirit as subject to
divine wisdom. In the Spirit's association with creation it
is the office of the Holy Spirit "to quicken, enliven, and
beautify all things."[22] The process is an expression of
divine self-love. The Spirit is "an infinitely sweet energy
which we call delight."[23] The results of the process, as
distinguished from the process itself, are objects of divine
love as well. The created order is the place where the Holy
Spirit continues to dwell. The Holy Spirit continues to
operate by bestowing its blessings of common and special
grace. Since "the blessing of the Holy Spirit is Himself,
communication of Himself,"[24] divine love for the world in
general and the particular creature (the results of the process) is an expression of divine self-love (the process
itself). The Holy Spirit as the love between the first and
second persons of the trinity is also the love of both for
the world. Indeed it is this quality that merits glory for
the Spirit equal with that of the other two persons.
Edwards states, "But there is equal glory due to the Holy
Ghost, for He is that love of the Father and the Son to the
world."[25] As divine communication, divine self-love
expresses itself through the act of creation and includes

love for the resulting created order. All that is, in this context of divine interaction, is a communication of divine being that is comprehended in the divine being. It is, therefore, the realm of grace.

Edwards most frequently characterizes the first person of the trinity as *being*, of which the Son and the Holy Spirit are self-communications as divine wisdom and divine love. Though being, understanding, and willing are distinguishable from one another as "persons" in Edwards' thought, they form a unity as well. For deity to be is for deity to know and will. Wisdom and love are constitutive of being; hence, through knowing and willing, being communicates itself. Since being is all there is, being knows and wills itself. This internal, triune communication of being overflows *ad extra* as divine creativity. Edwards' most frequently used metaphor for this overflow as divine self-communication is the fountain. Although this image occurs throughout his works, Edwards develops it as a dominating metaphor, elaborated in detail, specifically in the *Dissertation concerning the End for which God Created the World*.

This posthumously published treatise is a working out of the specific implications of Edwards' conception of the trinity concerning the meaning of God's creativity. Edwards' basic thesis is that the ultimate end for which God created the world is the glory of God. He begins with a discussion of the various meanings for the word "end." He proceeds by introducing the thesis that God created the world as an expression of self-glorification and defending it on the basis of what reason alone tells us. He continues to defend his thesis on the basis of a thorough examination and interpretation of what revelation communicates in scripture. He concludes with a magnificent vision of the over-

flowing of divine being *ad extra*, emanating glory in which
the saints participate in their ever-increasing union with
God by returning God's love in the form of praise. We are
left with the image of God as a fecund, recycling fountain
of water or light, ever enlarging itself by means of the
emanation and remanation of itself throughout eternity:

> The emanation or communication of the divine
> fulness, consisting in the knowledge of God, and
> joy in God, has relation indeed both to God and to
> the creature: but it has relation to God as its
> fountain, as it is an emanation from God; and as
> the communication itself, or thing communicated, is
> something divine, something of God, something of
> his internal fulness, as the water in the stream is
> something of the fountain, and as the beams of the
> sun, are something of the sun. And again, they
> have relation to God, as they have respect to him
> as their object, for the knowledge communicated is
> the knowledge of God; and so God is the object of
> the knowledge, and the love communicated is the
> love of God; so God is the object of that love, and
> the happiness communicated is joy in God; and so he
> is the object of the joy communicated. In the
> creature's knowing, esteeming, loving, rejoicing
> in, and praising God, the glory of God is both
> exhibited and acknowledged; his fulness is received
> and returned. Here is both an *emanation* and
> *remanation*. The refulgence shines upon and into
> the creature, and is reflected back to the lumi-
> nary. The beams of glory come from God, and are
> something of God, and are refunded back again to
> their original. So that the whole is *of* God,
> and *in* God, and *to* God, and God is the beginning,
> middle and end in this affair.[26]

The significance of the fountain is two-fold regarding
nature's role in divine self-communication. Edwards makes
explicit what creation is with reference both to the creator
and the creature. Creation, whether distinguished in terms
of act or consequence, is the ongoing communication of the
divine being *ad extra*, which is itself the glory of God.
Further significance lies in Edwards' use of related imagery for the creator, the creation in general, and the

human creature in particular, much of which is taken
directly from the natural order.

Edwards speaks of a natural inclination to self-
communication as God's motive for having created the world:

> [T]he disposition to communicate himself, or dif-
> fuse his own FULNESS, which we must conceive of as
> being originally in God as a perfection of his
> nature, was what moved him to create the world
> . . . . But the diffusive disposition that
> excited God to give creatures existence, was rather
> a communicative disposition in general, or a dispo-
> sition in the fulness of the divinity to flow out
> and diffuse itself . . . . Therefore, to speak
> more strictly according to the truth, we may
> suppose, *that a disposition in God, as an original
> property of his nature,to an emanation of his own
> infinite fulness, was what excited him to create
> the world; and so that the emanation itself was
> aimed at by him as a last end of creation.* [27]

He links diffusion, flowing, and emanation with communication as a definitive aspect of God's creativity. It
is essential to what it means to be God that God communicate
as God the creator.

The consequences of God's creativity represent God, are
images of their creator, and as such, yield knowledge of
divine being.[28] That God can be known through God's works
implies knowers. Though God's ultimate end in creating the
world is God's own glory, this includes rather than excludes
divine communication to the human creature. Properly
speaking, as created beings human creatures are included in
and the consequences of the divine overflow. As creatures
who seek union with God and who "remanate" back the glory of
God, human beings become participants in God's self-
enjoyment and, as such, sharers in God's ultimate end in
creation. Edwards thus distinguishes human being, defined
as capable of direct communication with the creator, from
the rest of visible creation.

It is the law of our species both according to "nature

and reason" and according to revelation that we seek to know
God's will through word and work and comply with it.   It is
this law, distinguishing us from both the creator and the
rest of creation, that defines our humanity and allows our
participation in divinity.[29]   Indeed, it is the fulfillment
of this law that makes us participants in the glory of God.
He states, "the manifestation of God's glory to created
understandings, and their seeing it and knowing it, is not
distinct from an emanation or communication of God's
fulness, but clearly implied in it . . . .   And thus we see
how, not only the creature's seeing and knowing God's
excellence, but also supremely esteeming and loving him,
belongs to the communication of God's fulness."[30]

Edwards goes on to identify God's external communication
through the creation of the world with the Holy Spirit or
God's internal self-communication between the first and
second persons of the Trinity.   He states, "God's external
glory is only the emanation of his internal glory."[31]
Divine creativity is divine *self*-communication.   Since
creation as both act and consequence, manifests or exter-
nalizes the divine glory, the manifestation of glory and the
human responses of seeing it, knowing it, esteeming God
supremely, and loving God are all genuine communications of
God's fullness.   In short, as consequences of God's inclination to communication through self-knowledge and self-love,
human creatures participate in and indeed augment divine
glory by knowing and loving God.   The human share in the
glory of God as both communication and communicant is to
glorify God.

The world, also a communication of divine creativity, is
in some sense a condition for the glory of God.   It is a
necessary condition for the human glorification of God.   We
do not know and love God apart from God's external com-

munication. Since human being is a part of the world and
since the human glorification of God further contributes to
the divine glory, Edwards is implying that the world is also
a condition for God's own self-glorification. The world is
at the very least the chosen, if not necessary, fulfillment
of a divine disposition to communicate itself. In any case,
the creation of the world is a means to an end -- a means
that   actually   accomplishes   now   and   will   continue   to
accomplish its end.   This makes the world of inestimable
worth:

> The glory of God, in being the result and con-
> sequence of . . . works of providence . . . is in
> fact the consequence of creation . . . . So that
> it is apparent that the glory of God is a thing
> that is actually the result and consequence of
> the creation of the world . . . . it [the glory
> of God] is what God seeks as good, valuable and
> excellent in itself . . . . God's glory there-
> fore, must be a desirable, valuable consequence of
> the work of creation. Yea, it is expressly spoken
> of in Psalm civ.3 . . . as an effect, on account
> of which God rejoices and takes pleasure in the
> works of creation.[32]

It is precisely because the world as a work of God is a
means by which God's glory is accomplished, or said another
way, it is because nature is divine communication, that
metaphors for the deity such as "sun" and "fountain" are of
much more than ornamental value.   These metaphors convey
truth from Edwards' perspective.

The kinds of images Edwards chooses indicate that it is
characteristic of Edwards' imagery that it maintains or preserves distinctions within an overall unity. Just as the
metaphor of the sun preserves and reflects both the distinctions among the three persons of the trinity and the unity
formed by their interrelations, so the metaphor of the fountain captures the creator-creating/creation-created distinction while preserving the basic unity of all being. This is

true not only of the dominating metaphor of the fountain but
of the less frequently used images Edwards associates with
the fountain.   There are many different images occurring
throughout the essay, natural images drawn from the Bible
(the corn of wheat), philosophical images (the agent), and
mechanical images (the watch).   In particular the images of
the chariot, the tree, and the human body indicate a
reciprocity between mechanism and organism, on the one hand,
and personalism, on the other hand.

For Edwards God is always creating the universe
ex nihilo and the end of creation is eschatologically conditioned.   Within this context he identifies *communication*
and *emanation* as definitive of creation. We tend to
restrict *communications* to the verbal realm and tie it
almost exclusively to human persons as agents, e.g., individual human beings' communicating by speaking to one
another.   We also tend to associate *emanation* with organic
phenomena (e.g., odors emanating from decaying food) and
with physical or mechanical phenomena (e.g., light emanating
from a lightbulb).   This restriction of categories is alien
to Edwards' thought because *communication* and *emanation* have
in common a diffusion or impartation of being.   Creation as
communication and emanation includes agential and personal
activity, on the one hand, and organic and mechanical activity, on the other hand.

Divine being creatively communicates itself as the
charioteer for whom the universe is a chariot.[33]   That same
being is also the roots and the life-giving sap of the universe viewed as a tree, an image of God's disposition to
diffuse being.[34]   In addition, communicating being is the
vital organs of the universe viewed as a cosmic human
body.[35]   Edwards explicitly connects the tree and body imagery with the fountain metaphor, and this connection is

also implicit in the chariot imagery, in the circular movement common to both wheel and fountain.

The focus in Edwards' thought is upon divine being
itself, understood as all-inclusive, all-comprehending.
Humankind is here to reverberate along with the rest of
creation the glory of God. While human consciousness allows
human being a special place in creation, the images associated with that specialness are not those of domination.
Organism and mechanism interact with personalism to call
into question exclusively anthropomorphic views of God and
anthropocentric views of the universe, on the one hand, and
the impersonalistic views of human existence in the universe, on the other hand.

Divine creativity portrayed in organic, mechanistic, and
personalistic imagery, is both the origin and the destiny of
the universe. The universe, whether viewed as grand machine
or organic whole, has no existence apart from its origin and
destiny:

> The first Being, the eternal and infinite
> Being, is in effect, BEING IN GENERAL: and compre-
> hends universal existence . . . . God in his
> benevolence to his creatures, cannot have his heart
> enlarged in such a manner as to take in beings that
> he finds, who are originally out of himself,
> distinct and independent. But he from his good-
> ness, as it were enlarges himself in a more
> excellent and divine manner. This is by com-
> municating and diffusing himself; and so instead
> of finding, making objects of his benevolence; not
> by taking into himself what he finds distinct from
> himself, and so partaking of their good, and being
> happy in them, but by flowing forth, and
> expressing himself in them, and making them to par-
> take of him, and rejoicing in himself expressed in
> them, and communicated to them.[36]

Here Edwards collapses the distance between creator and
creation altogether. "Making," rather than an act of fabri-
cation, takes on overtones of fecundity and nurture as the

"objects of benevolence" emerge from within the divine being as it enlarges itself. Furthermore, origin and destiny become unified as well:

> God aims at that which the motion or progression
> which he causes, aims at, or tends to. If there be
> many things supposed to be so made and appointed
> that by a constant and eternal motion, they all
> tend to a certain centre; then it appears that he
> who made them, and is the cause of their motion,
> aimed at that centre, that term of their motion, to
> which they eternally tend, and are eternally, as it
> were, striving after. And if God be this centre,
> then God aimed at himself. And herein it appears,
> that as he is the first author of their being
> and motion, so he is the last end, the final term,
> to which is their ultimate tendency and aim.[37]

Divine creativity is the process by which divine being enlarges itself by means of communicating its own fullness either directly through created consciousness or indirectly through the rest of the created order. Self-communication characteristic of the trinity in itself is identical with its overflow expressed through creativity. God's creative activity is God's self-communication. This communication is chiefly an act of love guided by wisdom that is characterized by a fecundity that nurtures its self-impartations. Images of organism, mechanism, and personalism interact to convey the power, order, and faithfulness of divine being and the intimacy of the relationship between creator and creation.

CHAPTER THREE

BEING'S SPECIAL COMMUNICATION

The human creature requires a special work of divine
self-communication in order to become a saint who
"remanates" the glory of God. This special work involves
two "moments" of divine self-communication: revelation and
the infusion of grace, divine love itself, into the human
heart. Although God's created works represent images of God
as their author, their full significance is not self-evident
apart from God's revelation. Scripture witnesses to the
incarnation of Jesus Christ, his crucifixion, and resurrection; it further reveals that nature itself is the language
of God. The condition for human acceptance of scripture as
authoritative is the indwelling of the Holy spirit or consent in human life. Edwards' religious anthropology
requires later, detailed discussion in its own right. The
issue at hand is an examination of divine communication in
relation to revelation and consent.

Edwards' conception of communication is that it is the
process by which being in general, as the triune principle
of all that is, imparts its fullness or glory through particularity. This impartation finds direct expression in the
creation of finite, embodied consciousness, and indirect
expression in the finite order. Finite consciousness, conditioned by sin, requires special communication, modelled on
conversation and manifested in scripture, in short, an
authoritative revelation.

Scripture reveals that divine communication through the
diffusion of being is supremely an act of love guided by

wisdom. This on-going act is eschatologically intended.
Being in general communicates itself through particularity
by pre-ordained agreement for the purpose of redemption.
Creation is thus the starting point for and first act of the
drama of redemption. Though being is absolute in relation
to nothing and perfect in its goodness, the fulfillment of
its glory remains to be accomplished. Fulfillment is its
destiny, and communication through time and space is its
mode of accomplishment. Divine consent relates all parts to
a greater whole. It is both the chief characteristic of
perfection and the means by which perfection is preserved
and extended. Divine consent, particularly as it is
experienced in human life, is the syntax for which history
is the grammar and nature the vocabulary.

Revelation

In his writings on revelation Edwards distinguishes between divine work and divine word, states why there is a
need for such a distinction, and further relates the two to
one another.[1] God's word, by which Edwards means specifically scripture, is a divine work distinguished from other
divine works by its special purpose. Divine work and word
are not disjunctive. Edwards as frequently compares scripture as a work with other divine works as he distinguishes
scripture as word having special primacy in contrast to
divine works in general. Scripture, creation, providence,
the natural order, and the human frame all fall under the
general category of "work," and they have in common that
they are unified systems pervaded by mystery.[2]

The difference between scripture and the natural order
is in part one of degree. Both communicate the divine will
in accordance with divine wisdom; however, scripture communicates it more directly whereas the natural order com-

municates it by inference and serves purposes other than communication alone. The model for scriptural communication is conversation, an exchange between minds.[3] Edwards connects conversation with God's moral government of human beings as distinct from God's "general government of providential disposal."[4] The latter does not require the conscious participation and cooperation of the human creature in the way that the former does. For example, gravity does not require human consent in order to be operative. Relations among human beings and between human beings and God require verbal exchange as is implied by the fact that intelligence and morality, understanding and will, are involved.

Edwards connects human intelligence and morality with the divine word in both a positive way and a negative one. Stated positively, part of what it means to be human is to be intelligent, social, and able to communicate verbally with the author of human being through scripture and prayer. Scripture and prayer interact as a running dialogue with divine being, a dialogue that reflects friendship. Revelation is God's part of a conversation among friends. Scripture is one of the greatest of God's works for human beings. It is central to all other works. There is a movement from very general divine activity to that activity most especially reserved for human/divine relationships that draws its intimacy from the image of friendship.[5]

There is also a negative reason for the necessity of God's revelation through scripture. God's word takes its particular form as scripture and as such has its peculiar authority because of human sin. Human reason by itself is insufficient for determining true human happiness, characterized primarily by Edwards throughout his works in terms of human delight in right relationship with or consent to

divine being. This insufficiency arises as a loss of previously constitutive capacities rather than a positive contamination of still-existing human faculties. Human
understanding and will have lost the governing capacity that
properly relates them to one another, as the soul to the
body, and orients the whole human being properly to divine
being.[6] Revelation, defined as an authoritative scripture,
becomes a necessary replacement for what is lost due to the
insufficiency of reason. Edwards describes scripture as a
testimony or witness given to compensate a lack of an organ
of sense or a faculty. He constructs the following hypo-
thetical situation:

> We could not conceive of the things of *sense*, if
> we had never had these external senses. And, if we
> had only some of these senses, and not others; as
> for instance, if we had only a sense of feeling,
> without the senses of seeing and hearing, how
> mysterious would a declaration of things of these
> last senses be! Or, if we had feeling and hearing,
> but had been born without eyes or optic nerves, the
> things of light even when declared to us, would
> many of them be involved in mystery, and would
> appear exceedingly strange to us.
>   Thus persons without the sense of seeing but
> who had the other senses, might be informed by all
> about them, that they can perceive things at a
> distance, and perceive as plainly, and in some
> respects more plainly, than by touching them; yea,
> that they could perceive things at so great a
> distance, that it would take up to many ages to
> travel to them. They might be informed of many
> things concerning colours, that would be all per-
> fectly incomprehensible, and yet might be believed;
> and it could not be said that nothing at all is
> proposed to their belief, because they have no idea
> of colour . . . .
>   . . . These, and many other things would be
> attended with unsearchable mystery to them, con-
> cerning objects of sight; and concerning which,
> they could never fully see how they can be recon-
> ciled to reason; at least, not without very long,
> particular, gradual, and elaborate instruction; and
> which, after all, they would not comprehend so as

clearly to see how the ideas connected in these
propositions do agree. -- And yet I suppose, in
such a case, the most rational persons, would give
full credit to the things that they know not by
reason, but only the revelation of the word of
those that see. I suppose, a person born blind in
the manner described, would nevertheless give full
credit to the united testimony of the seeing world,
in things which they said about light and colours,
and would entirely rest on their testimony.[7]

I have cited such a long passage because the passage itself
reflects how Edwards' mind characteristically works. In his
miscellanies, his sermons, and his formal, theological
treatises, he stresses the role played by the senses in
knowledge of God. In addition he typically constructs
experiments in thought that deal with the deprivation of one
or more sense whether he is discussing scientific knowledge
or religious knowledge. He further refuses to set reason
and revelation in opposition to one another.

In this thought experiment reason is analogous to the
sense of touch. The blind who know primarily by means of
touch do not give up their sense of touch just because they
have the testimony of those who see. Nor do they continue
to rely solely upon a sense of touch, and disregard the
testimony. The knowledge attained through touch is subordinated to the testimony of the sighted, and certainly the
testimony is authoritative, should the two come into irre-
concilable conflict. Edwards' point is that once the blind
have accepted the insufficiency of touch alone, it is incon-
sistent to turn around and make touch authoritative where
touch and testimony conflict. For revelation to be authoritative implies by definition that reason alone is not sufficient.

The relationship between human reason and divine
revelation as manifested by scripture parallels in some
respects the relationship between divine work in general and

divine word as a species thereof. Edwards refers to revelation as a lens that allows the eye of reason to see both
microscopically and telescopically what it might otherwise
miss.[8] He compares the relationship between God as revealer
by means of scripture and the community as recipient of
God's word to that of head with the rest of the body. His
primary point is that God's word informs us of the organic
unity in which society stands in relation to its governor.
Like the thought experiment cited at length these images of
lens and body convey distinction without disjunction.
Edwards' main emphasis is upon unity and continuity.

Edwards' main purpose is not to denigrate human reason,
rather he seeks to demonstrate what human happiness is and
how best to achieve it. He asks: what do we need to know
to be happy? He answers, "1st. The religion of nature or
the religion proper and needful, considering the state and
relations we stand in as creatures. 2d. The religion of a
sinner, or the religion and duties proper and necessary for
us, considering our states as depraved and guilty creatures,
having incurred the displeasure of our Creator."[9] Reason
apart from revelation through God's word is insufficient to
attain the knowledge necessary to human happiness in either
case.

Edwards is quite clear that the insufficiency of reason
alone is not due to an imperfection in the laws of nature
in themselves which he considers to be perfect as a work of
God just as God's word is a work of God; rather it is human
imperfection in relying solely on reason conditioned by sin
that prevents human happiness. As he succinctly puts it,
"What, according to the nature of things, is fittest and
best, may be most perfect; and yet our natural knowledge of
this, may be most imperfect."[10] The redemption of sinners
cannot be circumvented, and therefore, reason alone is not

sufficient even to yield full knowledge of the relation in which we stand as creatures. In like fashion divine activity in general is not fully apprehensible by human beings apart from revelation through the divine word.

Human reason, conditioned by sin, cannot by its own exertion recognize divine communication; therefore, human being cannot play its proper role in the divine destiny apart from redemption. What allows human participation in the divine destiny is the transformation of human life itself. Divine being effects this participation by communicating its own love to the human creature. Human being becomes an embodiment of divine love and thereby the highest visible expression of divine self-communication. *Consent* is Edwards' name for love, and it is to consent that we now turn.

Consent

Edwards' concept of *consent* as the means by which being communicates itself is inextricably connected to his concept of being, for *consent* is how being is proportion or relation in a philosophical sense for Edwards. Being sustains itself and generates the rest of reality by consenting to itself. Stated theologically, consent is divine self-love. Edwards wrote in "The Mind:"

> We shall be in danger, when we meditate on this love of God to himself as being the thing wherein his infinite excellence and loveliness consist, of some alloy of the sweetness of our view, by its appearing with something of the aspect and cast of what we call self-love. But we are to consider that this love includes in it, or rather is the same as, a love to everything, as they are all communications of himself. So that we are to conceive of the divine excellence as the infinite general love, that reaches all proportionally, with perfect purity and sweetness; yea, it includes the true love of all creatures, for that is his Spirit or, which is the same thing, his love. And if we take

> notice when we are in the best frames, meditating
> on divine excellence, our idea of that tranquility
> and peace which seems to be overspread and cast
> abroad upon the whole earth and universe naturally
> dissolves itself into the idea of a general love
> and delight everywhere diffused.[11]

Consent, then, in its supreme instance is divine activity.
It further involves a human response in kind. This response
in kind is distinguishable simultaneously as a recognition
of divine consent by human beings and a repetition of divine
consent in human life.

Divine consent is the ultimate form of resistance to
annihilation or the absoluteness of being in relation to
nothing. As divine love guided by divine wisdom, consent is
the anti-type for which gravity is the type.[12] The laws of
gravity that operate to hold everything together in the
natural order shadow forth the truth that divine consent
rules absolutely by providing the unity of all that is,
material and spiritual, as a single reality. Consent operates at all levels of being and occurs in the form of structural agreement, as the primary relationship between the
shadows or images of being and being itself. Divine communication through work and word, whether words of nature,
scriptural word, or Word become flesh manifests divine consent. Divine consent is the essence of all beauty which
consists in mutual consent of one thing with another or
with divine being itself.

Consent integrates divine understanding with divine
will. It provides the trinity with its dynamic internal
unity; that is, the three persons consent to their economic
ordering. Consent also characterizes divine creativity as
determined by the covenant of redemption. The first person
of the trinity consents to create the world to provide a
companion for the second person; Christ, the second person,
consents in turn to undergo incarnation. Indeed, the Word

become flesh or the Incarnation is what allows God to love
the regenerate as the regenerate love God and one another,
namely with passion.[13]   Consent, therefore, characterizes
the trinitarian overflow that precipitates this particular
creation with its peculiar destiny.

Edwards develops his conception of consent and its role
in the divine drama as that is played out in human life in
The Nature of True Virtue.   True virtue is being's consent
to being.   Consent to being in general is indwelling universal love that integrates the faculties and renders being
truly excellent.   Consent binds human beings to divine
being, to one another, and to the cosmos.

In Edwards' vocabulary the concept *being* is laden with
value.   Indeed it is the nature of being to consent.   In
"The Mind" he writes, "Disagreement or contrariety to being
is evidently an approach to nothing, or a degree of nothing
. . . and the greatest and only evil; and entity is the
greatest and only good.   And by how much more perfect entity
is, that is without mixture of 'nothing' by so much more the
excellency."[14]   Edwards then proceeds to define "being" as
proportion and "excellency" as "the consent of being to
being, or being's consent to entity.   The more the consent
is, and the more extensive, the greater the excellency."[15]
His point is that the extent to which being consents is the
extent to which it persists.   Consent is the ultimate mode
of resistance to annihilation or nothingness.

God is being which most supremely resists annihilation
-- being without admixture of "nothing."   As the supreme
"instance" of resistance to annihilation, God is
distinguishable as a being.   In addition, whatever else is,
is by virtue of the divine consent.   Whatever is, shares to
some degree the resistance to annihilation that characterizes God as supreme being.   This resistance itself *is*

divine consent. God is, then, being in general. God is the
most perfect being and the degree of resistance present in
all other being.   God is both a being and the universal
system of being.

For human being, to consent to being in general is to
consent with divine self-consent. True virtue consists in
such consent and is the conscious participation of human
being in the divine life. Human consent to being in general
not only enlarges the human heart, but as the presence of
the divine life in human life, human consent enlarges,
augments, or extends divine glory itself. As Norman Fiering
points out, true human virtue requires nothing less from a
human being than divine holiness.[16]

Divine Consent as Human Response

In the opening chapter of *The Nature of True Virtue*
Edwards describes true virtue as moral beauty or excellency.
"Beauty" and "excellency" signal immediately that virtue
requires some mode of perception.[17] "Moral" refers specifically to the qualities, exercises, and actions of the will,
disposition, or heart that are attended with worthiness of
praise or blame. To ask what the nature of true virtue is,
is to ask: What "renders any habit, disposition, or exercise of the heart truly beautiful."[18]

Edwards' question is two-fold in its implications and in
its answer. That true virtue is moral beauty implies that
virtue requires an integration of the human faculties that
is exercised as a habit of being or way of life. This habit
of being involves apprehension as well as activity and is
itself apprehensible by others.

Edwards' own answer is that true virtue is consent to
being in general. Consent in its first instance is good
will directed toward being in general and, in its second

instance, delight in response to benevolent being.   In
short, consent is all-comprehending love, visibly expressed
through particular manifestations.   The particular manifestations further generate love by an attraction that presupposes the apprehension of spiritual beauty.

Benevolence toward Being in General
    True moral beauty consists first and most essentially in
benevolence to being in general.   It is "that consent,
propensity, and union of heart to being in general, which is
immediately exercised in general good will."[19]   It is a
"disposition to love being in general."[20]

    By "being in general" Edwards here means, first of all,
all being as opposed to any particular being and, secondly,
intelligent being.   Most importantly he means being
irrespective of its particularity, its beauty or what it can
give the lover in return -- what he calls "being simply
considered."[21]   Benevolence to being in general is willing
the highest good for all intelligent beings without
reference to particularity, beauty, or ability to respond
in kind.

    The supreme instance of benevolence to being in general
is divine being whose benevolence or goodness is prior not
only to the beauty and particularity of other being, but
also to the existence of each and all other beings.   Divine
good will is the foundation for both the beauty and the
existence of all being, actual and possible.

    That there should be something rather than nothing pre-
supposes divine love that, for the truly virtuous, elicits a
response in kind, regardless of the particular manifestations of being.   Being, simply considered, and the love that
motivates its particular expressions are inseparable.   This
inseparability invests all its manifestations with worth

without considering the different qualities that adhere in
any given manifestation.

Benevolence toward being in general means that the
lover, human or divine, will seek the good of every individual "unless it be conceived as not consistent with the
highest good of being in general."[22] The "highest good of
being in general" is nothing less than the divine good
itself and should not be confused with the utilitarian formula of the greatest good for the greatest number where each
individual human being counts as one.

Edwards distinguishes among individual beings in terms
of their degree or share of existence. He states that the
degree of existence, "other things being equal," determines
the share of the affections of the lover directed toward
particular being.[23] What he means by "degree of existence"
is that one being may have more existence, that is, be
"further away from nothing"[24] than another being. The
example he gives is the contrast between the degree of
existence of an archangel and the degree of existence of a
worm. The being who has the greatest share of existence for
Edwards is, of course, God. God, one of a kind, as the
source, preserver, and end of all being, has the greatest
degree of existence "in comparison to which the sum of all
other beings is as nothing."[25] Therefore, God as the
object of benevolence deserves the greatest share of benevolence.

Edwards' distinction, "degree of existence," has several
implications for ethical theory. First of all, each individual being that helps to comprise being in general does
not count equally, as God, insofar as God is a being, counts
more than the rest of being. Secondly, his distinction,
"degree of existence," according to the examples he gives is
one of species. An archangel belongs to the species

archangel and a worm belongs to a different class altogether. The implication is that each human being, by virtue
of belonging to the human species, is equal in terms of
degree of existence. While Edwards is at this point
operating on the basis of a hierarchy of being, it is not a
hierarchy within the human species. So far the only
distinction he has made that can be construed as relevant to
differences among individual human beings is the distinction
between individual beings whose highest good is consistent
with being in general and those individual beings whose good
is conceived as not consistent with the highest good of
being in general.

So far Edwards has said that true virtue or moral beauty
is love of a specific kind, namely, good will, that has as
its object being in general, that is, being without respect
to individual qualities but with respect to degree of share
of existence.

Consent to Consenting Being

Edwards' reference to "other things being equal" refers
to the distinctions he proceeds to make with respect to
quality of beings and the kinds of responses on the part of
the lover that pertain to individual beings. Edwards
distinguishes within the category of love three different
but related affections. They are benevolence, complacence,
and gratitude. Benevolence is that affection by which the
lover seeks or wills the highest good of the beloved.
Complacence is the delight or joy the lover takes in the
particular beloved. It is the aesthetic dynamic of love.
Gratitude, the lover's thankfulness to the beloved, presupposes the beloved's benevolence to the lover. Complacence
and gratitude, in contrast to benevolence, share the premise
of a quality peculiar to the beloved that attracts the

lover. For Edwards this quality is benevolence itself. The
beloved's love for being in general renders the beloved
beautiful. Love renders one being beautiful to another.
This beauty is the secondary ground or object of true
virtue.[26]

One who is truly virtuous loves virtue in others. The
benevolence of a particular beloved further attracts the
lover. Consent to a particular consenting being is a
further consequence of consent in its first instance.
(Divine consent to particular consenting beings for their
benevolence subtly implies election.) In addition, consent
to consenting being augments the lover, enlarges the lover's
being, and this in turn increases consent itself. This
second instance of consent, this time to a particular being,
not only expresses a greater degree of benevolence on the
part of the lover, but is an expression of complacence or
delight in and gratitude toward the beloved as well.[27]

The benevolence of the beloved as the secondary ground
or object of virtue has several implications. Consent to
consenting being is an extension of quality whereby being
itself is augmented. Being further expands by attraction.
Love to benevolent being is love to particular being for its
benevolence. Within the context of benevolence toward being
in general Edwards is placing great value on particular
being and particular love as well.

The relationship between willing the good of being in
general, on the one hand, and further willing the good of
benevolent being in particular, enjoying benevolent being,
and appreciating or feeling gratitude toward benevolent
being, on the other hand, is complex. The benevolence of a
being as the secondary ground or object of true virtue has
as its condition benevolence to all being in general. This
distinction is a logical distinction rather than a temporal

BEING'S SPECIAL COMMUNICATION   71

one. Edwards is saying that when one loves or is truly virtuous, this love has an internal dynamic or logic with
reference to its objects and its affections for its objects.
If one truly wills the good of being in general, she or he
will necessarily attract and be attracted to other benevolent being for its benevolence to being in general; the
attraction presupposes benevolence to being in general on
the part of one who is attracted.

Edwards goes on to make further distinctions. Though
the benevolence of the beloved is the secondary object of
truly virtuous benevolence, it is the primary ground or
object of complacence and gratitude.[28] The beloved's benevolence as the object of consent is the lover's acceptance of
or consent to consent. Consent in its secondary instance
implies reciprocity and recognition. A benevolent being's
benevolence toward us is the ground of our joy, our value,
and the kindness we receive. While true love for Edwards
cannot be based first or solely on what the beloved does or
feels for us, the beloved's benevolence to being in general
validates both the lover's love and the lover. Further, the
lover's responses of delight and gratitude to benevolent
being are appropriate and valid as well. As long as the
context for love of benevolent being is love of being in
general, Edwards affirms delight and gratitude in particular
love. Indeed, for Edwards benevolence in the object of consent is the primary ground for all spiritual beauty.

Edwards distinguishes one benevolent being from another
in relation to the degree of being and the degree of benevolence. Two beings, each of whom has an equal share of both
existence and benevolence, are better than either alone;
however, one being can have a greater share of both
existence and benevolence than several beings taken
together.[29] Edwards is making the same move he made pre-

viously in respect to degrees of existence alone. God, of
course, has the greatest share of both existence and benevolence.

This move has different implications for what goes on
within any species of existence, however. For example, while
all members of the human species who exist at any given time
can be said to have an equal share of existence in itself,
all members are not equally benevolent. The less benevolence or consent to being in general one human being exercises, the more that human being stands in opposition to
being in general and deserves opposition rather than consent. In other words, the less consent, the more dissent.
Benevolent being as the secondary object of true virtue is
most importantly "the primary and most essential beauty of
everything that can justly be called by the name of
virtue."[30] Edwards distinguishes this primary beauty from
an inferior or secondary beauty or virtue, which he also
calls natural virtue and which he discusses at length in
subsequent chapters.

Edwards devotes the second chapter of *The Nature of True
Virtue* to distinguishing and relating true virtue as love to
created beings. True virtue as love for being in general
and as love for benevolent being in particular "most chiefly
consist in *love to God*, the Being of beings, infinitely the
greatest and best."[31]

Edwards' reference to "Being of beings" has at least two
senses. First God is a being among beings who, compared
with the rest of being in general, is the greatest and best
being. But God is also that by which all other being is.
God is thus being in general. In this particular text
Edwards goes on to say that God is that "from whom all is
perfectly derived, and through whom and to whom is all being
and all perfection; and whose being and beauty are, as it

were, the sum and comprehension of all existence and
excellence . . . ."[32]   God not only heads the universal
system of existence but includes it.   Divine consent provides the pattern for both human love for created beings and
human love for the divine being.

> The most proper evidence of love to a created
> being arising from that temper of mind wherein con-
> sists a supreme propensity of heart to God, seems
> to be the agreeableness of the kind and degree of
> our love to God's end in our creation, and in the
> creation of all things, and the coincidence of the
> exercise of our love, in their manner, order, and
> measure, with the manner in which God himself exer-
> cises love to the creature in the creation and
> government of the world, and the way in which God,
> as the first cause and supreme disposer of all
> things, has respect to the creature's happiness
> in subordination to himself as his own supreme
> end.[33]

In short, human consent is love first and foremost for God
and subordinately for any other and all other being.   This
love includes love for particular beings based on their particular beauty so long as that beauty is itself true virtue.

Anything less than an all-comprehending love of this
precise nature is less than true virtue.   In one way or
another it places the created system above God.   Edwards
goes on to distinguish private affections from true virtue
and private systems from the universal system of being.   A
private system is a part or circle of existence less than
the universal system of being.   Because the interests of the
object of a private affection, whether the object be a particular person or a private system, inevitably compete with
the highest good of the universal system of being, the owner
of the private affection ends up in a position contrary to
being in general.[34]

Benevolence to being in general is not simply a question
of numbers.   One human individual whose love consists

chiefly in love for God can call the interests of private
systems, however large in numbers they may be, into question
as violating the highest good. Genuine consent may require
either divine or human dissent to particular portions of
being on the basis of their dissent to being in general.
Furthermore, among created beings, consent is co-present
with varying degrees of dissent or contrariety to being in
any given human being.

True virtue or consent is, thus, socially binding among
human beings as well as binding between any given created
being and the supreme being. Human beings who consent to
being in general and benevolent being in particular by definition consent to one another.

Several questions remain. What is the source of private
affections and, more precisely, what are they? How do they
stand in relation to true virtue?

Apprehending Spiritual Beauty

Edwards distinguishes love to benevolent being as itself
a beauty that is "the primary and most essential beauty of
everything that can justly be called by the name of true
virtue." He adds, "I say 'the primary and most essential
beauty' because there is a secondary and inferiour sort of
beauty' which I shall take notice of afterwards."[35] Having
presented his vision of the nature of true virtue, Edwards
proceeds to examine the "secondary and inferiour sort of
beauty" by both contrasting it with primary beauty and
relating it to primary beauty.

Secondary beauty is the consent or agreement perceived
by the human mind in things and among things in the visible
creation. It is also the consent of the mind to the mutual
consents it perceives.[36] Its range includes aesthetic
appreciation of the visible order, secular or humanistic

justice and politics, self-love or self-consent, conscience or the moral sense, and human instincts such as pity. This beauty is secondary to true virtue or primary beauty in two senses of the word "secondary." Secondary beauty is secondary in a formal or metaphysical sense. That is, consent or agreement in things, among things, and to things in the visible creation bears the image of primary beauty.[37]

Secondary beauty is also secondary in that it is "inferiour" to primary beauty. There is a discontinuity between the two. What all secondary beauty has in common in addition to bearing the image of primary beauty is that, in the absence of primary beauty, its consent is a private affection directed toward a private system. It is an affection whose object is a particular person, quality, or system independent of or not subordinated to the universal system of being. Secondary beauty ungoverned by primary beauty is dissent to being in general. It is to some degree an approach to nothingness and therefore in opposition to or at enmity with being.

It is very important to recognize that Edwards views both secondary beauty or consent and all the objects of secondary beauty or consent as part of the universal system of being. The mutual consents among things that render them beautiful, the secular world of arts, sciences, and politics, the human self, the good and evil that the moral sense senses, and the results effected by various human instincts are each part of being in general as are the affections for them.

The secondary beauty that goes by the name of virtue in the world is mistaken for true virtue for good reason. Private consent bears a positive resemblance to the consent that is directed toward being in general and benevolent being in particular, for it involves benevolence, complacence, and gratitude towards its object.[38]

Further confusion arises because the beauties or virtues of secondary beauty have a negative moral goodness in them. They can serve for those in whom they are operative to prevent additional moral evil; for example, pity prevents cruelty. The effects produced by secondary beauty are frequently the same effects that true virtue produces. The particular private affections characteristic of secondary beauty are of the same denomination as the particular affections characteristic of primary beauty; that is, pity, whether it is private pity or holy pity, is still pity.[39]

What distinguishes primary from secondary virtue is first the inclusiveness of the affection, the inclusiveness of the object of the affection, and the role played by inclusivity. The distinction lies further in the condition necessary for divine consent to be actualized in human existence.

What is absent in secondary beauty that is the chief distinguishing characteristic of true virtue is God. As Edwards puts it:

> The reason why men are so ready to take these private affections for true virtue, is the narrowness of their views; and above all, that they are so ready to leave the divine Being out of their view, and to neglect him in their consideration, or to regard him in their thoughts as though he did not properly belong to the system of real existence, but was a kind of shadowy, imaginary being. And though most men allow that there is a God, yet in their ordinary view of things, his being is not apt to come into the account, and to have the influence and effect of a real existence, as it is with other beings which they see, and are conversant with by their external senses. In their views of beauty and deformity, and in their inward sensations of displicence and approbation, it is not natural to them to view the Deity as part of the system, and as the head of it, in comparison of whom all other things are to be viewed with corresponding

impressions.[40]

It includes further any belief in God where God is not
apprehended as present in the universal system of existence.
The absence of God, more than simple atheism, is the denial
of God's immanence, the reality of God's existence present
in daily, ordinary life.

Edwards' emphasis on the presence of God in the universal system is crucial to his concept of true virtue as
beauty. The human apprehension of divine excellency depends
in part upon the senses. Edwards states:

> That form or quality is called beautiful, which
> appears in itself agreeable or comely, or the view
> of which is immediately pleasant to the mind . . .
> when a form or quality appears lovely, pleasing,
> and delightful in itself, then it is called beauti-
> ful; and this agreeableness or gratefulness of the
> idea is *beauty*. It is evident that the way we come
> by the idea of beauty is by immediate sensation of
> the gratefulness of the idea called beautiful; and
> not by finding out by argumentation any conse-
> quences, or other things with which it stands con-
> nected; any more than tasting the sweetness of
> honey, or perceiving the harmony of a tune, is by
> argumentation on connections and consequences. The
> manner of being affected with the immediate pres-
> ence of the beautiful idea, depends not on any
> reasonings about the idea after we have it, before
> we can find out whether it be beautiful or not; but
> on the frame of our minds, whereby they are so made
> that such an idea, as soon as we have it, is
> grateful or appears beautiful.[41]

The anatomy of a judgment of beauty or excellency is that
one come to it by way of an immediate sensation of the
"gratefulness" or gracefulness of the idea called beautiful.
Human beings sense beauty. This sense is immediate; that
is, judgments of beauty are not the consequence of a
strictly cognitive process. The condition for whether one
senses beauty is his or her frame of mind.

Primary beauty is consent to being in general and benevolent being in particular. It involves "the immediate sen-

sation of the gratefulness of the idea called beautiful" in
several respects. Consent itself is an idea called beautiful by the beholder. The act of consent renders the one who
consents beautiful. The secondary ground or object of consent is the beloved's own consent to benevolent being. The
lover's consent to the beloved's benevolence that involves
the lover's complacence or gratitude is a response to the
beauty of the beloved. God as the most benevolent being
with the greatest degree of existence is by definition the
most beautiful or most virtuous of all being.

The point is that for Edwards *sensing* the beauty of
being, especially the being of God, is crucial to true human
virtue; hence, the presence of divine being in the system of
universal being is a necessary condition for true virtue.
Because virtue as delight or complacence in being's benevolence is the primary beauty by which all else is rendered
beautiful, the presence of divine being is a condition for
secondary beauty even though the divine presence itself is
not necessarily taken into account. Love grows in part by
the recognition or apprehension of love at work throughout
reality. Recognizing love at work throughout reality includes paying heed to love's self-revelation as the ground
of secondary virtue and the beauty of sensible reality.

The sense of divine beauty that is the ground of all
other beauty is the sense and taste for divine things that
was lost by the human fall into sin. This is a loss that
renders the human sense stupefied. It is a loss that cannot
be regained by the efforts of human nature alone.

The condition for its presence in human being, like the
condition for any sense of beauty, is "the frame of mind."
By "frame of mind" Edwards means affection. The condition
for sensing divine beauty is, then, benevolence towards
being in general, that frame of mind that wills the highest

good or loves all that is, in the first instance, simply
because it is. The sense of divine beauty is consent in the
second instance; it is love for benevolent being in particular. Benevolent being, in particular, whether human or
divine, elicits special good will, delight, and gratitude on
the part of the lover because benevolent being is virtuous
or beautiful being. The lover, to use one of Edwards'
favorite words, *relishes* the beauty. Hence love, itself a
beauty, is the condition for the human sense for divine
being, and the exercise of that sense gives love itself new
dimensions.

The loss of the human sense for divine beauty that is
present throughout creation results correspondingly in the
contraction or narrowing of the frame of mind or the positive affections. The condition for the exercise of this
sense is itself lost. The loss constitutes an approach
toward nothingness or annihilation. Although God is
omnipresent in the universal system of being of which
created being is a part, and of which the non-human creature
is an image or shadow, human being has no access to the full
significance and full appreciation of that presence. The
loss of the immediate sense of the gratefulness or gracefulness of divine being and the subsequent contraction of
the human frame of mind divorces the sensation of all other
beauty from its appropriate context. Thus, for example,
self-love that was initially intended as love for oneself as
a being included in the universal system of being becomes
self-love in opposition to or dissent from being in
general.[42] The moral sense senses less. The sense of
justice and the instinct of pity are reduced.[43] Beauty
itself is diminished. The diminution of human nature renders human being blind, deaf, and dumb to the divine presence. It is a loss of consonance with the divine destiny.

For Edwards, the human condition of sin is dissonance of the highest order. This dissonance renders humankind "the highest species with the lowest excellencies."[44]

Nature and Divine Consent

Edwards' doctrine of God characterizes God as dynamic being that communicates itself as origin, pattern, and destiny of all reality. The mode of self-communication is the divine will directed by divine wisdom. Edwards' term for this mode of communication is *consent*. Divine being consents to itself in its economic ordering and its creation and redemption of the world. Divine consent includes consent to all manifestations of being; indeed, it is how being in its plurality is made manifest. Human being, in particular, is invited to participate consciously as co-consenting being in divine consent.

For Edwards nature plays a dramatic role in this process of communication. Nature, understood as sensible reality, is the image or shadow of being. Nature provides us through the sun and the rainbow with images that represent God's trinitarian structure. The fountain, the human body, and the wheel shadow forth divine creativity.

Nature is the realm of common grace. Within this realm the human senses provide us with paradigms of the need for revelation. As the realm of common grace nature is the realm of secondary beauty or virtue. The consent within nature reflects divine consent or primary beauty. Under the proper conditions nature communicates or reveals divine consent to human being. This communication has implications for the relationship between God and nature and between human being and the rest of nature as well as human/divine relationships. Chief among them is that nature communicates daily the divine destiny and human participation in this destiny.

PART II

THE HUMAN CONDITION

CHAPTER FOUR

INCARNATIONS OF THE HOLY SPIRIT

For Jonathan Edwards every bush is a burning bush, every
rainbow a sign of the covenant, and every human being potentially an incarnation of the Holy Spirit.[1] In the "Personal
Narrative" Edwards refers to nature as the "words of God."
In his own experience natural phenomena communicated divine
being. He "felt God" or sensed God's presence in everything
while "singing forth, with a low voice [his] contemplations
of the Creator and Redeemer." His own experience of regeneration and his observance of the experience of others
around him came to serve as the basis for a complicated
religious anthropology. Understanding nature's role in the
drama of redemption requires a knowledge of his religious
anthropology and its relationship to his doctrine of God.

Edwards' religious anthropology answers the questions:
What does it mean to be human in the context of the drama of
redemption? Under what conditions does one become a participant in divine consent? His answer is christocentric.
The Spirit of Christ dwelling within makes human beings co-
consenters with divine being. To be human in the context of
redemption is to become an incarnation of the Spirit and
thereby a member of the mystical body of Christ.

Incarnation -- the Incarnation of Christ as the Son of
God and the continual incarnation of the Holy Spirit within
each saint -- provides the key to understanding not only the
relationship between Edwards' doctrine of God and his religious anthropology, but the role played by nature in the
drama of redemption as well. Nature, the realm of common

grace, includes body, created consciousness, and the laws
that govern both. Nature is, in effect, all sensible and
sensing reality. It is a means by which divine being communicates. The indwelling of special grace in the human
soul makes human being not only a means, but the subject and
object of divine communication as well. This indwelling has
the effect of allowing human being to apprehend nature,
including human nature as the language or words of God and,
thus, relates the saint to his or her creator.

Edwards' religious anthropology finds expression in his
epistemological and soteriological writings. His writings
on typology as a method for interpreting reality and his
apocalyptic writings, both of which are subjects of the next
chapter, provide the key to relating the salvation of individual saints to the redemption of the cosmos itself.

Edwards' epistemological and soteriological writings
have received extensive scholarly treatment. However, from
Perry Miller and John Smith in the past to the more recent
work of Wallace Anderson, Conrad Cherry, and Mason Lowance,
no one has analyzed the role played by Edwards' interpretation of the Incarnation of Christ in relation to his epistemology and soteriology. Though Cherry's earlier work, *The
Theology of Jonathan Edwards*, is an analysis of Edwards'
concept of faith, it contains no treatment of the relevance
of the Incarnation to faith in Edwards' thought.[2]

Incarnation as a concept is the theological, connecting link between nature and spirit in Edwards' thought.
It relates Edwards' doctrines of creation, providence, and
redemption. It further relates Edwards' christology to his
doctrine of the Holy Spirit. Though in terms of theological
value, the Incarnation of Christ is second in importance to
Christ's crucifixion and resurrection, Edwards' doctrine of
the Incarnation and his view of incarnation in general serve
as the condition for relating divine good to human good.

Creation, Providence, and Redemption

The end for which God created the world is the glory of
God.   Throughout his works Edwards stresses that God's
motive and end for creation is self-love.   In his trinitarian writings consent or love, in its first instance, is
consent between the first and second persons of the trinity.
This consent is the third person, the Holy Spirit or divine
inclination.   Divine creativity reflects a general inclination on the part of the deity to communicate itself.   This
inclination manifests itself in the form of this particular
universe by covenant agreement between the first and second
persons of the trinity.   This covenant, the covenant of
redemption, is logically prior to actual creation.   Edwards'
formulation of the covenant of redemption stresses that the
world was created for redemption.

One way to understand the relation between creation and
redemption, particularly as Edwards formulates these doctrines in his trinitarian writings and the *Dissertation concerning the End for Which God Created the World*, is to see
them as identifying two different aspects of the same process.   Edwards' understanding of providence presents us with
yet a third aspect of this process.   Edwards described providence or the preservation of the universe as continual
creation out of nothing:

> Since . . . body is nothing but the infinite
> resistance in some part of space caused by the
> immediate exercise of divine power, it follows that
> as great and as wonderful power is every moment
> exerted to the upholding of the world as at first
> was to the creating of it -- the first creation
> being only the first exertion of this power to
> cause such resistance; preservation, only the con-
> tinuation or the repetition of this power every
> moment to cause this resistance.   So that the uni-
> verse is created out of nothing every moment and if
> it were not for our imaginations, which hinder us,
> we might see that wonderful work performed con-
> tinually which was seen by the morning stars when

they sang together.[3]

Creation out of nothing that marks the initial actualization of divine creativity is ongoing. Divine creativity is ceaseless in its operations.

Divine being is a dynamic process by which love in accordance with wisdom works to bring reality into existence and give it shape. This process is creative and continual; it is also oriented toward a specific end (the glory of God). God's self-glorification as the chief end for which God created the world includes the good of the human creature. Edwards's theological way of expressing this motif is to stress that divine creativity is the diffusion of divine fullness itself. Edwards connects the diffusion of divine fullness directly to the church as a companion to Christ:

> So God looks on the communication of himself, and the emanation of the infinite glory and good that are in himself to belong to the fulness and completeness of himself; as though he were not in his most complete and glorious state without it. Thus the church of Christ (toward whom, and in whom are the emanations of his glory and communications of his fulness) is called the fulness of Christ as though he were not complete without her.[4]

Edwards went on to add that God's love for the human creature is part of God's self-love and therefore God's self-glorification because the human creature to whom God's own fullness is diffused is comprehended in divine being itself.

The communication of God's "glory and good" to the human creature is an extension of divine excellence. Divine being extends its excellency by communicating its consent to finite being. The communication of consent to the human creature is its redemption.

The process of continual creativity includes the perfecting of what is created. Redemption focuses on that aspect of the process by which divine being communicates its own good to what it continually brings into existence. The communication of the goodness of divine being to what it creates is gradual. This communication occurs through time and space and, therefore, takes time.

The Good of the Human Creature

In the *Dissertation concerning the End for Which God Created the World* Edwards distinguishes the good that divine being communicates to the human creature as knowledge of God, holiness, and happiness. Human knowledge of God consists in knowing at a finite level what God knows as God knows it; human holiness consists in loving what God loves as God loves it; and happiness consists in rejoicing in what God rejoices as God rejoices. What God knows, loves, and rejoices in is God or universal existence. God's knowing, loving, and rejoicing includes the human creature as its object. Human knowing, loving, and rejoicing constitute human participation in divine communication. In other words, divine being glorifies itself by communicating its own good to the human creature. Each aspect of the good communicated implies the other two. Nevertheless, human holiness or consent is the condition for knowledge of God and happiness.[5]

Edwards' anthropology, cosmology, and epistemology are so interconnected as to be inseparable and are dependent upon distinctions that overlap in meaning. Distinctions like *consciousness, mind, spirit,* and *soul* are fairly straightforward in meaning; however, such distinctions as *created, uncreated, image, shadow, idea,* and *body* depend for their meaning upon the context in which Edwards uses them. For example, we have seen that Edwards refers to both the sun and the human mind as images of the trinity. What makes

them both images is that both bear the triune structure of
the mind that created them. Nevertheless, they bear this
structure in different ways; the human mind, unlike the sun,
is conscious. Thus, the human mind bears the image of the
trinity more directly.

Throughout his writings Edwards distinguishes finite
existence from divine being in terms of creatureliness.
What all finite existence holds in common is that it is
created out of nothing. There are, however, differences
within the category of finitude or creatureliness. Unlike
the rest of the created order, the human creature is
conscious and subject to an immortality in which it
retains its unique identity. In addition, Edwards stresses
Christ's human creatureliness while maintaining his full
divinity.

All finite existence bears the image of its creator.
Divine being gives its own shape to the reality it brings
into existence. How finite existence bears the image of
divine being differs according to whether or not any given
bearer is conscious. Consciousness distinguishes the human
creature from the rest of created order and gives the human
creature a special place not only in relation to the rest of
creation but in relation to divine being.

The specialness of the human position has to do with the
difference between consciousness and material body and the
primacy Edwards gives consciousness. What makes the human
creature human *being* is human consciousness. In order to
understand what consciousness or spirit is, we must first
examine Edwards' writings on the relationship between
consciousness and its objects. This requires distinguishing
between divine consciousness and human consciousness,
describing the relationship between the two, and analyzing
the relationship between embodied consciousness and other

bodies.

In "The Mind" Edwards defines consciousness as "the
mind's perceiving what is in itself -- its ideas, actions,
passions, and everything that is there perceivable. It is a
sort of feeling within itself. The mind feels when it
thinks, so it feels when it desires, feels when it loves,
feels itself hate, etc."[6] Consciousness, whether perceiving, thinking, or feeling specific emotions, is apprehending or grasping its objects. The range of possible
objects includes both objects of perception and objects of
reflection.

What the divine mind perceives in itself is all that is,
including itself. The divine mind apprehends all reality.
Indeed, divine apprehension generates reality. It is in
this sense that material objects exist mentally:

> And indeed, the secret lies here: that which truly
> is the substance of all bodies is the infinitely
> exact and precise and perfectly stable idea in
> God's mind, together with his stable will that the
> same shall gradually be communicated to us and to
> other minds, according to certain fixed and
> established methods and laws: or in somewhat dif-
> ferent language, the infinitely exact and precise
> divine idea, together with an answerable, perfectly
> exact, precise and stable will with respect to
> correspondent communications to created minds, and
> effects on their minds.[7]

There are several issues involved in this passage: the
generation and composition of material bodies, the difference between the divine mind and created minds, and the
process by which created minds apprehend material bodies.

The generation and composition of all material bodies
requires the continual and direct exertion of the divine
will in accordance with the divine understanding. In this
passage Edwards formulates in philosophical language what he
expresses in theological language as his doctrines of
creation, providence, and the trinity. Wallace Anderson

argues persuasively in his introduction to Edwards' philosophical and scientific writings that Edwards in this
passage and other related passages consistently rejects any
notion of matter as constituted by some substance in addition to the divine mind itself. As Anderson further points
out, Edwards' rejection of substance as different in kind
from the divine mind is a rejection of both materialism and
dualism.[8] This means that the difference between physical
bodies and created consciousness is not one of origin, but
one of effect. Both originate and persist by the direct
exertion of the divine will in accordance with the divine
understanding.

The generation of body is its composition. Body
including the human body is a configuration of ideas (color,
extension, motion, solidity, etc.) that reduces in the last
analysis to resistance to annihilation.[9] This resistance to
annihilation, definitive of body, is, stated positively, the
process of divine exertion. Furthermore, material body
manifests the dynamics of this exertion to created
consciousness through the senses.

Herein lies the difference between material bodies and
created consciousness. Whereas material bodies repeat to
some degree the dynamic structure of divine mind (i.e., the
sun bears the image of the trinity), created consciousness
repeats at a finite level the activity of apprehension by
which the divine mind continually brings all its objects,
material and immaterial, into existence.[10] Created
consciousness neither creates out of nothing nor preserves
what exists; furthermore, it is as dependent upon the divine
mind as any other objects of the divine mind for its own
continued existence. Nevertheless, created consciousness,
like divine consciousness, communicates through knowing and
willing. Whereas material bodies are a means of com-

munication, consciousness, whether created or divine, is
both the subject and the object of communication. In "The
Mind" Edwards sets out the ontological relationship of body,
created consciousness and the divine mind in metaphysical
terms:

> As to bodies . . . they have no proper being of
> their own; and as to spirits, they are com-
> munications of the great original Spirit. And
> doubtless, in metaphysical strictness and
> propriety, he is and there is none else. He is
> likewise infinitely excellent, and all excellence
> and beauty is derived from him, in the same manner
> as all being and all other excellence is, in
> strictness, only a shadow of his.[11]

Material existence has no existence in its own right; its
existence is dependent upon the constant exertion of the
divine mind. Created spirit or consciousness, also dependent upon the divine mind, in this case, the Holy Spirit, is,
in contrast to body, an impartation of the divine mind
itself. Though they differ with reference to existence,
both shadow forth divine being more or less directly.

What gives animated bodies life is the Holy Spirit. In
"An Essay on the Trinity" Edwards states that the Holy
Spirit's operations with respect to creatures are "to
quicken, enliven, and beautify all things, to sanctify
intelligent [beings] and to comfort and delight them." He
further describes the Holy Spirit as the "energy of God."[12]
Translated into philosophical language, this means that animated bodies exhibit the exertion of the divine mind that
knows and wills them into existence. Animation, however, is
not to be confused with an impartation of the divine mind
itself.

Human being is created, embodied consciousness. Edwards
distinguishes sharply between the human body and the human
soul although he affirms their unity. In the *Treatise concerning Religious Affections* Edwards distinguishes between

the "animal spirits" of the human body and the human will.
The "animal spirits" of the human body which he associates
with the vital organs exhibit the same vivifying principle
common to all animated bodies regardless of kingdom or species.   The will, by contrast, is an activity of mind or
soul.   The distinction Edwards is making is between biological life and psychological life.[13]

Edwards grants that biology and psychology interact.
The condition of the life of the body affects the life of
the soul;   the condition of the soul affects the life of the
body.   Nevertheless, the soul governs the body.   The body
does not generate the affections of the will; nor is the
will ultimately dependent upon the body:

> The body of man is no more capable of being really
> the subject of love or hatred, joy or sorrow, fear
> or hope, than the body of a tree, or than the same
> body of man is capable of thinking and
> understanding.   As 'tis the soul only that thinks,
> so 'tis the soul only that loves or hates, rejoices
> or is grieved at what it thinks of.   Nor are these
> motions of the animal spirits, and fluids of the
> body, anything properly belonging to the nature of
> the affections; though they always accompany them
> in the present state; but are only the effects or
> concomitants of the affections, that are distinct
> from the affections themselves, and no way essen-
> tial to them; so that unembodied spirit may be as
> capable of love and hatred, joy or sorrow, hope or
> fear, or other affections, as one that is united to
> a body.[14]

This statement constitutes a refutation of any attempt to
reduce human affections to bodily generated effects.   This
is precisely Edwards' aim since his intention is to
establish the legitimacy of religious affections in their
own right.   Edwards stresses the primacy of the soul over
the body by emphasizing that the interaction between body
and soul is more likely to be one in which the will or
affections generate sensible effects in the body.   In theory

spirit does not require body at all.

What role, then, do human embodiment and body in general play in the process by which divine being communicates itself? Edwards does not attribute created consciousness or finite spirit as he defines it to any other species in the sensible order. The uniqueness of the human position as embodied soul makes human being a connecting point between the rest of the sensible order and divine being. This connection establishes human being's dominion over the rest of the created order.[15] Nevertheless, Edwards does not denigrate body, human or non-human, in itself. For example, in his doctrine of sin he refutes the notion that embodiment causes sin.[16]

While Edwards clearly distinguishes between the human body and the human soul, he does not directly translate this distinction into a nature/spirit dualism. The natural order does not end with bodies and the laws that govern them. It includes the laws that govern human consciousness and human behavior as well. As we have seen in the analysis of consent, the realm of nature includes incorporeal life as well as corporeal life. Secondary or natural virtue includes secular justice and a moral sense or conscience as well as the aesthetic appreciation of corporeal objects. Though consciousness, mind, spirit, and soul distinguish human life from the rest of sentient existence, these terms as they apply to the human creature do not remove it from nature. Instead, the human soul and its counterparts, under the right conditions, allow the human creature to apprehend the divine mind operating throughout the natural order and to participate in those operations as they work to fulfill the divine destiny.

Nevertheless Edwards' conception of body in relation to consciousness, human and divine, raises the issue of why

bodies exist at all. Could not divine consciousness have
communicated itself as a plurality of discrete human
consciousnesses without generating material bodies of any
kind? Edwards does not address this question directly, but
his answer is implicit in his formulation of the covenant of
redemption and his doctrine of redemption. The end for
which God created the world is the glory of God. The covenant of redemption establishes the method by which this end
is to be accomplished. The method includes not only the
creation of finite body and spirit but the incarnation of
God in human form as a condition for Christ's work of
redemption and the unleashing of special grace upon the
earth.[17] The implication is that *any* creature, whether
animated or unanimated, whether conscious or unconscious,
is, in its first instance, a means by which divine being
communicates glory. In addition, created, embodied
consciousness -- human being -- is potentially both the
object and the subject of divine communication as well as a
means. Human being is, therefore, both a means and a
penultimate end in God's self-glorification. To ask why
body exists is as relevant as asking why created
consciousness exists. Divine being accomplishes its own
ultimate end by means of finite existence.

Divine being's ultimate end, namely, the glory of God,
includes the good of the human creature. The ultimate end
for all human knowledge is to know what God knows as God
knows it. Edwards' epistemology is religious. Precisely
what this means will become clearer upon examination of
Edwards' soteriology.

Soteriology

Edwards' doctrine of redemption extends from the redemption of the individual saint to the redemption of the

cosmos. The saint, the communion of saints, and the universe are all subject to redemption. The redemption of the
individual saint is a discrete instance of a larger process
that is eschatologically conditioned and cosmic in its proportions.

Nature's primary role in this drama is typological.
Nature provides the types by which the individual saint
interprets redemption at work in his or her own life, the
corporate life of the communion of saints, and the life of
the cosmos itself.

Nature's typological role in the life of the saint
requires that the individual human being involved begin to
undergo the transformation effected by the Holy Spirit's
operation of special grace. Nature plays a role in this
transformation in addition to its role as type. It helps
prepare human being for possible sanctification by intensifying the conviction of sin. The work of special grace
effected by the Holy Spirit renders the saint receptive to
the truth of scripture. Scripture reveals that Christ as
divine being became incarnate as human being to atone for
human sin and proclaim the kingdom of God. The indwelling
of the Holy Spirit makes Christ's incarnation and atonement
real to the saint so that he or she is included in the
divine society. Nature, particularly as it is manifested in
Christ's human nature, is the means by which divine
excellency communicates itself. Scripture, typologically
interpreted, also reveals that nature itself is a book of
types. Properly interpreted, the types drawn from nature
augment scripture to reveal the divine destiny.

In his essay, on "The Being of God," Edwards wrote:

Things are so disposed to future ends, so perfectly ordered to bring about such and such
necessary and good ends, that there [is], as it
were, as exact and perfect [a] conformity, or

> rather correspondence, between means and the end,
> as there is between a stamp and the picture that is
> designed to be stamped with it, or as there is in
> the types in the press and the impression intended
> by it, or as there is between the letters and their
> combinations on paper and the words that are
> intended should be spoken by him that shall read
> them.[18]

Edwards also wrote in "The Mind" that God is the pattern of
all being.[19]   Nature is a pattern of relationships that
shadows forth or reflects this pattern of being.   The
resistance to annihilation by which Edwards defines body
shadows forth being's resistance to nothing as manifested in
consent.   As a shadow of the pattern of being, nature is a
means to the fulfillment of the glory of God.   It represents
the design of the stamp, the types, and the letters. It renders visible the invisible process by which being communicates itself.

The seen presents the unseen.   We have examined *consent*
and its related vocabulary of *virtue* and *beauty* for its
relevance to Edwards' doctrine of God.   We need now to analyze the significance of *virtue* and *beauty* in relation to
his religious epistemology. Edwards distinguishes the relationship between the visible and the invisible in terms of
primary and secondary qualities.   He makes this distinction
with particular reference to beauty:

> The beauty of the world consists wholly of sweet
> mutual consents, either within itself or with the
> Supreme Being.   As to the corporeal world, though
> there are many other sorts of consents, yet the
> sweetest and most charming beauty of it is its
> resemblance of spiritual beauties.   The reason is
> that spiritual beauties are infinitely the
> greatest, and bodies being but the shadow of
> beings, they must be so much the more charming as
> they shadow forth spiritual beauties.   This beauty
> is peculiar to natural things, surpassing the art
> of man.[20]

When Edwards focuses directly on the issue of beauty, he

uses the word *consent* to express the relationship between
being and shadows. Edwards distinguishes primary and secondary beauty from one another in *The Nature of True Virtue*.
Secondary beauty, also referred to as natural beauty, includes not only the strictly corporeal, but the incorporeal
as well. Justice, self-love, instinct, and any concept of
natural conscience, all are secondary beauties.[21]

Secondary beauty is distinguishable from primary beauty
with reference to the status of the consent involved on the
part of the perceiving subject and in terms of the object
perceived. What makes secondary beauty *secondary* is its
role in relation to primary beauty. The technical use of
the terms *primary* and *secondary* by most philosophers refers
respectively to that which inheres in the object perceived
(e.g., extension) and that which belongs to human perception
(e.g., color). Edwards, by contrast, uses *primary* and
secondary in relation to one another to refer to two different modes of subject/object relationships, one of
which *(secondary)* mirrors or reflects the other *(primary)*.
Consent on the part of a subject to beauty in an object is
involved in either case. The conscious apprehension and
appreciation of secondary beauty has the status of being a
natural law constitutive of all human being.[22]

Any human being by nature may apprehend beauty in the
world or in the soul. However, in order for this apprehension to be an apprehension of primary beauty, it must
include an apprehension of the principle by which secondary
or natural beauty is made manifest. This apprehension of
primary beauty as the "ground" or "rule" of the appreciation
of secondary beauty is not natural to human being.

Primary beauty as the ground of secondary beauty includes secondary beauty. The difference between the two in
relation to divine activity is one of degree rather than

kind. Secondary beauty is an image of primary beauty. The
relationship between the two is, itself, one of agreement
and consent. There is no disjunction between the two in
relation to divine consent.[23]

Nevertheless, Edwards concludes with reference to the
effects produced in the human heart:

> Though it be true, that there is some analogy in it
> [secondary beauty] to spiritual and virtuous beauty
> -- as far as material things can have analogy to
> things spiritual of which they can have no more
> than a shadow -- yet, as has been observed, men do
> not approve it because of any such analogy per-
> ceived. And not only reason but experience plainly
> shows that men's approbation of this sort of beauty
> does not spring from any virtuous temper, and has
> not connection with virtue . . . . It is evident,
> in fact, that a relish of these [material] things
> does not depend on general benevolence at all to
> any being whatsoever, any more than a man's taste
> for honey, or his being pleased with the smell of a
> rose.[24]

We have already seen in the analysis of consent, that
beauty, *excellency*, and *virtue* are interchangeable terms in
Edwards' vocabulary. Edwards' point in this passage is that
the apprehension of secondary beauty or virtue, apart from
its context of primary beauty, reflects a lack of true or
primary virtue on the part of the apprehending subject.

Full apprehension of divine beauty manifested throughout
the natural order requires that the apprehending subject
know as God knows, will as God wills, and rejoice as God
rejoices. Thus, the apprehending subject must consent as
divine being consents.

Stated in more philosophical terms, what Edwards is
saying is that the human will qualifies its apprehension of
the objects present to consciousness. This is what he means
when he defines consciousness as "a feeling within itself
. . . [that] feels when it thinks, . . . desires, . . .
loves." For human being to consent as divine being consents

requires an alteration or transformation of the human will.
This alteration adds a further dimension to human apprehension by expanding it:

> We know how those things appear which we behold
> with waking eyes. They appear real because we have
> a clear idea of them in all their various mutual
> relations and concurring circumstances, modes, and
> dispositions -- the consent of the simple ideas
> among themselves, and with the congery of beings,
> and the whole train of ideas in our minds, and with
> the nature and constitution of our minds them-
> selves, which consent and harmony consists in ten
> thousand little relations and mutual agreements
> that are ineffable. Such is the idea of religion
> (which is so exceedingly complex) in the minds of
> those who are taught by the Spirit of God.[25]

Because human being is conditioned by sin, human apprehension is truncated. All humankind shares the capacity to
apprehend beauty or virtue in this truncated fashion; this
is in part what common grace means. The alteration of the
human will so that it is governed by the Holy Spirit is special grace. It is the indwelling of the Holy Spirit in the
human will itself. The movement from consent in nature to
divine consent presupposes spirit first in both the order of
being and the order of knowing in Edwards' thought. Human
being cannot apprehend nature as image, shadow, or type of
spirit apart from intimate relationship with divine being.
There is no direct movement from a known nature to knowledge
of spirit. Nevertheless, although the transformation of the
will is an operation of special grace, common grace or
nature plays a dramatic role in the process of transformation.

Nature and the Holy Spirit

For Edwards sin is a condition of human nature that
results in wickedness and only secondarily in particular
acts themselves. It is a condition from which no human

being escapes whether his or her particular actions are more
or less wicked on the whole. Because of the peculiar nature
of the condition it requires special grace in order for it
to be overcome.

Special grace for Edwards is necessarily above nature
for several reasons having to do with nature. The sense for
divine things is lost to human nature. It can no more be
regenerated by human nature than the human body can grow a
new limb after an amputation. Non-human nature cannot regenerate this sense, either. As the language of God it is
the object of the human sense. For non-human nature to
restore to full capacity the diminished senses would be the
same as color restoring vision to the blind and sound
restoring hearing to the deaf. Moreover, human and non-
human nature are as interconnected in Edwards' thought as
nature and grace. All nature is implicated to some extent
in the fall of human nature. Furthermore, for Edwards the
human condition requires not only the regeneration of the
lost sense, but the atonement for the wickedness ushered in
by its loss. Redemption must therefore include atonement as
part of regeneration.

For Edwards the work of redemption that effects salvation is the incarnation of Christ as that is made alive and
real for the saint by the special presence and operation of
the Holy Spirit within the saint. In "An Essay on the Trinity" Edwards wrote, "'tis God of whom our good is purchased
and 'tis God that purchases it and 'tis God also that is the
thing purchased."[26] By this he meant that the second person
of the trinity became flesh to purchase human redemption by
way of atonement to the first person. Human acceptance of
the atonement requires a regeneration of the lost sense of
divine things that regenerates totally; this regeneration
effected by the Holy Spirit regenerates the whole person.

It is human good.   It is the Holy Spirit dwelling in the
saint.

Redemption occurs in time and space.   God became flesh
in time and space through Christ's incarnation.   God becomes
flesh or takes over the whole individual human being in time
and space through that human being's experience of saving
grace.   Not only did God become human and dwell among us,
but the Holy Spirit possesses us and dwells within us daily.

For Edwards every human being is potentially an incarnation of the Holy Spirit.   In other words, divine consent
becomes the governing principle of an embodied soul.
Edwards' records of the spiritual transformation, his sermons on the subject, and his formal treatises and miscellaneous notes on the process of spiritual transformation
reflect in one way or another his formulation of how individual human being comes to consent to being in general.
What all these works share in common is the issue of what
makes a person or people love universal existence.[27]

Edwards' distinction between special grace and common
grace accounts in part for the presence and absence of consent as the governing principle of the soul.   Consent to
being in general is neither natural to human being nor is it
self-generated by human being; yet, the expansion from a
love based solely on self-interest to a more inclusive love
can and does occur in human life.   Furthermore, how this
expansion takes place is not solely dependent on a particular human being's immediate environment.   The transformation whereby consent to being in general becomes the
governing principle in one's life can occur in the most
unexpected souls regardless of how one defines expectation.
In Edwards' language the Holy Spirit initiates the transformation and the transformed are the elect.

Divine love as the governing principle of the human soul

is human participation in the divine life. Human consent to
being in general is loving as God loves and is the condition
for both knowing as God knows and rejoicing as God
rejoices.[28]

We have seen in the examination of Edwards' distinction
between "animal spirits" and the affections that the affections of the will govern the interaction between body and
soul that issues in their unity. We have also seen in the
examination of his distinction between primary and secondary
beauty that the apprehension of primary beauty is dependent
on the presence or absence of consent in the apprehending
subject. Thus, the will qualifies both bodily sensation in
the apprehending subject and the apprehension of the objects
of consciousness.

In the *Treatise concerning Religious Affections* Edwards
distinguishes the faculty of understanding from the faculty
of will. The understanding is the faculty by which the soul
"is capable of perception and speculation, or by which it
discerns and views and judges things."[29] The will is the
faculty by which the soul is inclined or disinclined toward
the objects presented to it by the understanding.[30] The
exercises of the will differ in degree according to the
vigor, intensity, and duration of the inclination or
disinclination. The range of possibilities extends from
slightly more than indifferent pleasure or displeasure to
the affections, for example, love or hatred.[31]

In miscellany 782 Edwards spells out the significance of
the primacy of the will in its governance of sensation and
apprehension in his distinction between speculative and sensible knowledge. His focus is upon spiritual knowledge and,
therefore, the objects of consciousness in this case are the
ideas of reflection. However, his distinction between speculative and sensible knowledge is equally applicable to

objects of perception.[32]

Speculative knowledge is knowledge yielded by the understanding apart from any involvement of the will. It is "a kind of mental reading wherein we don't look on the things themselves but only those signs of them that are before our eyes. This is a *mere cogitation* without any proper apprehension of the things thought of."[33]

In contrast to speculative knowledge, sensible knowledge is *"apprehension* wherein the mind has a direct *ideal view* or contemplation of the things thought of."[34] Sensible knowledge refers to the operations of the understanding in conjunction with the will and, therefore, involves pleasure or displeasure in response to the having of an idea. Edwards calls this apprehension "having a sense."[35] His paradigm for this mode of knowing is God's knowledge, including God's self-knowledge. This knowledge consists in the actual, immediate, and perfect presence of ideas in all their relations.

One example will suffice to point out the differences between speculative and sensible knowledge. A sensible knowledge of love as an idea of reflection present to consciousness includes having a sense of what love is. This "having a sense" is an actual repetition of the affection itself. In miscellany 238, Edwards states, "Those ideas of reflection, all ideas of the acts of the mind (as ideas of thought, of choice, love, fear, etc.) -- if we diligently attend to our own minds we shall find they are . . . repetitions of these very things over again."[36] This repetition of the ideas of reflection itself is missing in speculative knowledge. A speculative knowledge of love is analogous to reading the word *love* on a written page and going on to the next word and the next in order to get through the page. One never pauses to apprehend the full meaning that the word love signifies.[37]

Edwards devotes the rest of miscellany 782 to an explication of sensible knowledge. Sensible knowledge, as it
involves the will, is the knowledge of the good or evil of
its object. It is "the sense or kind of inward tasting or
feeling sweetness or pleasure, bitterness or pain, that is
implied primarily in [the object] or arises from it."[38]

Sensing the good or evil of an object involves both the
"sweetness or pleasure, bitterness or pain" that arises from
the object and the condition of the will itself. The will
in which consent to being in general is absent knows the
good or evil of objects within the limitations set by this
absence.

Edwards distributes sensible knowledge into natural and
spiritual. He makes this distinction in terms of how we
come by the sensible knowledge we have and in terms of the
different nature of the objects themselves.

Natural sensible knowledge is the ideal apprehension of
objects that takes place "by the laws of nature."[39] The
knower "by mere nature [may] come to have a sense of the
importance or terribleness or desirableness of many
things."[40] The knower knows its object in terms of its
natural good and evil.[41] Edwards defines natural good and
evil as:

> All that good and evil which is agreeable or
> disagreeable to human nature as such, without
> regard to the moral disposition -- as all natural
> beauty and deformity such as visible, sensible pro-
> portion or disproportion in figures, sounds, and
> colors; any good or evil that is the object of the
> external senses; and all that good or evil which
> arises from gratifying or crossing any of the
> natural appetites; all that good and evil which
> consists in gratifying or crossing a principle of
> self-love and consisting in others' esteem of us
> and love to us, or their hatred and contempt; and
> that desirableness or undesirableness of moral

> dispositions and actions so far as arising from
> hence; and all that importance, worth, or terrible-
> ness arising from a relation to this natural good
> or evil.[42]

It is important to note that what constitutes natural good
in this passage is basically the same as what constitutes
natural or secondary beauty or virtue in *The Nature of True
Virtue*.

The realm of time and space is the chief concern of one
who has a sense of the natural good and evil of things.
Mere human nature assisted by common grace can achieve such
a knowledge. In addition this knowledge extends to "things
of religion . . . with respect to the natural good or evil
that attends them."[43] Natural knowledge yields a sense that
God is, that God is great and powerful as manifested in
God's works and word, that sin is heinous, that we are
guilty of sin, that God is merciful, and that salvation is
desirable.[44]

Spiritual knowledge, by contrast, is new knowledge not
based on nature alone, particularly human nature even with
the assistance of the Holy Spirit co-working with natural
principles. Spiritual knowledge is an extraordinary operation of the Spirit of God. It extends to the eternal and
yields a sense of the spiritual good or evil of the things
of religion. It requires that the Spirit of God perform
"something above nature."[45] The "something above nature"
that the Spirit of God performs that is peculiar to the
saint is a "saving conviction" of the truth of divine
things. This saving conviction is "a sense of the divine or
spiritual excellency of the things of religion."[46] In other
words, the Spirit or love of God becomes the principle
governing force of the human will. The saint, governed by
divine love, apprehends not only what the rest of nature has
been communicating through human nature about the things of

religion, but in addition, divine excellency or love itself
as the broader context for the things natural to religion.

The spirit of God dwelling within the human will or
heart makes the excellency or consent of Christ vivid, real,
and alive to the saint. This indwelling is an alteration or
transformation of the saint's will so that it consents,
senses with, the divine will. The saint in his or her own
measure knows and wills as divine being knows and wills.
This operation of special grace attunes the human soul to
divine consciousness.

This transformation is above nature because human nature
is conditioned by sin. Left to its own devices, the human
soul has "a natural stupidity."[47]   Sin is a "stupefying
influence" that makes us blind to the spiritual context
within which all else occurs.[48]

Sensible knowledge or ideal apprehension requires
inspiration, the inbreathing of the Spirit of God. Edwards
defines inspiration as an intuitive, absolute certainty of
truth.[49]   The saint, to a lesser degree, shares this
intuition with the prophet. This ideal apprehension, or
sense of the excellency of divine things, distinguishes the
saint from human beings who have a natural, sensible
knowledge of the things of religion in a way that actuality
is distinguished from desirability or potentiality. The
saint is convinced by his or her apprehension that divine
excellency or consent is ultimate truth or reality; without
the special operation of the Holy Spirit the human creature
who has a natural knowledge of religion is convinced, at
best, only that the saint's conviction is desirable.

Nevertheless, as Edwards points out, both knowers share
conviction in common. The sense of divine things depends in
part on a sensible knowledge of what is natural in religion
as a preparation of the mind for a sense of spiritual

excellency. Edwards calls "those things that are natural in religion . . . the substratum of this spiritual excellency."[50] Edwards goes on to elaborate:

> Thus a sense of the excellency of God's mercy in forgiving sin depends on a sense of the great guilt of sin, the great punishment it deserves; a sense of the beauty and wonderfulness of divine grace does in great measure depend on a sense of the greatness and majesty of that being whose grace it is, and so indeed a sense of the glory of God's holiness and all his moral perfections; a sense of the excellency of Christ's salvation depends on a sense of the misery and great guilt of those that are the subjects of this salvation. And so that saving conviction of the truths of things of religion does most directly and immediately depend on a sense of their spiritual excellency; yet it also, in some measure, more indirectly and remotely depends on an ideal apprehension of what is natural in religion, and is a common conviction.[51]

For Edwards, ideal apprehension of those things natural to religion works to foster a conviction of sin, a necessary condition to receiving special grace. Without this conviction of sin, Christ's atonement is meaningless and Christ's own excellency inaccessible to human understanding. What the conviction of sin and the special grace of the Spirit yield for Edwards is that the way to salvation revealed by scripture is "perfectly agreeable to reason and the nature of things."[52] If the saint experiences the sense for divine things as prepared for by the sense for things natural to religion, no doubt remains that scripture provides what human reason alone can never provide and is therefore "certainly a contrivance of superhuman excellent wisdom, holiness, and justice, and therefore God's contrivance."[53]

The process Edwards describes in miscellany 782 reflects his soteriology, religious psychology, and epistemology combined. Human salvation depends upon a reception of special grace. What saves human being is an indwelling love that

extends to include universal existence. The indwelling of
this love is a condition for appropriate human love. The
presence of this love is a condition for apprehending the
full import of reality. Indwelling love, as the governing
principle of the will, is the condition for apprehending the
atonement and the revealed truth of scripture. Indwelling
love is the condition for apprehending that a bush burns
with the presence of God and that a rainbow is a sign of the
covenant.

The psychology of the alteration of the will regenerated
by special grace is marked by the transition from guilt and
fear to a sense of the excellency of divine things.
Nature's role is to intensify the conviction of sin or guilt
in preparation for salvation and to provide the paradigm or
metaphor for the operation of special grace itself, namely,
the new *sense* for divine things. To apprehend the
excellency of divine being is to sense it in a way analogous
to ordinary seeing, hearing, touching, tasting, and
smelling. One's having a sense or grasp of spiritual
excellency is a repetition of the excellency itself. To
have a sense or apprehension of universal love is to love
universally.

All genuine knowledge, whether it be of spiders, the
laws of gravity, or the excellency of Christ, is first and
last sensible knowledge. It is fundamentally gained through
experience. This locates it directly in the realm of time
and space. Under the proper conditions, namely, the Holy
Spirit's operations of both common and special grace, human
beings experience relationship with divine being. To
experience this relationship means for Edwards that the
temporal/spatial order is a manifestation of eternal and
infinite order. Any given moment of the time/space continuum is laden with positive meaning and value. Every

moment carries significance for the dynamic movement of the
whole in its struggle toward perfection.

Edwards held no misgivings concerning the inner
struggles characteristic of the life of the saint. His
account of his own religious experience reflects this
struggle at a heightened pitch and he did not restrict his
observations to his own experience.[54]   Edwards' point is
that the saving grace of the Holy Spirit operating in the
human will marks the beginning of an ongoing process of
transformation that must be supported, sustained, and nurtured by a community of saints undergoing the same process.
This process is not without its setbacks. Edwards'
"Personal Narrative" and his types drawn from nature for the
life of the individual saint and the people of God give
ample evidence of the difficulties involved in sanctification.

For Edwards it is not natural in light of human sin for
human creatures to love God. Although it is natural for
them to apprehend God's natural excellencies, namely, greatness and wrath, through human nature's interaction with non-
human nature, it is not natural for them to apprehend nature
as a communication of God's spiritual excellencies, chiefly,
the complexity of God's love itself. From Edwards'
perspective, the human apprehension of the meaning of divine
love requires the indwelling of divine love itself. Because
the natural state of human affairs without special grace is
conditioned by sin, the human situation is one of stupidity
of the senses regarding both the full significance of physical objects and the meaning of spiritual excellency. At
best, human nature left to its own devices appreciates
natural beauty for its own sake and fears the wrath of God.

The best example of this situation is from Edwards'
"Personal Narrative." As we have seen, Edwards originally

regarded thunder as a manifestation of the wrath of God.
Its occurrence filled him with terror for the future of his
own soul.   His own religious transformation allowed him to
place the wrath of God into the larger context of God's
grace.   Thunder became for him a welcomed phenomenon that
manifested God's majesty conjoined with God's grace.
Edwards' response was to sing back to the thunder that once
terrorized him.   Both prior to his transformation and
following it Edwards apprehended thunder as a divine communication.   The transformation of his own affections or
will, what he calls the indwelling of special grace, allowed
him to apprehend divine wrath in relation to divine grace.
Non-human nature communicated divine being to him in both
instances, but his own human nature required a transformation he himself could not generate in order for him to
apprehend the full significance of the communication.

His original apprehension of thunder as a communication
of divine wrath convinced him only of his sinful condition.
It offered him no release from it.   The day that apprehension changed to an apprehension of the conjunction of God's
majesty and grace marked the beginning of decreasing concern
for his own condition, his increasing focus on the
excellency and glory of God, and his growing desire to
become conformed to Christ.

Nature and the Incarnation of Christ

A conviction of sin and an indwelling of special grace
allow the saint to apprehend the efficacy of Christ's atonement, Christ's excellency, and the authority of scripture.
Edwards' christology emphasizes both Christ's atonement for
human sin and his messianic role as herald of the kingdom of
God.

In *Types of the Messiah* Edwards emphasizes Christ's

messianic role as herald of the kingdom.[55] In *An Humble
Attempt to Promote Explicit Agreement and Visible Union of
God's People in Extraordinary Prayer* Edwards includes in
Christ's messianic role the deliverance of the non-human
creature from the abuse it has suffered as a consequence of
human sin. This deliverance begins with the first coming of
Christ and will be accomplished when Christ comes again on
earth in the final millennium.[56]   Thus, the Christ event
has implications for all of nature. Christ's atonement for
human sin is efficacious for the non-human creature as well
as the human creature.

     Incarnation is the condition for the atonement. In *A
History of the Work of Redemption* , Edwards wrote:

> Christ's incarnation was a greater and more wonder-
> ful thing than had ever come to pass; and there has
> been but one that has ever come to pass which was
> greater, and that was the death of Christ which was
> afterwards. But Christ's incarnation was a greater
> thing than had ever come to pass before. The
> creation of the world was a very great thing, but
> not so great a thing as the incarnation of Christ.
> It was a great thing for God to make the creature,
> but not so great as for God, as for the Creator
> himself, to become a creature . . . . When Christ
> was born, the greatest person was born that ever
> was, or ever will be born.[57]

In this passage on the greatness of the Incarnation Edwards
stresses the connection between incarnation, creatureliness,
and birth. Edwards' emphasis upon Christ's human creatureliness is as characteristic of Edwards' christological writings as his emphasis upon Christ as the perfect sacrifice
for human sin. One of the finest examples of Edwards'
interweaving of these two themes is his sermon, "The
Excellency of Christ."[58]

     Edwards' most succinct definition of *excellency* is:
"The consent of being to being, or being's consent to
entity. The more consent is, and the more extensive, the

greater is the excellency."[59] The excellency of Christ lies
chiefly in his own consent both to deity and to human being.
It manifests itself in Christ's assumption of full human
nature along with his fully divine nature. His assumption
of human nature includes his incarnation, his death as perfect sacrifice for sin, his bodily resurrection, and his
exaltation.   In other words, Christ's assumption of human
nature is never relinquished.[60]

In "The Excellency of Christ" Edwards' concern is to
demonstrate how the excellencies of divinity and perfected
humanity conjoin in the person of Christ and to show what
application the conjunction has for the salvation of sinners.   What   is   significant   about   this   sermon   to
understanding the role of nature in Edwards' thought as a
whole is: his stress on incarnation, his depiction of
atonement, his portrayal of Christ's exaltation after the
crucifixion, and his appeal to human creatures to accept
Christ on the basis of Christ's own creatureliness.

Although Edwards stresses equally both the divinity and
the humanity of Christ, from Christ's incarnation to his
exaltation Edwards uses vivid body imagery to show how divinity and humanity converge. The issue he is addressing is
the significance of the Word made flesh to dwell among
us.[61]   Edwards draws a graphic picture of the lowliness of
Jesus' birth, the material poverty of his family, the
poverty throughout his life, and the bodily as well as
psychological torment and suffering he endured from
Gethsemane to crucifixion.   He stresses that even in
Christ's exalted state now in heaven Christ remains fully
human throughout eternity.   Consistent throughout Edwards'
description of Jesus' birth, life, crucifixion, and exaltation is his emphasis upon Christ's suffering as the medium
by which divine being reveals its nature.   It is Jesus

Christ's perfected, embodied humanity that communicates the divinity of a triune God.

Nowhere is this more clearly the case in the sermon than the point at which Edwards addresses the atonement:

> Then was Christ in the greatest degree of his humiliation, and yet by that, above all other things, his divine glory appears. Christ's humiliation was great, in being born in such a low condition, of a poor virgin, and in a stable: his humiliation was great, in being subject to Joseph the carpenter, and Mary his mother, and afterwards living in poverty, so as not to have where to lay his head, and in suffering such manifold and bitter reproaches as he suffered, while he went about preaching and working miracles; but his humiliation was never so great as it was in his last sufferings, beginning with his agony in the garden, until he expired on the cross. Never was he subject to such ignominy as then; never did he suffer so much pain in his body, or so much sorrow in his soul; never was he in so great an exercise of his condescension, humility, meekness, and patience, as he was in these last sufferings; never was his divine glory and majesty covered with so thick and dark a veil; never did he so empty himself, and make himself of no reputation, as at this time; and *yet never was his divine glory so manifested by any act of his, as in that act of yielding himself up to these sufferings.* When the fruit of it came to appear, and the mystery and ends of it to be unfolded in the issue of it, then did the glory of it appear; then did it appear as the most glorious act of Christ that ever he exercised towards the creature.[62] [Emphasis mine]

Just as Christ's bodily pain and sorrowing soul manifest the divine glory, so his love to his enemies manifests divine love: "That blood of Christ that was sweat out, and fell in great drops to the ground, in his agony was shed from love to God's enemies and his own. That same and spitting, that torment of body, and that exceeding sorrow, even unto death, that he endured in his soul, was what he underwent from love to rebels against God, to save them from hell, and to purchase for them eternal glory."[63]

As perfect sacrifice for our sins Christ bears witness
to divine justice: "Revenging justice then spent all its
force upon him, on the account of our guilt that was laid
upon him; he was not spared at all; but God spent the
arrows of his vengeance upon him, which made him sweat
blood, and cry out upon the cross, and probably rent his
vitals, broke his heart, the fountain of blood to
water . . . ."[64]

These sufferings afflicted upon the embodied Christ not
only atone for human sin but also constitute the past
experience of a now exalted Christ. In his exalted state
Christ intercedes for the saints "as one that has had
experience of affliction and temptation; he has not forgot
what those things are; nor has he forgot how to pity those
that are subject to them."[65] Edwards stresses Christ's own
experience several times throughout the sermon. His point
is that Christ's human experience provides the means by
which Christ identifies with human suffering in order that
human beings might draw near to him and receive the benefits
of his divinity. Edwards asks his congregation, "And would
you not only have him near to God, but also near to you,
that you may have free access to him?"[66]

Edwards assumes human misery and human fear for the
future as facts of life. He addresses his sermon to those
facts. That divine being would identify itself with human
misery in order to transform it is certainly a major part of
his message. Even more important, however, is that the
transformation of bodily and psychic pain, affliction, hu-
miliation, weariness, and hunger is available to the human
creature as creature. Christ's very appeal to human
creatures lies in his own creatureliness; Edwards states,
"but there is this to encourage and embolden the poor

sinner, that Christ . . . is a creature as well as Creator;
and he is the most humble and lowly in heart of any creature
in heaven or in earth."[67]

The accessibility of Christ due to his humanity and the
availability of the transformation of misery to the human
creature establishes the possibility for human/divine relationships. In the application of his sermon to human life,
Edwards characterizes this relationship as one of friendship
based on abiding intimacy.

Friendship is the major theme of Edwards' application of
his sermon on Christ's excellency although Edwards refers to
Christ as friend throughout the sermon. He makes explicit
the full meaning of that friendship by using examples and
metaphors that stress a social and familial intimacy dependent upon bodily contact. (This quality of intimacy also
becomes a major theme of his types drawn from nature.)

Edwards preaches that Christ is a friend to the saint
because he is like human creatures in his humanity. He is
the sharer of human circumstances.[68] Though Christ is
fully divine in a way that escapes finite comprehension, he
is accessible to finite comprehension because his "human
excellencies are but communications and reflections of his
divinity."[69] Edwards goes on to add: "As the glory of
Christ appears in the qualifications of his human nature, it
appears to us in excellencies that are of our own way and
manner, and so, in some respects, are peculiarly fitted to
invite our acquaintance and draw our affection."[70]

For Edwards even the exaltation of Christ after his crucifixion reinforces the intimacy of the human/divine
friendship. Because Christ remains fully human as well as
divine throughout eternity instead of shedding his humanity
after the resurrection, Christ "is not exalted that he may
be at a greater distance from [the saints] but that they may

be exalted with him."[71]

The saint in his or her humanity will be made like
Christ in his full humanity. Edwards concludes his sermon
by stating:

> Christ has brought it to pass that those that the
> Father has given should be brought into the house-
> hold of God; that he and his Father, and his
> people, should be, as it were, one society, one
> family; that the church should be, as it were, ad-
> mitted into the society of the blessed Trinity.[72]

In the sermon Christ's humanity from birth to death
includes both body and soul. In his depiction of the atonement Edwards uses body imagery (birth, blood, spit, broken
heart, rent vitals, and the physical agony of the crucifixion) to make vivid the suffering of Christ's soul. He
emphasizes Christ's creatureliness in his appeal to the
human creature. In his depiction of friendship with Christ
in Christ's exaltation he draws upon the biblical imagery of
parent and child, husband and wife, and head and body
relationships.[73] Time spent with Christ in heaven will be
spent "with the most friendly familiarity," eating and
drinking together.[74] Again the human body lends concreteness to Edwards' dominating theme of Christ as friend.
Throughout the sermon Edwards consistently uses body imagery
to exhibit or render concrete the human excellencies of
Christ that communicate, in turn, divine excellency.

The sermon is nothing less than an invitation to the
hearer to join "the society of the blessed Trinity," to
become an incarnation of the Holy Spirit.[75] The invitation
is dependent for its persuasiveness and effectiveness in
large part upon the concreteness Edwards' use of body imagery gives to Christ's atonement and exaltation. While his
use of body imagery is a rhetorical device aimed at awakening the new sense for divine things in the heart or will of
the hearer, it is not solely a rhetorical device. Edwards'

use of body imagery reflects his own conviction that body, indeed all nature, is divine communication. In an early miscellany Edwards interpreted Psalm 96:13 as a prophesy of the Incarnation in which he observes God had to come embodied in order to be real and continuing for human redemption. The Incarnation serves as both a condition for God to love the saint with passion, and as the "object" by which the saint knows all other objects to be divine communication.[76] Or as Edwards stated elsewhere, "the beauties of nature are really emanations or shadows of the excellencies of the Son of God."[77]

The question remains: *How* do the beauties of nature emanate or shadow forth Christ's excellencies? Stated another way, what is the method by which these excellencies are communicated and to what specific end? Whereas Edwards' doctrine of the Incarnation provides the substantive connecting link that relates human and divine being to one another, (the link between anthropology and theology), *incarnation* as a general concept presupposes, in addition, a structure of meaning within creation itself. It is to this structure of meaning as method of divine communication, especially its prophetic character, that we now turn.

CHAPTER FIVE

NATURE AS A BOOK OF TYPES

Divine communication is revelatory. The infusion of special grace makes scripture authoritative in the life of the saint. Edwards' method for interpreting scripture is typological. He argues by the authority of scripture for a typological interpretation of nature. Nature, like scripture, is a book of types; nature, like scripture, is divine communication. It follows that for scripture to become authoritative in the life of the saint, nature must take on typological meaning for the saint as well. The sense of the excellency of divine things includes the apprehension of primary beauty in and through secondary beauty or the natural order. Nature in light of scripture reveals to human existence the presence of divine being at work, extending its fullness.

The communication of God's fullness, that is, the continual redeeming creativity by which divine being communicates itself, is eschatologically conditioned, and therefore historical. The glory of God is fulfilled in a kingdom of God that begins on earth. This kingdom is present in part here and now with the regeneration of each new saint. It will be fulfilled in the future on earth during the final millennium and will continue eternally after the final judgment at the end of time itself. In Edwards' apocalyptic writings redemption takes on cosmic proportions as new creation. Nature's role in this drama is to bear and deliver *new creation*. Like a woman in travail, nature groans as it awaits delivery. History becomes in Edwards' thought the record of the birth pangs of the ages as they issue forth the kingdom of God.

I have already noted at some length in the introduction the recent scholarship on Edwards' use of typology. That Edwards extended typology as a method of interpreting scripture to include interpreting nature is by now a truism. Specifically how he did so and what allowed him to do so are still matters of debate. Whereas Conrad Cherry contrasts Edwards' use of typology with allegory, Mason Lowance describes Edwards' modification of typology as an allegorization of the type.[1] In contrast to both Cherry and Lowance I argue that Edwards' modification and application of typology is anagogic.

Anagogic interpretation has its roots in the Medieval fourfold scheme of meaning: literal, allegorical, moral, and anagogic. *Anagogy* refers specifically to the spiritual, ordinarily hidden significance of reality. Northrup Frye defines anagogy as that point in which nature, rather than container of reality, becomes contained. He goes on to add that anagogy focuses upon "the conceivable or imaginative limit of desire, which is infinite, eternal, and apocalyptic."[2] In other words, in the context of anagogy nature becomes the body of infinite, eternal spirit -- it is historicized. Blake and Yeats are perhaps the most familiar examples of modern visionaries whose works require anagogic interpretation.

Edwards, like Blake and Yeats, was a visionary. An analysis of his writings on typology in conjunction with his apocalyptic writings demonstrates the anagogical character of his employment of typology, and it is anagogy that distinguishes Edwards' employment of typology from that of his contemporaries and most of his immediate predecessors. His writings on typology as method, taken with his apocalyp-

tic writings, present Edwards' view of the cosmos and
thereby set the stage on which human/divine relationships
occur. An examination of these writings, therefore, com-
pletes the process preliminary to a discussion of Edwards'
types drawn from nature.

Typology as Method

Much of Edwards' reflection upon typology is found in a
treatise entitled *Types of the Messiah*, the major thesis of
which is: "That the things of the Old Testament are Types
of things appertaining to the Messiah and his kingdom and
salvation, made manifest from the Old Testament itself."[3]
Included under the rubric of Old Testament type are ritual,
law, similitude, figure, symbolical representation, symbol,
allegory, emblem, parable, and proverb. The type is a
future-oriented event in the world, divinely ordained and
therefore prophetic. The domain of the type as it occurs in
the Old Testament includes all visible phenomena from dreams
and visions such as Ezekiel's wheels and Isaiah's call, to
"things that had an actual existence," namely in nature,
history, and the law.[4]

God communicates to human beings through the type. This
communication, due to its connection with things that
actually happen, is extended to include other ancient
nations as well as the Hebrews. Typological communication
is God's language in general.[5]

This last point is confirmed in Edwards' exegesis of
John 10:34-36: "Now types are a sort of words: they are a
language, or signs of things which God would reveal,
point forth, and teach, as well as vocal or written words,
and they are called the word of the Lord, in Zech. IV.6 &
X.11."[6] Part of the content of revelation in scripture
for Edwards is that God communicates through the type

throughout reality. This divine communication in general is revelatory.

The point of divine communication through the type is of course, the antitype. Edwards' christology is profoundly eschatological and prophetic. The future determines the present and therefore the past. As we have seen, Edwards focuses on divine ends from the most minute material particles at the first moment of creation to the ultimate spiritual purpose of creation, and all such ends converge upon the glory of God from the most minute to the grandest. The very word *end* is charged with apocalyptic overtones throughout Edwards' thought, and it is a serious mistake to interpret Edwards' discussion of ends as referring to purpose, goal, design, or destiny in some atemporal sense.

His christology is as focused upon the kingdom of God ushered in by the Messiah as it is upon the person of the Messiah. He believed in the second coming of Christ, his thousand-year reign upon the earth, followed by the judgment of the world and its destruction. He writes, for example, of Ezekiel's wheels, "The third and greatest wheel begins its revolution at the creation, and finishes it at Christ's second coming to judge the world and destroy heaven and earth, in a literal sense."[7]

If the Old Testament prefigured and prophesied the New Testament in Edwards' thought, to the extent that the kingdom of God was not accomplished upon this earth now, the New Testament prefigured and prophesied as well. Christ's parables, the groaning of creation in Romans, and, of course, the book of Revelation fed Edwards' mind with prophetic types no less than the Old Testament histories, the Psalter, the prophets, and the law. Indeed, of all the books of the Bible, only Revelation merited a separate, almost word by word commentary.[8] Futhermore, sixty-six ser-

mons upon Revelation remain extant.[9] Of the Messiah and the
kingdom to come Edwards writes:

> 'Tis spoken of abundantly as the greatest and most
> glorious event beyond all that eye had seen, ear
> heard, or had entered into the heart of man; at the
> accomplishment of which not only God's people and
> all nations should unspeakably rejoice; but the
> trees of the field, the hills and mountains, the
> seas and dry land, and all heavens and earth,
> should rejoice and shout for joy; and in comparison
> of which the greatest events of the Old Testament,
> and particularly the two most insisted on, the
> creation of the world and the redemption out of
> Egypt, were not worthy to be mentioned of or to
> come into mind.[10]

The relationship between type and antitype in Edwards'
thought is classically that of temporal prefiguration and
fulfillment. Type and antitype structurally "agree," to use
Edwards' own words. Edwards includes in his *Types of the
Messiah* a detailed catalogue of Old Testament types roughly
a hundred pages long that begins with Genesis and covers
virtually every book including the Levitical codes and
Numbers in the Old Testament. He ends by giving special
attention to Hebrews and Galatians as authoritative prece-
dents for his typological interpretation of the Old
Testament. The most frequently recurring word he uses with
reference to the relationship between type and antitype is
agreement, followed by alternative references to *similitude*
or *resemblance*. Paragraph after paragraph begins "The
remarkable agreement between . . ."[11] "The things that are
said of the burning bush do wonderfully agree . . ."[12] and
"There is yet a more remarkable, manifest, and manifold
agreement . . . ."[13]

In the cosmological order "agreement" between type and
antitype refers to the fact that the type is an image of its
antitype. We have seen that the relationship between divine
consciousness and its objects is a unity of spirit and

matter such that the structure of matter repeats, represents, and shadows forth spirit. The type as an event or
thing that actually happens belongs to that overflow of
being *ad extra* as a produced effect. The end for which
matter is, is that it serves as type for spirit and it can
do so because the difference between spirit and matter in
terms of origin is one of degree and visibility, not kind.
For the type to agree with the antitype means that the type
presents us with the antitype.

In the order of being the agreement between type and
antitype means that the truth of the type functioning as
divine word or language manifests perfectly the truth of the
antitype understood as perfect self-understanding or divine
wisdom. Though human apprehension of the type as divine
self-knowledge is partial at best, from the divine perspective the type agrees with the antitype by expressing its
truth perfectly.

As it concerns human redemption, *agreement* refers to the
communication between divine and human being. The types as
images or shadows of divine being are divine revelation.
The way to recognize the antitype is through the type. This
recognition is apprehension, a characteristic of human
nature: "The principles of human nature render TYPES a fit
method of instruction. It tends to enlighten and illustrate
and to convey instruction with impression, conviction, and
pleasure, and to help the memory. These things are confirmed by man's natural delight in the imitative arts, in
painting, poetry, fables, metaphorical language, & dramatic
performances. This disposition appears early in children."[14]

What occurs in the order of being is repeated in human
psychology. Human delight in the imitative arts confirms
human consciousness' repetition of divine ideas. Hence we
were made to consent and agree as parts of a greater reality

that itself expresses divine consent and agreement. Agreement of type with antitype provides human being with an access to divine consciousness that parallels the primary human access to other human minds, namely, language. Types function as God's language in Edwards' thought, and because their agreement, resemblance, or similitude with the anti- type is divine self-knowledge, the agreement would qualify as experience as Edwards understands it. Because redemption and sanctification involve human consent to being and the type is a means by which we understand the full, eschatolo- gical significance of redemption, human apprehension of the agreement between type and antitype is essential to the salvation of the soul and communion with the society of the trinity. Salvation depends in part upon human agreement repeating the divine agreement occurring between type and antitype. This divine agreement from God's perspective is God's self-knowledge and from a human perspective is revela- tion.

That revelation would be mysterious, enigmatic, or am- biguous to human beings, saved or otherwise, made perfect sense to Edwards for at least two reasons: namely, his view of the human condition and his understanding of the role of types in God's overall design. Edwards argued that revela- tion is required even for a religion of nature because of the loss of an original, God-given capacity or "organ" by which to sense or know divine being. Comparable to blind- ness, this lack of a sense for divine being makes scripture necessary and authoritative. Although human reason is insufficient by itself for apprehending divine being directly, the human heart can, when infused by the Holy Spirit with special grace, begin to cultivate and exercise the newly-given sense so that it can strengthen and grow. That scripture is authoritative means that it is the abso-

lute beginning point and continuing companion throughout the
growth or educational process. The ability to apprehend the
meaning and truth of scripture is itself subject to development. With the indwelling of the Holy Spirit the believer
cultivates an increasingly better understanding of scripture
in particular and revelation through natural phenomena in
general. Thus, meaning and truth in the type appear most
hidden in the beginning to the novice and gradually become
more and more uncovered or disclosed with practice as part
of the general process of sanctification.

In addition to religious epistemological considerations,
Edwards also understood mystery as a necessary component of
revelation and therefore constitutive of the type by definition, quite apart from considerations of the human condition. "It is evident by John 11:50-52 that occurrences in
the history of the New Testament as well as Old have a
mystery in them, and that they are ordered on purpose to
represent and shadow forth spiritual things."[15] The type,
by virtue of being a temporal-spatial event that prophesied
or prefigured another as yet unfulfilled event, its antitype, carried a content that was necessarily enigmatic and
ambiguous. This was as much due to the fact that the type
is not the antitype, but the image of the antitype, as it
was to the faulty vision of the beholder, however less
faulty that vision became over time.

Edwards alternately referred to types as images or shadows of their antitypes. Type, antitype, and the agreement
between the two formed a unity in Edwards' mind that was
both ontological and epistemological. In Edwards' theory of
types, the events that happen and the things that exist that
serve as types render the antitype visible and present to
the human eye in much the same way that physical objects are
the effects, carriers, and media of simple ideas. As with

ideas, so with the antitypes, all could be reduced ultimately to divine direct operation. Nevertheless, just as a
physical object is subject to an analysis that distinguishes
it as visible object from what constitutes it, namely ideas,
so a type is subject to an analysis that distinguishes it as
visible object from what constitutes it, namely its antitype
or spiritual meaning and truth. In the latter case the act
of analysis is interpretation or the discovery of how type
and antitype agree. This means that from the human perspective there are differences between type and antitype.

The first obvious difference is the visibility of the
type and the invisibility of the antitype. A type can be
seen without one's recognizing that it is a type whereas an
antitype cannot be seen without the aid of the type. This
is again like physical objects and the ideas by which they
are constituted. Just as physical objects are the occasions
for their constitutive ideas, so types are the incarnation
of their antitypes.

A second difference between type and antitype has to do
with the frequency or repeatability of the type as
distinguished from the one-time occurrence of the antitype:

> Images of divine things. It is with many of the
> images as it was with the sacrifices of old: they
> are often repeated whereas the antitype is con-
> tinual and never comes to pass but once. Thus
> sleep is an image of death that is repeated every
> night; so morning is the image of the resurrection;
> so the spring of the year is the image of the
> resurrection which is repeated every year. And so
> of many other things that might be mentioned, they
> are repeated often, but the antitype is but once.
> The shadows are often repeated to show t[w]o
> things, vis., [1.] that the thing shadowed is not
> yet fulfilled, and 2. to signify the great impor-
> tance of the antitype that we need to be so
> renewedly and continually put in mind of it.[16]

Another major difference is that the type in itself is the
shadow, not the substance of the antitype, or as Edwards

puts it, "Things are said to be true in Scripture in contra-
distinction to what is typical: the type is only the representation or shadow of the thing, but the antitype is the
very substance and is the true thing."[17] Pursuing the shadow metaphor used here is important. Just as a shadow presupposes, is considered part of, yet is not identical with
that of which it is a shadow; so, a type presupposes, is
considered part of, yet is not identical with its antitype.
The shadow bears the shape of that of which it is a shadow.
Conversely there is nothing perceivable that does not cast a
shadow, yet, to confuse the shadow with that which casts it
is an error with potentially severe consequences. Edwards
goes on to give examples taken from the Bible, and it is
clear from the examples that the major distinction he is
making is between the literalness of the type and the
"truth" of the antitype. One example will suffice here.
Interpreting John 6:32 Edwards says, "So Christ is said to
be the true bread from heaven, in opposition to the manna
that was typical, though that was literally bread from
heaven . . . ."[18] The complicated point he is making here
is that what is literal bread has its significance not only
in its being what it literally is, but in its conveying the
message that Christ is life-giving food for the human soul.

Bread works as an image or shadow of Christ for at least
two very important reasons. Bread is not literally Christ.
Bread is food, and food is necessary for life. Were we to
have Christ present at this moment, we could recognize the
import, truth, or significance of his presence for us if he
were to pick up a loaf of bread and say, "I am the true
bread for which this loaf is a type." Truth is communicated
precisely because of the literal differences between bread
and Christ which command our attention by disrupting our
ordinary assumptions, on the one hand, and the common func-

tion (i.e. life-giving) shared by both, on the other hand. Bread as the type is the image or shadow of Christ the anti- type, and the agreement between the two is that both give life. The bread bears or carries the burden of com- municating that truth. "I am" unaccompanied by "true bread" leaves out the most important information we need to hear. As Edwards himself put it, "Christ often makes use of repre- sentations of spiritual things in the constitution of the [world] for argument, as thus: the tree is known by its fruit. These things are not merely mentioned as illustra- tions of his meaning, but as illustrations and evidences of the truth of what he says."[19] The type, rather than being merely ornamental and dispensable, is the necessary vehicle for communicating truth.

Nevertheless, a type is a shadow of its antitype. If the truth were self-evident or if the event that is the antitype were fulfilled, it would need no type to serve as a vehicle. The type represents the antitype not by substi- tuting for it and somehow loosely corresponding to it, but by rendering the shape of the antitype or unfulfilled event visible in a way similar to which *montage* operates. By positioning visible objects properly in relation to one another (spatially in the same frame or temporally in a suc- cession of frames) one can communicate through photograph, film or videotape highly complex meaning in split seconds. This is precisely how a type operates. The truth is present (though not in the literalness of the objects taken in themselves), and it constitutes the type in the sense that the type has no reason for being a type unless it com- municates the truth of its antitype. The truth communicated is neither self-evident nor is it recognizable apart from the type. It is hidden within the fabric of the type.

This last major difference between type and antitype pertaining to mystery also concerns time. Types prophesy.

The temporal status of the antitype is proleptic. The antitype is temporally present in the type as its meaning or
significance; nevertheless, as an event in its own right the
antitype has not yet occurred.

The lack of fulfillment of the antitypes makes the type
necessarily parabolic rather than emblematic, or as Edwards
would say: "a parable . . . a mystical, enigmatical speech
signifying spiritual and divine things . . . ."[20] "Repent!
The kingdom of God is at hand!" proclaims Jesus. And by the
very proclamation the kingdom becomes simultaneously present
in the here and now and yet in its incompleteness a lure and
a hope for the future. The course of history is changed as
events now gravitate toward a heretofore unsuspected
future, and the events of the past take on new meaning only
latent within them at best at the time they actually
occurred. In this manner, the future pulls the present into
existence. The shadowy or imagistic quality of the type,
placed in a context where it is the future that determines
the present, takes on connotations of foretaste or glimpse
of something hitherto untasted or not seen, something new
and so powerfully attractive as to give the present and all
that preceded it their true shape and meaning. This
"something" for Edwards was the second coming of Christ, his
thousand year reign upon earth, the judgment of the quick
and the dead, and the final communion of saints with God.

Based on his typological interpretation of scripture,
the content of which convinced him that the coming kingdom
of God on earth was imminent, Edwards concluded that revelation (in scripture) proclaimed itself to be ongoing beyond
the pages of the Bible such that natural phenomena provided
a continuing source of types by which the divine mind communicated or revealed itself to human being. In the notebook he kept in which he collected images or types taken

from natural phenomena and in his notes on the Bible there
are several occasions where he argues for the validity of a
typological interpretation of natural phenomena and historical events based on scriptural authority.[21]

Edwards moved from biblical typology to natural typology
without ever giving up the centrality and authority of
scripture.[22] Nevertheless, though scripture determined what
in nature was a type, both scripture and nature were equally
books and the types in both cases equally God's language.[23]
Although God spoke through scripture, God did not restrict
conversation to scripture alone:

> It is very fit and becoming of God, who is
> infinitely wise, to order things that there should
> be a voice of his in his works, instructing those
> that behold them and painting forth and showing
> divine mysteries and things more immediately apper-
> taining to himself and his spiritual kingdom. The
> works of God are but a kind of voice or language of
> God to instruct intelligent beings in things per-
> taining to himself. And why should we not think
> that he would teach and instruct by his works in
> this way as well as in others, viz., by repre-
> senting divine things by his works and so painting
> them forth, especially since we know that God hath
> so much delighted in this way of instruction.[24]

For Edwards the purpose of God's speaking throughout the
created order was spiritual instruction; the motive, God's
delight. Human being was the recipient of this instruction:

> If we look on these shadows of divine things as the
> voice of God purposely by them teaching us these
> and those spiritual and divine things, to show of
> what excellent advantage it will be, how agreeably
> and clearly it will tend to convey instruction to
> our minds, and to impress things on the mind and to
> affect the mind, by that we may, as it were, have
> God speaking to us. Wherever we are, and whatever
> we are about, we may see divine things excellently
> represented and held forth. And it will abundantly
> tend to confirm the Scriptures, for there is an
> excellent agreement between these things and the
> holy Scripture.[25]

The types that occur in nature are parables that God speaks
to us "wherever we are and whatever we are about." Just as
Jesus taught his immediate contemporaries by speaking to
them in parables, so God continues to teach by speaking
parabolically through natural phenomena. Ordinary human
existence and its environment shadow forth divine things as
did the mustard seed, the planting of a field, and the lost
sheep.

Edwards lived in what was virtually a wilderness. The
economy of the Connecticut River valley was predominantly
agrarian.[26] In many respects his own immediate environment
resembled Nazareth and Galilee, if not Jerusalem and Rome.
(For the counterpart to Jerusalem and Rome one would have
had to travel east to Boston.) He, therefore, did not have
to make the same imaginative leap that people who live in
technologically advanced societies have to make to
reconstruct the *sitz im leben* of biblical times.

Nature is the God-given form of all visible existence
--God-given both objectively and subjectively. If nature
owes its existence to the willing and knowing operations of
divine consciousness, it also represents that consciousness.
Nature "agrees" with the divine mind and therefore communicates it. It bears the shape of the consciousness that
created it.[27]

A comprehensive discussion of nature's status as divine
communication includes how nature as a whole operates as the
"typical world" and this requires an examination of Edwards'
understanding of the term *analogy*. Edwards most frequently
uses the term *analogy* to refer to the shared structure of
all existence as it devolves from divine spirit
to mineral element. Although he will on occasion use
analogy interchangeably with the terms *type* and *image*,
it is clear from the types that Edwards actually drew from

nature that *analogy* and *type* are not identical in meaning.
Though both share in common an ultimate reference to images
or shadows, the role of an image as a type assumes but is
not exhaustively defined by *analogy*.

Just as the type "agrees" with its antitype, so the different manifestations of being agree, resemble, or imitate
one another in spite of obvious differences and however
faintly:

> Again it is apparent and allowed that there is a
> great and remarkable analogy in God's work. There
> is a wonderful resemblance in the effects which God
> produces, and consentaneity in His manner of
> working in one thing and another throughout all
> nature. It is very observable in this visible
> world; therefore it is allowed that God does pur-
> posely make and order one thing to be in agreeable-
> ness and harmony with another. And if so, why
> should we not suppose that he makes the inferiour
> in imitation of the superior, the material of the
> spiritual, on purpose to have a resemblance and
> shadow of them. We see that even in the material
> world, God makes one part of it strangely to agree
> with another, and why is it not reasonable to sup-
> pose he makes the whole as a shadow of the spiri-
> tual world?[28]

He later added:

> If there be such an admirable analogy observed by
> the creatour in His works through the whole system
> of the natural world, so one thing seems to be made
> in imitation of another, and especially the less
> perfect to be made in imitation of the more per-
> fect, so that the less perfect is as it were a
> figure or image of the more perfect, so beasts are
> made in imitation of men, plants are [a] kind of
> types of animals, minerals are in many things in
> imitation of plants. Why is it not rational to
> suppose that the corporeal and visible world should
> be designedly made and constituted in analogy to
> the more spiritual, noble, and real world? It is
> certainly agreeable to what is apparently the
> method of God's working.[29]

The analogy of one thing to another in the visible world
confirms and underpins spatially what the types, revealed in

scripture, promise both spatially and temporally. "It is very observable in the visible world " that the skeletal structures of different classes of animal species resemble one another. Unlike the type and antitype, we have all the different skeletal structures present on the basis of which to compare with one another; like the type in relation to its antitype, the shared resemblances of the different classes taken together are evidence of an unseen order.

For Edwards *analogy* refers primarily to a spatial structuring and interrelating of the whole of reality without reference to particular events. If the parts of the whole did not resemble one another in some way, the visible taken as a whole or any particular selected instance of the visible order could not embody proleptically the invisible. Analogy operates, then, as a comparative term by focusing on what holds in spite of differences of particularity. He uses analogy primarily with reference to a hierarchy or harmony of all being. If *type* and *analogy* were identical in meaning and, therefore, interchangeable, adequacy and usefulness of a particular type would depend greatly upon where it stood in the hierarchy of being relative to divine spirit, and Edwards certainly on occasion implies this:

> IMAGES of divine things: There are some types of divine things, both in Scripture and also in the works of nature and constitution of the world, that are much more lively than others, everything seems to arise that way; and in some things the image is very lively, in others the image but faint and the resemblance in but few particulars, with many things wherein there is a dissimilitude. God has ordered things in this respect much as He has in the natural world. He hath made man the head and end of this lower creation, and there are innumerable creatures that have some image of what is in men, but in an infinite variety of degrees. Animals have much more of a resemblance of what is in men than plants, plants much more than things inanimate. Some of the animals have a very great

> resemblance of what is in men, some in some
> respects, and others in others, and some have much
> less. Some are so little above plants that there
> is some difficulty in determining whether they be
> plants or animals. And even among plants, there
> are numberless in some things there seems to be, as
> it were, only some feeble attempts of nature
> towards a vegetable life, and it is difficult to
> know what order of being they belong to. There is
> a like difference and variety in the light held
> forth by types as there is in the light of the
> stars in the night. Some are very bright, some you
> can scarcely determine whether there be a star
> there or no, and the like different degrees, as
> there is the light of twighlight, signifying the
> approaching sun.[30]

From this passage one might conclude, for example, that
images taken from the animal world would supply us with
types of Christ more adequately than images taken from the
vegetable or plant world. This is simply not borne out by
the images or types of Christ Edwards himself drew from
nature. Images such as vine, rose, tree, and bread are as
frequently explicated as animal imagery or types like lion
and lamb. In addition, Edwards does not associate sin with
plants as he does with some animals.

Although it is a mistake to read into Edwards' use of
such terms as *analogy* and *type* rigid definitions that differ
in kind from one another, it is equally a mistake to blur
the distinctions that exist between Edwards' attention to
analogy in relation to typology and the types he actually
collected. What type and analogy have in common is the
voice of God operating through the image. They differ,
however, in several ways. Analogy operates in space apart
from considerations of time, mystery, and the attitude of
the beholder. Typology, though it assumes analogy, emphasizes resemblance in terms of detail and complexity. The
type is parabolic and, therefore, more specific. The proleptic quality of the type in relation to antitype and the

ensuing mystery inherent in both are not requisite to
Edwards' conception of analogy.

The difference between analogy and type has to do with
the degree of directness with which divine being is
involved. In other words, divine being communicates itself
more directly through the type. Any human being, regardless
of the condition of sin, can perceive analogies within the
structure of sensible reality and may infer on the basis of
the analogies a creator to whom sensible reality bears a
resemblance. Human reception to divine communication
through the type, however, requires an attunement of human
being to divine being, the chief condition for which is
human redemption. Types discerned in nature communicate
God's ongoing revelation which is redemption history or the
divine destiny itself.

Nature's Role in the Divine Destiny

As we have seen, God created the world for redemption.
In the *Treatise concerning the End for Which God Created the
World* and in his trinitarian writings Edwards argues that
the world was created to provide a companion for Christ. In
his trinitarian writings he further spells out the covenant
between the first and second persons of the trinity
regarding the incarnation as the particular method agreed
upon prior to actual creation by which to redeem created
being. Edwards is, to put it bluntly, supralapsarian. That
is to say, the human fall into sin, however much human
beings are accountable for sin, is included in the divine
plan. What follows the fall itself is the gradual redemption of humankind. The most notable single event that has
taken place so far is the Christ event, although the Holy
Spirit continually works through all sensible reality as
divine communication to bring it to its ultimate destiny.

Edwards' apocalyptic vision is his interpretation of what
that destiny is.

The *Apocalyptic Writings* contain much of the content of
Edwards' vision although the vision is implicit in many of
his writings and more or less explicit in some of his
miscellanies, his sermons preached on "Revelation," and some
of his types or images drawn from nature. The *Apocalyptic
Writings* include his notebooks commenting on "Revelation,"
two collections of noteworthy news items that signified to
him the coming kingdom of Christ on earth, extracts on
Lowman (another apocalyptist), and his treatise arguing for
prayer in concert for an outpouring of the Spirit entitled
*An Humble Attempt to Promote Explicit Agreement and Visible
Union of God's People in Extraordinary Prayer.* The collection of news items communicates the urgency and fervor of
Edwards' eschatology. The commentary on "Revelation" gives
us a rough idea of Edwards' view of the progression
of events that culminate in a new heaven and earth. The
Humble Attempt indicates in part the role played by nature
in the drama.

Stephen Stein's introduction to the *Apocalyptic Writings*
includes a discussion of Edwards' theology of the apocalypse. He rightly emphasizes the revivalistic context for
Edwards' apocalypticism, the christocentricity of the
millennium, and the gradualness of the historical
progression toward the millennium. He touches only briefly,
however, upon the role played by nature in this process and
the significance of some of its more violent aspects. As a
consequence, he does not entertain either the possibility of
nature resurrected as the new heaven and earth or the
inference in Edwards' thought that nature is in some sense
the body of God.[31]

What Stein has titled respectively "Notes on the

Apocalypse" and "The Apocalypse Series" represent notebooks
of commentary on the book of Revelation begun by Edwards as
early as 1723 and continued throughout his lifetime. Like
his collection of types drawn from nature they are fragmen-
tary and exhibit the working and reworking of particular
themes with which Edwards was concerned. For example,
Edwards, like other apocalyptic thinkers before him, assumed
that the record of events in Revelation did not necessarily
occur in chronological order in the scriptural account
itself. He attempted to untangle the scriptural record and
reorganize it chronologically. The time schedule at which
he initially arrived was subject to change throughout the
course of his commentary. Nevertheless, the actual
progression of divine events themselves remained the same
regardless of any change in his projected schedule.[32]

The actual progression of events in terms of earthly
history ranged from initial creation to the incarnation of
Christ through the millennium itself. They included the
breaking of the seven seals, the blowing of the seven trumpets, and the pouring out of the seven vials, the seventh of
which introduced the final millennium. Edwards read back
into history and tried to align particular historic events
with particular seals, trumpets, and vials. He further
tried to project into the future a timetable that would
estimate when the final millennium would occur.[33] It was
this timetable that he periodically revised.

What remained the same regardless of revision was the
progression of history toward a final victory over the
anti-Christ that would culminate in the second coming of
Christ and the initiation of his kingdom on earth.
Subsequent to the final triumph of good over evil, Christ
would rule over the elect upon the earth for a thousand
years. Thereafter, the final judgment would occur; this

heaven and earth would be destroyed; and all the saints
would undergo bodily resurrection in a new heaven and earth
where they would enjoy everlasting communion with one
another and God.

The issues raised by Edwards' apocalyptic writings that
are relevant to an examination of the role played by nature
in Edwards' thought are several. They include the significance of the presence of sin in this world and its effects
on nature; the millennium itself; the status of this heaven
and earth; and the significance of the resurrection of the
body. These issues pose two questions. What is the
character of Edwards' other-worldliness? What role did
Edwards' apocalyptic vision play in his daily living?

The Presence of Sin and Its Effects on Nature

Satan, or the devil, and his minions play an active role
in Edwards' thought, most notably in his apocalyptic writings. Since many of the writings are private notebooks, it
is clear that Edwards' view of the devil is serious and not
dismissable as merely allegorical. In the apocalyptic writings Edwards assumes the powerfulness of Satan as an active
force working through the world, particularly through human
agency. In his types drawn from nature, this force is what
corrupts and misdirects impulses toward authentic being and
is in some ways a counterpart to the Holy Spirit's common
and special operations that bring what is into full
existence.

This corrupting force differs from the Holy Spirit's
operations of common and special grace in that the
corrupting influence is not ultimately triumphant. It is
also confined in its operations strictly to the earth's
atmosphere and all that is below the atmosphere.[34] As the
corruptor of being, Satan is powerful and real for Edwards.

Nevertheless, Satan's primary function is privative, that
is, to direct being toward non-existence. Evil, properly
speaking, does not itself exist, and sin names the human
tendency to succumb to less than full existence and to
destroy or contaminate other existence, human or non-human.
Although God cannot be said to create that which aims being
toward non-existence, God does permit the corrupting
influence to operate. In *The Freedom of the Will* Edwards,
in a radical departure from Calvin, argues that God permits
rather than directly wills evil as a means to a greater
good.[35] Satan is thus subordinated to the divine will
during the life of this world, and is defeated once and for
all at the final judgment.

Sin as the tendency toward corruption of being has
significance for non-human existence.[36] Edwards' *Humble
Attempt* includes a long passage in which he interprets
Romans 8:19-22.[37] The Pauline text refers to the groaning
and travail of the whole creation as it awaits the final
redemption of the human body.[38] Edwards connects the anticipation of the creatures both with the second coming of
Christ and the final day of judgment.[39] Edwards interprets
the text thus:

> This visible world has now for many ages been sub-
> jected to sin, and made as it were a servant to it,
> through the abusive improvement that man, who has
> the dominion over the creatures, puts the creatures
> to. Thus the sun is a sort of servant to all
> manner of wickedness, as its light and other bene-
> ficial influences are abused by men, and made sub-
> servient to their lusts and sinful purposes. So
> the rain, and the fruits of the earth, and the
> brute animals, and all other parts of the visible
> creation; they all serve men's corruption and obey
> their sinful will; and God doth in a sort subject
> them [the creatures] to it; for he continues his
> influence and power to make them be obedient,
> according to the same law of nature whereby they
> yield to men's command when used to good purposes.
> 'Tis by the immediate influence of God upon things,

acting upon them, according to those constant
methods that we call the laws of nature, that they
are ever obedient to man's will, or that we can use
them at all. This influence God continues, to make
them obedient to men's will, though wicked. Which
is a sure sign that the present state of things is
not lasting: it is confusion, and God would not
suffer it to be, but that he designs in a little
time to put an end to it, when it shall no more be
so. Seeing it is to be but a little while, God
chooses rather to subject the creature to man's
wickedness, than to disturb and interrupt the
course of nature according to its stated laws: but
'tis, as it were, a force upon the creature; for
the creature is abused in it, perverted to far
meaner purposes than those for which the author of
its nature made it, and to which he adapted it.
The creature is as it were unwillingly subject; and
would not be subject, but that it is but for a
short time; and it, as it were, hopes for alteration. 'Tis a bondage the creature is subject to,
from which it was partly delivered when Christ came
and the gospel was promulgated in the world; and
will be more fully delivered at the commencement of
the glorious day we are speaking of; and perfectly
at the day of judgment.[40]

There are at least three major issues at stake in this
lengthy passage: Edwards' anthropology, the status of non-
human nature in relation to the human fall, and the implications of God's permission of wickedness.

Regarding anthropology, Edwards, in this passage as in
other similar passages, attributes dominion over the visible
creation to human beings.[41] In *The Nature of True Virtue*
dominion is a consequence of intelligence.[42] Human being is
at the top of a hierarchy of visible being, the lower limit
of which is inanimate being, namely, dust, rocks, and so
forth. The initial fall into sin entailed the loss of the
appropriate use of the human senses; hence, the need for
revelation (the scriptures) and its superiority to human
reason. The capacity to reason, though corrupted, was not
lost, and, from the passage just cited it is clear that

dominion was not lost either. The human capacity to
discover and use the laws of nature, in other words, human
reason, and therefore, dominion, is, however, perverted by
sin. As a consequence, the laws of nature discovered by
reason are put to wicked as well as good purposes.

As a consequence of the human fall the status of non-
human nature is ambiguous. The natural laws, "the immediate
influence of God upon things," are, because they are divine
acts, good. The consequent product of those laws, the non-
human creature, is "perverted to far meaner purposes than
those for which the author of its nature made it." This is a
"force" and a "bondage" upon the creature who waits in hope
for "alteration."

Human being, non-human nature considered as a product,
and the process that produced non-human nature are interconnected. This interconnection is irrevocable. As a consequence of human sin, we have used our dominion over
sensible reality to abuse it. To the extent that we have
abused non-human nature through the misuse of natural laws,
non-human nature suffers our sin and becomes corrupted.
Human beings have corrupted the rest of nature, itself the
realm of common grace, and will pay for the abuse. The non-
human creature is the unwilling victim of this corruption
and groans, travails, and awaits in hope for deliverance
from the bondage imposed.

In the passage just cited Edwards makes it clear that
the second coming of Christ, the millennium and the judgment
day not only deliver the elect from the bondage of sin but
all of non-human nature as well. Indeed, the deliverance
began in part with the first coming of Christ. Edwards
says, "'Tis a bondage the creature is subject to, from which
it was partly delivered when Christ came and the gospel was
promulgated in the world; and will be more fully delivered

at the commencement of the glorious day [the millennium] we
are speaking of; and perfectly at the day of judgment."
Edwards understood the message of Christ's incarnation and
atonement to include significance for *all* nature, non-human
as well as human. God became flesh and suffered for human
sin that human beings might recognize the presence of grace
or divine communication throughout all existence.   This
moment of recognition of the full significance of revelation
marks the beginning of the restoration of all sensible
reality.   Edwards is implying an epistemological point concerning the structure of reality.   The salvation of the
human senses marks the beginning of the deliverance of sensible reality from the bondage of human sin.

This passage sheds some light on the character of the
divine permission of wickedness.   Edwards is acknowledging
the empirically verifiable reality that natural laws continue to operate regardless of human misuse of them.   We
will take the consequences of our actions even at the
expense of the non-human creature.   There is no divine
suspension of natural law to mitigate against abuse of our
environment until the second coming and the millennium, and
on the day of judgment we will be held accountable.
Nevertheless, non-human nature will be delivered.

His point is that non-human nature has a reality and
worth apart from its subjugation to human abuse.   In the
larger scheme of things, God permits this abuse rather than
suspend the laws of nature only for a "short time" or a
"little while." God's permission of the abuse is "a sure
sign that the present state of things is not lasting:
. . . and God would not suffer it to be, but that he designs
in a little time to put an end to it, when it shall no more
be so."   God's "permission" reflects in part both the
interrelatedness and the interdependence of human and non-

human nature.

Edwards has more to say about the response of the creature to human abuse:

> Though the creature is thus subjected to vanity,
> yet it don't rest in this subjection, but is
> constantly acting and exerting itself in order that
> the glorious liberty that God has appointed at the
> time we are speaking of, and as it were, reaching
> forth toward it. All the changes that are brought
> to pass in the world, from age to age, are ordered
> in infinite wisdom in one respect or other to pre-
> pare the way for that glorious issue of things,
> that shall be when truth and righteousness finally
> prevail, and he whose right it is shall take the
> kingdom. All the creatures, in all their opera-
> tions and motions, continually tend to this. As in
> a clock, all the motions of the whole system of
> wheels and movements, tend to the striking of the
> hammer at the appointed time. All the revolutions
> and restless motions of the sun and other heavenly
> bodies, from day to day, from year to year, and
> from age to age, are continually tending hither; as
> all the many turning of the wheels of the chariot,
> in a journey, tend to the appointed journey's end.
> The mighty struggles and conflicts of nations and
> shakings of kingdoms, and those vast successive
> changes that are brought to pass, in the kingdoms
> and empires of the world, from one age to another,
> are as it were travail pangs of the creation in
> order to bring forth this glorious event. And the
> Scriptures represent the last struggles and changes
> that shall immediately precede this event, as being
> the greatest of all; as the last pangs of a woman
> in travail are the most violent.[43]

Creation not only anticipates a redemption that extends to all nature, it dramatically brings it forth from within. Creation gives birth to redemption. The grandeur of Edwards' vision as expressed in this passage ranges from the creature, to the motions of the heavens, to the coming-to-be and passing-away of human empires. All that is, wicked and good alike, works together like a clock and like a chariot, but most of all, like a woman in labor and delivery to give birth to full and perfect being. Groaning and travailing, ever active, the whole creation aims toward deliverance.

The two passages, cited at length and taken in conjunction, make clear that Edwards understood the deliverance of
the creature in two senses of the word *deliverance*. The
non-human creature is to be delivered from the bondage of
human abuse. In addition, the non-human creature, as participant in the whole of creation is to labor actively and
to help deliver the very redemption that is to free it as
well as human being from its bondage to human sin. *Creation
and redemption are inseparable in Edwards' thought.* At work
in every natural and social process, whether the process is
perverted or not, the force of redemption is present and
gradually coming into fulfillment -- through ceaseless
struggle and pain that itself intensifies as the process of
redemption nears completion. The rhythmic contraction and
expansion of the ages, the temporal measure of the divine
destiny, will finally bring forth a new and perfect birth
that will include the restoration of all existence. Nature,
human and non-human, is both the object of deliverance and
the bearer of deliverance.

The Millennium

The inseparability of creation and redemption in
Edwards' thought receives more explicit treatment in his
portrayal of the millennium in his commentaries on the book
of Revelation. In the "Apocalyptic Series," note 77,
Edwards identifies the final triumph of redemption and the
subsequent millennium with the pouring out of the seventh
vial. Edwards refers to the millennium as "the sabbatism of
the church, or the time of her rest."[44]   In both the
Humble Attempt and note 77 of the "Apocalyptic Series"
Edwards compares the travail of non-human nature with that
of the church.[45]   The triumph of redemption with which the

millennium begins includes the conversion of all nations to
Christianity as well as the restoration of non-human nature.
The millennium itself is the "day" of rest following other
millennia of heavy labor and delivery. In note 77 Edwards
compares this millennial seventh "day" with the seventh day
in the Genesis account of creation:

> We may further argue from the first sabbath, or
> seventh day of creation, which was a type of this.
> God's great works in making the world were all
> wrought and finished before this, and on this day
> God saw all completely done. He beheld them very
> good, and rested and was refreshed. No part of
> creation was done on the seventh day; there was
> nothing then to do but to rest, and rejoice in
> what was done and completely finished before. So
> in the millennium, which will begin in the seventh
> thousand years, God's spiritual work, his new
> heavens and new earth, so far as to be finished in
> this world will be completely finished. The work
> of bringing the world into subjection to Christ,
> and establishing Christ's kingdom in the world
> will be done; and Christ and his church will then
> rest, beholding the work done, and all very
> good, rejoicing in it, as being now absolutely
> completed.[46]

The Genesis account of God's initial creation is a type for
the process of redemption spread over seven thousand years.
Hence, redemption itself is a continuation of the initial
creation. As we have previously noted, God's providence or
preservation of the world is a process of continual creation
ex nihilo. Creation, preservation, and redemption become in
Edwards' thought different ways of distinguishing the same
divine activity. Creation focuses on existence as opposed
to non-existence; providence or preservation focuses on the
divine nurturing of existence; and redemption focuses on the
processes of divine healing and perfecting of existence
through existence itself.

Edwards also stresses divine evaluation of the consequences of creation and redemption. God's great works are

in both cases "very good." It is precisely the goodness present in the type that assures us that the fulfillment of the antitype in the millennium will be at least as good.

In addition, both the typical and antitypical seventh days are days of rest and rejoicing. Again, it is the type that conveys this information about its antitype. Nevertheless, the process works two ways. While it is the type that tells us what to expect in the fulfillment of the antitype, there is the implication that the divine activity of initial and continued creation out of nothing requires an energy and fecundity analogous to the groaning and travailing that brings forth redemption. In any case, the process requires a period of rest and refreshment as well as rejoicing.

Finally, Edwards indicates that it is precisely what is going on in this heaven and earth that will introduce or bring into being in some way the new heaven and earth. The millennium marks the completion of God's spiritual work, the new heavens and earth, so far as they can be finished in this world. The new heavens and new earth are in some way continuous with this heaven and earth rather than a means to circumvent their reality.

This World as Type

This heaven and earth are a type for which the new heavens and earth are the antitype. Edwards is consistent in this interpretation throughout his apocalyptic writings and makes reference to the status of this world as typical on several occasions. The typical status of this world allows for him to argue for the typical status of events in the world. The movement from this world to some particular instance within it is characteristic in the "Apocalypse Series." For example, Edwards begins his interpretation of

the scriptural text, "And there was no more sea," by stating: "As the creation of the world was a type of the new
creation or work of redemption, so the dark chaos which is
called 'the water' [Genesis 1:27], is a type of the sin and
misery which we are brought out of in the new creation which
is begun by causing the light to shine out of the
darkness."[47]   This passage not only reflects Edwards'
characteristic move from the world as a whole as type to a
part of the world as a type, it stresses the connection between the initial divine work of creation and the work of
redemption as "new creation," another characteristic of
Edwards' thought.

Two questions remain.   What role does nature play, if
any, in the new heaven and earth?   How does this world
differ from the new heaven and new earth?

The difference between this heaven and earth and the new
one sheds some light on the role played by nature.   The new
heaven and earth are the subject of Revelation 21.
Edwards' text of Revelation 21:1 reads, "And I saw a new
heaven and earth: for the first heaven and the first earth
were passed away, and there was no more sea."[48]   Edwards
returns again and again to this particular passage in his
notebooks of exegesis, in part to attempt to determine the
character of the new heaven and new earth.   In one instance
Edwards speculates, "'Tis probable 'tis called by the name
of the new earth, because 'tis the place of the habitation
of bodies as well as souls, a place wherein their bodily
senses shall be exercised.   There shall be that whereon they
shall tread with their feet, and an expanse over their
heads."[49]   The "new earth" is a new *earth* because its
reality will be able to be sensed.   It will be in some
manner spatially located.   Insofar as nature is sensible and
sensing reality, the new heaven and new earth are a new

nature.

What then is the difference between the old and the new
and what is the need for a new heaven and earth?   Edwards
refers repeatedly to the new heaven and earth as spiritual.
For example, he states, "What is here called a new heaven
and new earth, we are not to understand of a literal heaven
and earth, but a spiritual and mystical heaven and earth,
meaning no more than that new state of things in the spiritual world or in God's church, that was typified and represented by the old or literal heaven and earth.   The new
heaven and earth signifies the church."[50]   He goes on to
stress again and again the typological relationship between
old and new creation.   The type is a shadow of its antitype.
The antitype represents the perfected and fulfilled state
only latent in the type.   What, in part, makes the new
creation new is that it will be inhabited only by the people
of God where they will dwell in eternal bliss with God.

In an earlier note he argues that the new creation is
new with respect "to matter as well as form."[51]   From the
passages it is clear that "spiritual" excludes corruptibility which is a quality of body as we know it in this
world.   It is also clear, however, that the new creation
that is "spiritual" includes some concept of body, both
human and non-human, that takes up space, is perfect, and
therefore, is incorruptible.   In other words, *body*   and
sensibility transcend the distinction between *literal* and
spiritual.

The corruptibility of this heaven and earth, even in its
restored condition during the millennium, necessitates the
new creation.   Restoration of this creation to its initial
goodness is not sufficient.   As Edwards puts it:

    'Tis not probable that this [new creation] is
    materially the same earth that we now live upon,
    but only purged by fire and renewed; though perhaps

> it might well be so-called, according to the
> language of Scripture in parallel cases. But yet
> we do not find that this earth is called another,
> different from what was before the flood or fall.
> This place, if it be the *eternal* abode of the
> blessed, as it seems, it will doubtless be vastly,
> immensely more glorious than it was before the
> fall. But, it seems to me, fire by purging could
> not more than bring it to its primitive state; and
> it would be good as a new creation to make it so
> glorious. It likewise seems . . . that this globe
> with all its appurtenances is clear gone, out of
> the way; and this is a new one materially as well
> as in form.[52]

Edwards here considers the possibility that new creation
might mean only restoration of this creation and rejects
that position. He supports his position not only on the
grounds that the new creation will be eternal and more
glorious than this one, but also on the grounds that the new
creation will differ materially as well as formally from
this one. He consigns this world to termination after its
restoration or the millennium.[53] Perfection includes
restoration but also goes beyond it. In both cases, perfection includes some concept of matter.

From the passages just cited, it is clear that the world
will come to an end; however, it is not clear that nature
itself comes to an end. *World* and *nature* differ in Edwards'
vocabulary although the two frequently overlap in meaning.

Edwards' use of the word *world* varies in his writings as
does his use of the word *nature*. In miscellany 1038 Edwards
argues that the entire universe is corruptible and will come
to an end.[54] This indicates that *world* refers to anything
having to do with body and that, because all bodies as we
know them are corruptible, body will universally perish. In
the "Notes on the Apocalypse" *world* is associated with
anything having to do with time or change.[55] In the
"Apocalypse Series" *world* refers more to this globe and its

immediate   atmosphere   or   this   planet   and   its   visible
heavens.[56]

In the "Apocalypse Series" Edwards attempts to locate
the new heaven   and earth: "'Tis clear certain that this
place shall be remote from the solar system, that is, it
will be distant from it, and therefore, not in the same
place in any sense that is ever want to be used, in
Scripture or in the world."[57]   He goes on to add that
wherever the new heaven   and new earth will be located, they
will be an *eternal* abode.   It is not clear whether this new
location is within or without the universe, for Edwards uses
references to other places within the universe to express
the difference in spatial locality between this world and
the new one.   What is clear is that *world* minimally refers
to sensible reality as we presently sense it to a greater or
lesser degree depending on the condition of our senses.   It
is furthermore a place of probation that will first be
restored, then destroyed.[58]

A similar ambiguity is present in Edwards' use of the
word *nature*.   To the extent that *nature* refers to sensible
reality and the human senses, it is interchangeable with
world.   It is also interchangeable with "being in general"
and, therefore, by implication, with God.[59]   We have already
seen that *nature* refers to common grace.   With reference to
human nature as conditioned   by sin, nature is "the true
tendency . . . or innate disposition of man's heart, which
appears to be its tendency when we consider things as they
are in themselves, or in their own nature without the inter-
position of divine grace."[60]   *Nature* also refers to the
material order as typical of the spiritual order.[61]

The major difference between *world* and *nature* in
Edwards' vocabulary is that *nature*, unlike *world*, seems
to include in its meaning a connotation of incorrupt-

ibility. *World* refers to a specific place whereas *nature*
refers to a mode of activity. This world is conditioned by
time and, therefore, perishability. Though a new world in
the form of a new heaven and earth may be eternal, it will
be located in a "place" where imperishability is its nature.

One way to interpret Edwards' references to the
resurrection of the human body and the new materiality of
the new heaven and earth is to understand them in the context of the Holy Spirit's operations of common grace. The
Holy Spirit will not cease with the end of time itself to
quicken, enliven, and beautify whatever is. Divine being
will not cease to have material means by which to communicate itself. Corruptibility, as a chief characteristic
of these means, will cease; the *world*, insofar as that term
refers to reality, taken as a whole and conditioned by
corruptibility, will end.

In his "Notes on the Apocalypse," Edwards interprets
Revelation 10 and its references to the end of time as
meaning "that the time should be no longer, that is, the
time of those long, numerous, and tedious changes."[62] On
the basis of his apocalyptic writings in general as well as
this text in particular, nature, insofar as nature has to do
with temporality, corruptibility, and tendencies of the
human heart left to its own devices, is, as Perry Miller
described it, "unpityingly consigned . . . to an ultimate
conflagration on the Day of Judgment."[63] Edwards consigns it
to such a fate in the firm belief, based on his interpretation of Revelation, that it has served its purpose of
bringing into birth a new creation not subject to corruptibility -- in short, a new and perfect sensible and sensing
reality, or nature.

Resurrection of the Body

Edwards ultimately defines body as that which resists

annihilation.   Bodies   are   pockets   of   resistance.   These
pockets   of   resistance   are   subject   to   corruption   and
annihilation in time.   Edwards characteristically uses the
word   *body* in at least three senses.   *Body* of course refers
to the human body.   *Body* also refers to all sensible reality
for which humankind is the collective consciousness.   *Body*
furthermore refers to the church or the communion of saints
as the body of Christ.   Because nature for Edwards includes
body and because Edwards' apocalyptic vision focuses on the
resurrection of   the body, it   is somewhat   more than mere
speculation to suggest that the new heaven and new earth
include the resurrection of non-human nature as well as the
human body.   An examination of representative writings on
the resurrection of the body as well as writings in which he
associates body with sensible reality supports this position.

In   the *Miscellaneous Observations on Important Theo-*
logical Subjects Edwards   argues   as   follows   for   the
resurrection of the body:

> The   reasonableness   of   the   doctrine   of   the
> resurrection,   will   appear, if we suppose, that
> union with a body is the most rational state of
> perfection of the human soul; which may be argued
> from the consideration, that this was the con-
> dition in which the human soul was created at
> first; and that its separation from the body is no
> improvement of its condition, being an alteration
> brought on by sin, and was inflicted under the
> notion of evil, and expressly as punishment, upon
> forfeiture of a privilege.   From whence we must
> conclude, that the former state of union to the
> body, was a better state than the disunion that
> was threatened.   Sin introduced that death that
> consists in the separation of body and soul.   The
> state of innocency was embodied: the state of
> guilt was disembodied.   Therefore as Christ came
> to restore all the calamities which came from sin,
> it is most reasonable to suppose that he will
> restore the union of soul and body.[64]

The bifurcation of body and soul reflects the human condition of sin. Body and soul unified are better than soul
alone. Sin introduced the perishability of the body as well
as contamination of spirit, and Christ will restore the body
to its intended union with the soul to the benefit of the
soul.

What kind of bodies will resurrected bodies be?
According to the passage previously cited in which Edwards
dwelt on the significance of "new earth," resurrected bodies
will be bodies that exercise their senses, bodies with feet
to tread the new earth and heads to view the expanse above
them. In the chapter on a general judgment and future state
in the *Miscellaneous Observations on Important Theological
Subjects* Edwards gives this description: ". . . and their
bodies shall be immortal, and as secure from perishing, as
the world is to which they are translated."[65] The resurrection of the body occurs on judgment day, following the
millennium. Those saints living at the time of the general
judgment will be immediately translated to join with all
saints of previous generations in the new heaven and earth.
In the "Apocalypse Series" Edwards interprets Revelation
20:5, 14, references to two resurrections and two deaths, by
saying:

> We read here of the first and second death and of
> the first and second resurrection. The first
> resurrection and the second death answer to one
> another . . . . I think 'tis evident, the first
> resurrection is a spiritual resurrection, and the
> second death is a spiritual and eternal death. The
> first death is a natural death and the second
> resurrection is a natural resurrection. He that is
> partaker of the first resurrection or regeneration,
> a resurrection to spiritual life - however he must
> die the first death, a natural death, yet he shall
> never die the second, or the spiritual and eternal
> death. As there is a spiritual resurrection, a
> first resurrection, of particular believers, so
> there is a coming spiritual resurrection of the

world in general, spoken of in this chapter, a won-
derful renovation of the world upon spiritual
accounts.[66]

Here Edwards distinguishes "spiritual" and "natural" from
one another. However, the contrast is between a spiritual
resurrection and a natural death, on the one hand, and a
natural resurrection and a spiritual death, on the other
hand. The saints will enjoy spiritual resurrection or regeneration during their lives on this earth, though they
will suffer natural death like the rest of the race. Their
final reward will be a natural resurrection as opposed to
the eternal spiritual death suffered by the damned.
"Natural resurrection" here refers to the resurrection of
the body that is elsewhere described as immortal. Nature as
defined in terms of the human body clearly has a place in
the new heaven and earth though body is shed of its characteristic perishability on this earth.

Edwards further compares the spiritual resurrection or
regeneration of the saints on this earth with an impending
spiritual renovation of the present world during the final
millennium. Read in conjunction with Edwards' interpretation of the groaning of creation, this passage reflects by
implication that the spiritual renovation during the millennium includes the restoration of nature to its initial condition prior to the human fall.

Finally, though Edwards does not make it explicit in
this particular passage, the spiritual resurrection or renovation of the world during the final millennium carries
implications of a natural resurrection of the world as body
to imperishability which is the new creation or new heaven
and earth itself. Edwards makes this connection between the
spiritual renovation of this heaven and earth with the new
heaven and earth more explicit elsewhere in the "Apocalypse
Series" in his lengthy interpretation of Revelation 21-22:

> These two chapters describe the happy state of the
> church after the resurrection. But there are two
> resurrections: the first or the spiritual resurrec-
> tion, and the literal resurrection, and a happy
> state of the church succeeds both. And respect is
> had to both these happy states in this description;
> this is a description of the church in the new
> heaven and new earth, after the former heaven and
> earth are passed away. But there shall be a new
> heaven and earth in two senses. First the heaven
> and the earth is to be renewed as to the spiritual
> state of things. The spiritual renovation of the
> world is in Scripture sometimes called creating a
> new heavens and a new earth. And secondly this
> heaven and earth will literally pass away; and the
> people of God will have a new habitation, a new
> world to them in the room of it.[67]

In this passage Edwards draws a parallel between what happens in the life of the church and the destiny of sensible
reality. Just as the saint and communion of saints undergo
spiritual regeneration of the body, so this heaven and
earth undergoes a renewal in time and space and a literal
passing away that is superseded by a "new habitation" in
which the saints will dwell. Creating a new heaven and
earth begins with the renovation of this one just as the
spiritual regeneration of the saint begins in time and
space. Edwards' use of "new" and "spiritual" refers to the
perfectability, hence, imperishability of bodies, human and
cosmic, rather than to their exclusion.

Nature as comprehended in being is divine communication
for Edwards.[68] It should come as no surprise that, shed of
its perishability, nature extends beyond this world to the
next. In reference to this world Edwards viewed nature also
as the body of human consciousness, taken collectively.
This world as the body of a collective human consciousness
functions to enhance rather than detract from nature's role
as communication. The two are not mutually exclusive in his
thought.

That Edwards could view the human race collectively in terms of consciousness is in part reflected in his doctrine of original sin.[69] Damned or regenerated, we are all one race whose chief distinguishing characteristic relative to other created life in this world is an intelligence that bears more resemblance to its creator's than any other form of sentient being as we know it. In the *Miscellaneous Observations on Important Theological Subjects* Edwards states, "Reasonable creatures are the eye of the world, they are capable of beholding the beauty and excellency of the Creator's workmanship, and those displays of himself, which he has made in his works; and therefore, it is requisite, that the beauty and excellency of the world, as God has constituted it, should not be kept secret."[70] In arguments for the immortality of the soul in the miscellanies Edwards refers to intelligent beings as "consciousness of creation."[71] This consciousness must exist in order for the world to have being at all and must continue to exist after this earth is destroyed in order for its existence not to have been in vain.[72] The collective memory of this perishable world plays a role similar to Christ's memory of his past earthly existence in his present exalted state. The communion of saints translated at the end of time remains human, therefore subject to experience and memory, their membership in the divine society notwithstanding. Although it is clear that this earth like our present individual bodies ceases to be, it is equally clear that immortality extends to the body as well as the soul and will be enjoyed in a new, imperishable "habitation." Furthermore, that the "eye," bodily resurrected, would not continue to behold God's beauty and excellency in a new creation that is in some way sensible is inconceivable if Edwards' apocalyptic vision is to be taken seriously. Just as resurrected human bodies will be new in the sense of being perfect and imperishable, so the new creation is nature resurrected perfect and imperishable.

Edwards' "Otherworldliness"

Edwards' focus on the final millennium, the final judgment, and the new heaven and new earth was hardly escapist. Nor did that focus allow him to denigrate life on this earth. On the contrary, the only way to the new heaven and new earth was through the birth pangs of this world. He was, thus, more attuned to the significance of the beauty and the ugliness, the joy and the pain, of this world as it struggled to bring new creation into existence.

Edwards' apocalyptic vision performed many roles in his personal life, his ministry, and his thought. I will note only a few of them at this time. In regard to nature, Edwards' apocalyptic vision lent his interpretation of all events in his life an urgency and an intensity that would otherwise be missing. His vision affirmed his extension of prophecy beyond Old and New Testament alike to include all sensible reality.

His eschatology, based as it was on scripture and extended to include all sensible reality, provided in part the motive for his collecting the types drawn from nature. While he was indeed seeking eternal truths and the divine presence as manifested in nature, this included his seeking verification in the old creation that a new one was being born. He was listening and watching for that continual divine communication that was the divine destiny itself. If this creation was in the process of giving birth to a new one, for Edwards it was equally the case that anticipation of new creation brought to birth the full significance of this present and past. For Edwards, as for the Jesus of

Nazareth portrayed by Albert Schweitzer, the ultimate events of the future lured the present into existence.[73] This creation as a type for new creation meant that particular events and processes within this creation also served as types that bore witness to that event.

Edwards' apocalyptic vision also provided him a context within which to evaluate sensible reality. He could walk the fine line between excessive asceticism and excessive sensuality. His interpretation of God's overall destiny allowed him to validate the human senses and all sensible reality as the language of divine communication. However, he could discriminate the good news from the bad in the communication. Nature as divine communication communicated both corruption and beauty, damnation and salvation.

Edwards' apocalyptic vision further provided him with a means by which to interpret the significance of divine activity at work in the cosmos for the individual and corporate life of the saints as expressed in daily existence. The types drawn from nature addressed specifically *how* the communion of saints embodies the Holy Spirit. As the embodiment of the Holy Spirit, the saints participate consciously in the actualization of the kingdom of God on earth. This process of actualization, manifested in nature, both human and non-human, has spiritual implications for human society in its own resistance to annihilation, and it is to these implications that we must now turn.

PART III

IMAGES OF DIVINE THINGS

CHAPTER SIX

THE DRAMA OF REDEMPTION

Edwards kept a notebook in which he recorded his observations of specific natural phenomena as typical of spiritual meaning. The notebook contains two hundred and twelve
entries. It was later edited by Perry Miller and published
as *Images and Shadows of Divine Things*. Edwards himself
gave this notebook several titles: "The Images of Divine
Things," "The Shadows of Divine Things," "The Book of Nature
and Common Providence," and "The Language and Lessons of
God."[1] No systematic analysis with interpretation of the
types has ever been published. Conrad Cherry's treatment of
them in *Nature and Religious Imagination from Edwards to
Bushnell* is extremely brief. In a mere three pages he
describes them chiefly by distinguishing light imagery from
water imagery. His overall concern is primarily Edwards'
sensationalist psychology rather than Edwards' cosmology.
In addition, though Cherry addresses the issue of hell in
the context of Edwards' psychology of religion, his failure
to take seriously Edwards' eschatology as an ongoing
historical process reinforces a static, "otherworldly" (in
the pejorative sense) interpretation of the relation between
spirit and nature in Edwards' thought. Likewise Mason
Lowance's concerns in *The Language of Canaan* are with
Edwards' transformation of typology as method in relation to
his religious epistemology rather than with Edwards'
theology of nature, or cosmology, in its own right.[2]

These entries do, in fact, contain a theology of nature.
They characteristically stress the presence of God in the

created order. They also validate the human senses and,
therefore, human experience. The types or images Edwards
collected, when taken as a whole, demonstrate Edwards' conviction that sensible reality manifests or communicates
concretely a pattern of spiritual meaning. This pattern
is divine being extending its good throughout reality. The
content of the communication is redemption or new creation.

The images address a variety of specific issues involved
in the process of communication. We have noted that some of
the entries focus upon the status of nature as the source of
types and analogies and the scriptural justification for
this status.[3] Nature, like scripture, is divine language,
and as divine language has positive value apart from the
behavior and attitudes of the human recipients of the
language. Nevertheless, the divine purpose for the language
of nature is to communicate with human being. Human beings,
regardless of the shared condition of sin, are the crown of
creation. The context for divine communication through
nature is the human/divine relationship. Hence, the
collected images focus more on what nature tells us about
that relationship than on nature apart from that relationship. The interconnection between human and non-human
nature permeates the types as does the interconnection of
all nature with divine being. Edwards, however, does not
address the subject of non-human nature considered apart
from its relationships to divine being and to human nature.
This is consistent in light of Edwards' doctrine of God, his
doctrines of creation and redemption, and his apocalyptic
vision. Considered apart from the centrality of God, there
is no nature, human or non-human, for Jonathan Edwards.

The lack of consideration for a non-human nature in its
own right makes a certain epistemological sense outside
Edwards' particular intellectual framework as well. If

human beings are truly part of natural existence, it is dif-
ficult to imagine how humans could consider the rest of
existence unmodified by their own.   This is in part a
problem of human consciousness.   Non-human nature is nature
filtered always by human consciousness.   The fact of human
consciousness does not so much provide a license to commit
mayhem, although indeed that has been done, as it confirms
Edwards' stress on human accountability for the shabby way
human beings have abused the non-human creature by sub-
jecting it to human wickedness.   The human consciousness
that abuses nature requires redemption if nature is to be
restored.   Redemption includes the transformation of human
consciousness in its relation to the rest of nature.
Redemption includes the restoration of nature.

Edwards' images from nature are theocentric.   They
emphasize what in relation to divine being human beings are
to look for, listen to, touch, taste, feel and contemplate
in nature.   The theocentric emphasis serves to reinforce the
need for human redemption rather than the glorification of
the human condition such as it is.

The issues Edwards addresses in addition to the status
of nature are the beauty of nature in the context of redemption, genuine as distinguished from false conversion and
sanctification, the ongoing struggles inherent in sanctification, the power of sin and evil, the meaning of human
affliction, and the place of civil and ecclesiastical
authority in human life.   It is clear from the content of
the images dealing with commerce and government that Edwards
considered the social arena to be an extension of nature,
rather than a separate realm.   His overriding point
throughout the images is that all life -- non-human, human,
and divine -- is interconnected.

This interconnection points out yet another charac-

teristic of the types or images. From the images portraying
sin we learn that for Edwards sin includes the human rending
asunder of the interconnection between non-human nature and
divine being. We have taken nature out of its context of
divine communication and have sought nature's goods for
their own sake. This abuse has not only contaminated non-
human nature but has wrought destruction in human life.

For Edwards one of the consequences of this abuse is to
render the status of body in general and the status of earth
and the human body in particular ambiguous. Body as a communication of spirit presents us with lively images of
corruption as well as redemption. The earth, corruptible
and corrupted, also corrupts. The water that presents us
with a lively image of God's providence presents us with an
equally lively image of sin. The moon that presents us with
an image of the church also presents us with the image of
the corruption of material prosperity. The human body whose
heart presents us with the image of spiritual transformation
also contains bowels and dung, the image of our spiritual
corruption and its earthly consequences.

All these images communicate spiritual truth and value;
however, spiritual truth is not univocal. Spiritual truth
includes the evaluation of the conditions of sin and damnation as part of the process of redemption or new creation
for Edwards. Edwards' negative evaluation of bowels, dung,
ravens, snakes, and so forth indicates his awareness of the
ambiguity of human nature and human appetites in relation to
non-human nature, stripped of its interconnection with
divine good. These negative evaluations do not appear to
reflect a denigration of matter in itself, or an ambivalence
toward body on Edwards' part. To make such a judgment
reflects a confusion of ambiguity based on context with sub-
jective ambivalence. That some of the images vary in what

they communicate according to the context in which they
occur reflects Edwards' awareness of the ambiguity of the
human condition as it is qualified by sin. That some images, for example, serpents and spiders, bowels and dung,
consistently communicate impending damnation indicates
Edwards' own judgment, as opposed to Origen's, that there is
sin that is unredeemable. The divine response to sin of
this kind is, from Edwards' perspective, eternal wrath.

What nature as divine communication communicates is the
spiritual meaning of resistance. The unifying theme of the
images is a rhythm of resistance -- resistance to annihilation or nothingness set in opposition to resistance to full
or authentic being. The images vibrate with the conflict
produced by friction, tension, and organic and physical
change. Edwards' most dominant concern is with the meaning
of incarnation and the processes that produce or corrupt it.
How nature communicates the meaning of resistance is through
the interplay of light and shadow. Nature shadows forth or
reflects divine wisdom, love, and judgment.

The typical arena for this rhythm of resistance is
nothing less than the heavens and the earth. As Edwards
puts it, "There are most representations of divine things in
things that are most in view or that we are chiefly concerned in: as in the sun, its light and other influences
and benefits; in the other heavenly bodies; in our own
bodies; in our state, our families and commonwealths; and in
this business that mankind do principally follow, viz.,
husbandry."[4] Edwards' horizon includes his observations of
the behavior and significance of heavenly bodies, earth,
air, fire, and water; color, metal, and weather; plants and
animals; birth and death in general; the human body; human
familial, vocational, and political relationships; and human
technology. The antitypes for which nature provides the

types include Christ and the church, the life of the saint
on this earth, sin, the devil and his minions, damnation and
final judgment, the millennium, the new heaven and earth,
and the resurrection of the body to everlasting life.

The process by which Edwards connects a particular type
with its antitype is scriptural. That is, Edwards examines
the phenomena and processes of common grace with his
thorough knowledge of scripture in the forefront of his
consciousness. He characteristically interprets nature or
common grace by reference to scripture. His direct observations of natural phenomena augment his understanding of
scripture, but Perry Miller is correct to point out that for
Edwards scripture for the most part confirms nature rather
than the contrary.[5]

Edwards' method of interpreting nature by means of
scripture reflects the application of his claim that revelation is superior to reason. His method also reflects the
application of his apocalyptic vision that this creation is
in the process of giving birth to new creation. The types
themselves bear witness to Edwards' belief that the human
arts and sciences form an integral whole with human religious experience and that it is the task of theology to make
explicit the character of this integration.[6] The content
of the types and the method taken together, reflect how
seriously Edwards takes the incarnation of Christ and his
willingness to extend its significance beyond the strictly
human realm.

The breadth of the content of the images or types and
their number make it impossible to do an exhaustive explication of each one. Instead I have selected those types which
most extensively represent what I understand to be characteristic of the types as a whole, namely the rhythm of
resistance. I have arranged the representative types

according to what I interpret to be Edwards' major concerns.
These are: the presence of sin and evil in the world, the
redemptive beauty of nature and its focus on the new heaven
and new earth, and the individual and corporate life of the
saint.

The life of the saint as an individual who is a part of
a larger body, the communion of saints, is the paradigmatic
instance of new creation or redemption as the final destiny
of all creation. Edwards devotes the largest portion of his
types drawn from nature to the life of the saint. This concern is his greatest and requires separate treatment in the
concluding chapter.

Resistance to Being

Edwards addresses roughly a quarter of his images to the
subject of sin.   The images fall into three categories.
They are the human condition, the devil, and the wrath of
God. Edwards devotes the largest portion of these images to
the human condition.

Sin as a Shared Condition

For Edwards sin is the shared, human, spiritual condition of resistance to full or authentic being. In human
nature this condition is manifested by a confusion of the
senses and a subsequent misdirection of the affections and
appetites that concludes in the acquisition of those things
that yield material and spiritual prosperity for their own
sakes rather than for the glory of God. This acquisition
does violence to all life and is an affront to God. The
natural processes that communicate illusion, decay, pollu-
tion, corruption, prey, and perishability to which all
bodies are subject shadow forth this human spiritual condition. Edwards regards sin as a psychological condition in
respect to each individual human being, and he regards sin

as a corporate or social condition of the race taken as a
whole. In the images that address sin he is particularly
concerned with those who are in "high places" in terms of
earthly and spiritual prosperity, and, as we shall soon see,
the devil is in part the spiritual head of the social body
of human sin.

Edwards characterizes sin as the loss of the ability to
sense or to recognize what is truly good:

> The water, as I have observed elsewhere, is of a
> type of sin or the corruption of man and of the
> state of misery that is the consequence. It is
> like sin in its flattering discoveries. How smooth
> and harmless does the water oftentimes appear, and
> as if it had paradise and heaven in its bosom.
> Thus when we stand on the banks of the lakes or
> river, how pleasant does it oftentime appear, as
> though under more pleasant and delightful groves
> and bowers, and even heaven itself wrought to tempt
> one acquainted with its nature to descend thither.
> But indeed it is all a cheat; if we should descend
> into it, instead of finding pleasant delightful
> groves and a garden of pleasure and heaven in its
> clearness, we should meet with nothing but death, a
> land of darkness, or darkness itself, etc.[7]

This type renders the complexity of Edwards' psychology of
sin. Evil and misery are the consequences of human confusion concerning the good. We do not seek evil for its own
sake; rather we seek the good as we have misperceived it.
Rather than regard the reflection of good as a divine communication of being or goodness, we mistake the reflection
as an object, appropriable in itself. In our reaching for
what we perceive as goodness instead of its reflection, we
plunge headlong into misery and non-existence. In another
image Edwards wrote:

> If persons have dirt in their eyes it exceed-
> ingly hinders their sight. This represents how
> much it blinds men when their eyes are full of the
> world or full of earth. In order to the clearness
> of our sight we had need to have our eyes clear of
> the earth, i.e., our aims free from all things be-

longing to this earthly world, and to look only at
those things that are spiritual, agreeable to what
Christ says: If thine eye be single, thy whole
body shall be full of light, but if thine eye be
evil, the whole body shall be full of darkness.[8]

Edwards' point is that if our senses are functioning properly, our "aims" will be directed properly. Conversely, if
our aims are directed solely toward the things of this earth
for their own sake, this indicates that our senses are
distorted and deranged. Dirt in the eye is a type of spiritual blindness or sin.

Why is the acquisition of earthly good for its own sake
not good enough? What is it about true good that makes the
earthly good that is its shadow not good enough?   The
thirty-sixth image states simply, "See notes on Eccles. 1.5,
etc."[9]   Edwards' notes on this scriptural passage which
begins, "The sun also rises . . . ," consist of a long
passage on the imperfection of earthly good. I will cite
only parts of this text.

It is good that is sought by the labour of the
creature, by the labour of the sun and wind and
streams, they are labouring for good. But by their
restlessness therein, still continuing to labour,
it appears that they don't fully attain their end,
they don't attain any sufficient good. If they
did, they would leave off labouring as having
attained what they labour for . . . .
        And as it [continual laboring] shows the
unsatisfying nature of earthly good, so it shows
its exceeding fleeting, fading nature. It is an
evidence of the great imperfection in it [earthly
good] that after it has been enjoyed a little while
it don't only perish in the enjoyment but turns to
ill, to that which is loathsome, so that the
contrary is desired. After the light of the sun
has been enjoyed a little while, it is troublesome
and darkness is desired. After we have been awake
a little while, it is burdensome, we want sleep,
and then we are weary of that and want to be awake
again. When a man eats that which gratifies his
appetite, it presently grows irksome, he desires no
more of it for the present.[10]

As in his *Humble Attempt* and other of the apocalyptic writings Edwards here attributes the continual labor for good to all creation. It is this continual labor that portrays the divine good itself. The continual labor for the good that characterizes all creation including the human creation is, because of its changeability, an image or shadow of the divine good rather than the divine good itself. What the human creature perceives to be the good for which he or she labors does not endure. The goodness of food, wakefulness, and sleep are subject to human need. The rivers that water the earth also flood it. The sun whose heat is necessary to germination and warmth also produces heat waves and drought. Edwards' point is that whatever is truly good in itself endures, transcends any change in circumstances. The eternal character of the divine good limits the appropriateness of human pursuit of the things of this earth. Human sin is a condition characterized by the loss of the ability to discriminate what is appropriate. Evil and wickedness are the consequence of our laboring for good without the ability to discriminate what good truly is. Misguided intentions produce spiritual and material excess. This loss of the ability to discriminate what is appropriate and pursue it, is a condition no human being escapes. It is partly for this reason that the human will can never be said to be free.

While no human being escapes the condition of sin, for Edwards those in "high places" are more subject to corruption than others. Several of the types deal with the significance of heights and high places with special reference to human sin as a fall.[11] Those in high places include the materially prosperous, the earthly powerful, the highly educated, the famous and honored, and the spiritually prosperous:

> The higher anything is raised up in the air, the
> more swift and violent is its fall. And the higher
> any body falls from, if it falls into the water,
> the more violently and deeply it is plunged. Thus
> it is in religion. Thus it is with backsliders
> and hypocrites, and them that are rested high
> in knowledge, wealth, and worldly dignity, and
> also in spiritual priviledge and in profession and
> in religious illuminations and comforts.[12]

Edwards distinguishes here among human beings in terms of
earthly and spiritual power. Those who are recognized on
earth as powerful in any way are especially vulnerable to
excessive abuse of those powers. If they place their happiness solely in the things of this life, even in the spiritual things of this life, they, like bubbles, will burst
into non-existence at the moment of death.[13] They are the
hogs who feed off the earth and are good for nothing until
the slaughter.[14] Of the appropriate relations between the
powerful and those whom they govern Edwards says, "The head
supplies, animates, and directs the body, but the body supports and bears the weight of the head. This is an image of
what should be between civil and ecclesiastical heads of
societies and their people."[15] For Edwards, pursuit of
power for its own sake, like pursuit of any earthly good for
its own sake, is a corruption of being. Once achieved,
power, if it is abused, corrupts the social body as well as
its powerful head. Those who are "heads" are far more subject to corruption than the rest of the body, and the
effects are far more devastating; for the corruption of the
head extends beyond the head itself to destroy the entire
body which it governs. For Edwards, sin is a condition of
the human spirit that is social and political as well as
individual in its implications and consequences. Nature
warns us through the operation of gravity in high places
that God will not tolerate social injustice.

The Devil

> It is observed of the CROCODILE that it cometh
> of an egg no bigger than a goose egg, yet it grows
> till he is fifteen cubits long (Pliny says thirty).
> He is also long-lived and grows as long as he lives
> (See Spencer's *Similes and Sentences*, p. 68). And
> how terrible a creature does he become, how
> destructive and hard to be destroyed. So sin is
> comparatively crushed easy in the egg, taken in its
> beginning; but if left alone, what head does it
> get, how great and strong, terrible and destructive
> does it become, and hard to kill, and grows as long
> as it lives. So it is with sin or Satan's interest
> in particular persons. So it is with his interest
> in towns, countreys, and empires and the world of
> mankind. How small was Satan's interest in the old
> world, beginning in Cain's family, but what did it
> come to before the flood? How small was idolatry
> in its beginnings after the flood, but how did it
> carry the world before it afterwards, and held it
> for many ages, growing stronger and greater and
> worse and worse? So it was with the kingdom of the
> anti-Christ, and so it was with Satan's Mahometan
> kingdom, and so it will probably be with the last
> apostasy before the end of time.[16]

The birth and life of the crocodile is a type of the birth
and life of sin as encouraged by Satan. In his development
of this image Edwards emphasizes the corporate as well as
the individual character of sin, its distinctive manifestation as idolatry, and its continued growth through the ages.
Sin is equated with "Satan's interests." From the passage
it is clear that for Edwards "Satan" names a force that permeates human individuality and exceeds it. It is a social
force that has an organic life of its own in which individual human beings participate. Collective human wickedness, in short, is the body of the devil.

Edwards detects Satanic forces at work chiefly and
characteristically in the behavior of specific animals. The
crocodile is only one example. Ravens preying upon rotting
human flesh; the cat preying upon the mouse; the lion, the
tiger, and the crocodile that elicit human horror, the

little foxes   destroying the grapes, and beasts of prey in
general, all serve as instances that embody the Satanic
forces for corruption and destruction.[17]   The most frequently occuring type for Satan, however, is, not surprisingly, the serpent.[18]

That serpents who had no feet could lure their victims
into their mouths and devour them fascinated Edwards.   For
him this phenomenon epitomized temptation.   Most of all the
phenomenon epitomized the temptation of those sinners who
have already heard the gospel preached:

> In the manner in which birds and squirrels
> that are charmed by serpents go into their mouths
> and are destroyed by them, is a lively represen-
> tation of the manner in which sinners under the
> Gospel are very charmed and destroyed by the Devil.
> The animal that is charmed by the serpent seems to
> be in great exercise and fear, screams and makes
> ado, but yet don't flee away.   It comes nearer to
> the serpent, and then seems to have its distress
> increased, and goes a little back again, but then
> comes still nearer than ever, and then appears as
> if greatly affrighted, and runs or flies back again
> a little way, but yet don't flee quite away, and
> soon comes a little nearer and a little nearer with
> seeming fear and distress that drives them a little
> back between whiles, until at length they come so
> [near] that the serpent can lay hold of them and so
> become their prey.   Just thus often times sinners
> under the Gospel are bewitched by their lusts.
> They have considerable fears of destruction and
> remorse of conscience that makes them hang back,
> and they have a great deal of exercise between
> while, and some partial reformations, but yet they
> don't flee away.   They will not wholly forsake
> their beloved lusts but return to them again.   And
> so, whatever warnings they have and whatever checks
> of conscience that may exercise them and make them
> go back a little and stand off for a while, yet
> they will keep their beloved sin in sight and won't
> utterly break off from it and forsake [it], but
> will return to it again and again and go a little
> further and a little further, until Satan remedi-
> lessly makes a prey of them.   But if any one comes
> and kills the serpent, the animal immediately es-

> capes. So the way in which our souls are delivered
> from the snare of the Devil is by Christ's coming
> and bruising the serpent's head.[19]

This passage reflects the psychological dynamics of prey,
seduction, and destruction that require the cooperation of
human self-deception and addiction. For many who have been
warned, resistance to annihilation is only temporary and
serves to heighten the intensity of the temptation to self-
destruction unless grace intervenes in an abrupt and dramatic manner.

The serpent never so much as has to make a move. Its
effect on its victim is hypnotic. Squirrels that easily
could flee in the other direction and birds that could take
to the air in flight do a dance of advance and retreat and
in spite of all protests to the contrary finally succumb to
their destruction. Edwards makes a similar point regarding
the complicity of the victim in his image of the cat and the
mouse. The mouse retreats, but not far enough, only to be
devoured in the end.

In a later entry Edwards stresses the gradualness of the
actual destruction:

> Serpents gradually swallow many of those ani-
> mals that are their prey; they are too big for
> them to swallow at once, but they draw them down
> little by little, till they are wholly swallowed
> and are past recovery. This represents the way in
> which Satan destroys multitudes of men that have
> had so good an education or so much conviction and
> light and common grace that they are too big to be
> swallowed at once. It also livelily represents his
> way of corrupting and prevailing against Christian
> countreys and churches, and against even some of
> the saints with respect to some particular errours
> and corruptions that he draws them into for a
> season.[20]

It is worth noting that Edwards includes Christians among
the possible victims, and that victimization can be temporary, that is, "for a season." He further stresses that

Satan's power to attract his victims lies in part in baiting
the trap with what is agreeable to the appetite of the
intended victim, whether it be material or spiritual bait.[21]

The destruction is nothing less than the eternal spiritual death of the victim for which natural death for all
human beings is a type:

> Ravens, that with delight feed on carrion,
> seem to be remarkable types of devils, who with
> delight prey upon the souls of the dead. A dead,
> filthy, rotten carcass is a lively image of the
> soul of a wicked man, that is spiritually and
> exceeding filthy and abominable. Their spiritual
> corruption is of a far more loathsome savour than
> the stench of a putrefying carcass. Such souls the
> Devil delights in; they are his proper food.
> Again, dead corpses are types of the departed souls
> of the dead and are so used. (Isa. 66.24.) Ravens
> don't prey on the bodies of animals until they are
> dead; so the Devil has not the souls of wicked men
> delivered into his tormenting hands and devouring
> jaws till they are dead. Again, the body in such
> circumstances being dead and in loathsome putrefac-
> tion is a lively image of a soul in the dismal
> state it is in under eternal death. (See Image
> 151.) Ravens are birds of the air that are
> expressly used by Christ as types of the Devil in
> the parable of the sower and the seed. The Devil
> is the prince of the power of the air, as he is
> called; devils are spirits of the air. The raven
> by its blackness represents the prince of darkness.
> Sin and sorrow and death are all in Scripture
> represented by darkness or the colour black, but
> the Devil is the father of sin, a most foul
> and wicked spirit, and the prince of death and
> misery.[22]

Though eternal death does not occur until after the final
judgment, it is clear from the passage that the wicked often
get a foretaste of that eternal death in the here and now,
just as the redeemed undergo a spiritual resurrection in
part in this life.

More to the point, Edwards presents us here with a picture of the devil as a power and a spirit, "the father of

sin, a most foul and wicked spirit, and the prince of death
and misery" and associates the devil with "blackness."
Whatever else the devil may have meant to Edwards, for him
it is the devil who originated "sin and sorrow and death."
Though sin requires the cooperation of human beings and no
human being escapes the condition of sin or accountability
for it, it does not reduce to individual human being alone.

Edwards' association of the devil with darkness and
blackness is biblically rooted and represents his attempt to
make vivid the power of the devil's lure of being into annihilation or nothingness. Edwards' main point is that the
devil preys on human being and consumes it through its own
wickedness. The wickedness itself is a gradual ceasing to
be.

For Edwards, the devil serves as the spiritual agency
that corrupts and destroys human being, both individual and
social. This agency transcends individual human agency
although it requires individual human participation in order
to be effective. This agency is an active force in human
life. It is personal in that it appeals directly to human
personality as its objects; it is organic in that it grows
by consuming its victims. Human sin feeds the devil and
sustains and increases the devil's power through the ages.
This power engages in a constant struggle against being.
Temptation and seduction are its chief characteristics. Its
relative success is dependent upon the human appetite for
and addiction to that which destroys human being. The appetite itself, not its spiritual or material object, is
deranged. The interaction between Satanic seduction and
human addiction to excess takes place gradually and not
without resistance on the part of the seduced or addicted.
Nature exhibits this process daily in the violence of non-
human animal life and the rotting of human corpses. These

phenomena communicate in vivid detail what the devil is, how
the devil operates, and the price the sinners who succumb
will finally pay -- eternal death. For Edwards those sinners who are in high places and abuse their position and
those, high or low, whose hearts are hardened in response to
hearing the gospel preached are chief among all other sinners.

Though the devil is triumphant regarding the souls of
the damned, the devil as a force for the destruction of
being ultimately fails. We know from Edwards' apocalyptic
writings that Edwards is no Manichaean. Nor can God be properly said to have created sin and evil; as a force or
forces against existence sin and evil themselves do not have
positive existence. From Edwards' images drawn from nature
we learn that God curses evil and sin and triumphs over them
in part by incorporating them into the process of bringing
forth new creation. Even the forces for chaos and destruction are in the last analysis subjugated to the divine
destiny.

There are two instances of this subjugation in the images regarding the devil in particular. As Edwards could
not detect the natural laws by which serpents lured mobile
prey larger than themselves into their very jaws, he, therefore, concluded that the phenomenon went beyond the laws of
nature and had the status of miracle. In images 16 and 43
he states:

> I don't know but that there are some effects
> commonly seen in the natural world that can't be
> solved by any of the general laws of nature, but
> seem to come to pass by a particular law for this
> very end to represent some spiritual thing, par-
> ticularly that of serpents' charming of birds and
> squirrels into their mouths.[23]
> It is a great argument with me that God, in
> the creation and disposal of the world and the
> state and course of things in it, had great respect

> to a shewing forth and resembling spiritual things,
> because God in some instances seems to have gone
> quite beside the ordinary laws of nature in order
> to it, particularly that in serpents' charming
> birds and squirrels and such animals. The material
> world, and all things pertaining to it, is by the
> creatour wholly subordinated to the spiritual and
> moral world . . . . So, to show how much He
> regards things in the spiritual world, there are
> some things in the ordinary course of things that
> fall out in a manner quite diverse and alien from
> the ordinary laws of nature in other things, to
> hold forth and represent spiritual things.[24]

God communicates through nature even if it requires what
appeared to Edwards to be the extraordinary, but regular,
suspension of natural law in order to warn us of the significance of human sin and its ultimate subordination to the
divine will. What Edwards views as a suspension of natural
law only gives the warning more urgency. Regardless of the
fact that we may now be in a better position to account for
the natural lawfulness by which serpents devour their prey,
the communication in the form of a warning still holds.
Prey, unsuccessful resistance to annihilation and the suc-
cumbing of the victim, observed in all its violence in non-
human nature, bear witness to their counterparts in human
nature. The consequences, while destructive in both cases,
are damning in the human arena. For Edwards non-human
nature warns us concerning human nature left to its own
devices without the intervention of grace.

The question remains: Why personify the forces for sin
and evil if evil is privative? While this is in fact a
larger question regarding certain strains of Christian tradition, particularly Augustinian, throughout Christian
history, Edwards' doctrine of God presents us with clues in
regard to why Edwards himself persisted in the conviction of
Satan's reality as personal, however privative. The answer
lies in a formal comparison of Edwards' doctrine of God with

his view of Satan. Both Edwards' doctrine of God and his
view of Satan depend on a concept of *person* that is not
restricted to human being. In addition, both his doctrine
of God and his view of Satan depend upon a dialectical
balance between personal and impersonal characteristics. We
have examined the significance of these factors in Edwards'
doctrine of God. Regarding his view of sin and evil, Satan
as personification symbolizes minimally that persons or subjects are responsible to and accountable for resisting
authentic being. In short, for Edwards, Satan as a personification stresses that evil masquerades as structure and
meaning that deeply affect human spiritual life by seeking
its annihilation. Just as the word *God* emphasizes the personal character of being in general, so *Satan* stresses the
personal implications of annihilation.

The Wrath of God
     The types focused on divine wrath serve as warnings that
God curses and ultimately dooms the forces for the corruption and destruction of being. Edwards interprets the
cursing of the serpent in the Genesis account as testimony
that all of nature, including snakes, is ordered by the
divine will to render images of spiritual things.[25] The
wailing of dragons and the mourning of owls communicate the
misery that the devils experience.[26] Edwards, who so
skillfully employed the image of the spider to portray the
damnation of sinners in his sermon "Sinners in the Hands of
an Angry God," uses the image in the notebooks on nature to
represent the ultimate fate of the devil or devils. He
writes, "As spiders when shut up together so that they can't
catch flies devour one another, so devils, after the day of
judgment when they shall be shut up in their consumate
misery and can devour the miserable sons of men no more,

will be each other's tormentors."[27]

Divine wrath directed toward the prince of evil and his minions has its counterpart with respect to human responsibility for sin. Nature's stormy seas, fierce heat from the sun, and lightning, bear witness to God's wrath toward human sinners.[28] Again, however, Edwards distinguishes degrees of sinfulness. He states, "Lightning more commonly strikes high things, such as high towers, spires, and pinnacles, and high trees, and is observed to be most terrible in mountainous places, which may signifie that heaven is an enemy to all proud persons and that God especially makes such the marks of His vengeance."[29]

That wickedness and sin excite God's wrath or anger is unambiguous in Edwards' writings; however, divine wrath itself has an ambiguous quality about it:

> As the SUN is an image of Christ upon account of its pleasant light and benefits, refreshing lifegiving influences, so it is on account of its extraordinary fierce heat, its being a fire of vastly greater fierceness than any other in the visible world, whereby is represented the wrath of the Lamb. This is a very great argument for the extremity of the misery of the wicked, for doubtless the substance will be vastly beyond the shadow, as God's brightness and glory is so much beyond the brightness of the sun, His image. Thus the sun is but a shade and darkness in comparison of it; so His fierceness and wrath is vastly beyond the sun's heat.[30]

There are several issues at stake in this passage: the contrast between shadow and substance, the implications of Edwards' use of the same image to represent both divine wrath and divine grace, and the implication that the wicked experience a misery while on this earth that foreshadows a greater misery to come.

The contrast between shadow and substance highlights the prophetic role of Edwards' images. The image of the sun

tells us not only what is presently true, but what will come
to pass. It is the sign of a promise. Present human
wickedness and the misery that will be its consequence play
the same role in relation to one another.

Even more striking is the implication that God's wrath
and God's grace are one and the same and differ depending on
the relative position or perspective of the recipient rather
than on some quality inherent in the divine character
itself. This interpretation is consistent with Edwards'
doctrine of sin as involving the distortion of the human
senses and his formulation of conversion as a new sense of
the heart for divine things. Whether we experience the
"extraordinary fierce heat" of the sun or its "refreshing
life-giving influences" is dependent upon where we are relative to the sun. The sun continues to behave in sun-like
fashion regardless of our location.

The implication is that the misery we experience as the
wrath of God, albeit that it truly is the wrath of God, is
the logical or natural outcome of our wickedness that
extends beyond the presently-felt misery into future reper-
cussions. The misery to which he refers is the misery of
acquisitiveness, the excessive appetite that never can be
filled, and the loss of authentic being that can sense and
taste divine things. Edwards is not connecting all human
suffering of pain and sorrows with divine punishment. On
the contrary, his type concerning the fall of those in high
places indicates that those who cause the suffering of
others especially elicit divine wrath.

Resistance to Annihilation

The whole material universe is preserved by
gravity or attraction, or the mutual tendencies of
all bodies to each other. One part of the universe
is hereby made beneficial to another; the beauty,
harmony, and order, regular progress, life, and

motion, in short, all the well-being of the whole
frame depends upon it. This is a type of love or
charity in the spiritual world.[31]

Gravity, or attraction which accounts for that resistance to
annihilation that is definitive of body, governs the relationship of one body to another, and operates to bring about
the human fall from high places, is for Edwards the gravity
of divine love. A direct operation of the divine will, gravity, whether it brings about existence or the fall of human
existence, shadows forth divine consent. Without gravity
there is no "beauty, harmony, and order, regular progress,
life, and motion . . . ."

> The meat and drink of mankind comes down
> from heaven in the rain, and even our clothing and
> habitations, and even the substance of our bodies,
> and is mostly of the very substance of the rain,
> which naturally leads us to the fountain of all
> mercies, and teaches us that we are fed and main-
> tained by those things that are wholly the fruits
> of God's bounty and are universally and entirely
> dependent on Him.[32]

The waters that flood the face of the earth from time to
time that exemplify human misery, and that comprise the
bubbles of human pride that burst into nothingness, are in
the last analysis the waters of divine mercy.

Nature's role as divine communication of spiritual
corruption and perishability is dependent upon its contrast
to nature's role as communication of divine beauty. This
relationship of contrast is one in which beauty, goodness,
or perfection will triumph over corruption and perishability
rather than a relationship of equal and opposing forces.
The destiny of this creation is to bear and deliver new
creation or redemption.

The process of perfection by which good overcomes sin
and evil is primarily one of attraction or resistance to
annihilation. We have already seen that Edwards defines

body as resistance to annihilation. This resistance is an
exertion of divine will in accordance with divine
understanding. The structure of body repeats or agrees
with, however faintly, the structure of the divine mind that
generates it. This structural agreement is an image or shadow of divine consent to its own being, to a fecund communication of its being through creativity, and to a nurturing
communication of its own good (its own consent) through
redemption or new creation.

New creation or redemption is in a process of becoming
fulfilled. Spiritual resistance to annihilation is a process whereby good transforms sin and evil and integrates
them into itself, or good, giving birth to more good,
simultaneously sheds sin and evil. The processes of generation and corruption in the natural order shadow forth this
process of spiritual resistance. This shadowing forth is
how the non-human creature participates in a redemption that
includes its own deliverance from bondage.

Edwards focuses on resistance as a transformation of sin
and evil in his types that are images of God's providence
and his types that shadow forth the beauty of redemption
itself. The types for which providence is the antitype
exhibit resistance to annihilation as a process of integration whereby convergence, synchronization, and contrast work
together to sustain and expand being. The types for which
divine beauty as redemptive is the antitype stress the
attractive power of beauty itself as a form of resistance to
annihilation.

Edwards emphasizes resistance to annihilation as fecundity coupled with an overt destruction of sin and evil in
his types that are more straightforwardly apocalyptic in
terms of their antitypes. Those who resist transformation
through integration, attraction, and regeneration suffer

eternal damnation. We have seen how resistance to authentic
being operates in the here and now in the examination of
Edwards' types of sin and evil. Resistance to authentic
being takes place on a cataclysmic scale prior to Christ's
second coming. This ultimate resistance to being is para-
doxically part of the final triumph of being itself. At the
final judgment, that which aims toward nothingness finally
succeeds. Only being, now perfected, remains.

Providence, the Integrating Factor

For Edwards God's providence or preservation of the universe is God's continual creation of it out of nothing. In
the apocalyptic writings Edwards spells out the specific end
or destiny for God's continual creation of the universe out
of nothing as redemption or new creation. All creation participates in the process which gives birth to new creation.
The new heaven and new earth will begin at the time of the
millennium with the restoration of this heaven and earth to
its primitive condition prior to the human fall. The
"creature" will be delivered. After the final judgment this
world will end, and the saints, bodily resurrected, will be
transported to a new "habitation." The saints will be
immortal and dwell in an eternal abode. God's providence or
preservation of the world is both God's ongoing process of
redeeming the world and God's redemption of human beings
through the world.

In the images drawn from nature that shadow forth God's
providence Edwards characteristically emphasizes convergence, synchronization, and contrast. The images characterized by convergence and synchronization communicate that
God's providence is the integration of complex natural processes directed toward a specific end. The images characterized by contrast serve to orient human being with

reference to what specifically shadows forth the end itself.

One image for divine providence as characterized by convergence is water. Type 77 is a lengthy exposition of how
branches empty into streams, streams into rivers, and rivers
into the ocean. The converging of these various bodies of
water represent the "course of God's providence."[33] This
process whereby smaller bodies of water converge with and
empty into increasingly large ones represents "how all
things tend to one, even to God, the boundless ocean."[34]
In vivid, visual imagery Edwards portrays the dendritic
character of water bodies as "the various dispensations of
divine providence."[35] Edwards elaborates:

> Some of the constituent branches of the main river
> have their head or source at the greatest distance
> from the mouth, and so all along there are new
> heads or sources beginning, from the head to the
> mouth of the main river. Some of these branches
> run directly contrary to others, and yet all meet
> at last. And the same branches don't keep the same
> course; their course is not continually in a right
> line, that which appears to us the directest course
> to the main river, but sometimes they run one way,
> sometimes another, sometimes their course is
> directly contrary to what it is at others.
> Sometimes, instead of going towards the main river
> they tend to, they run for a considerable space
> right from it, but yet nothing is lost by this but
> something gained; they nevertheless fail not of
> emptying themselves into the main river in proper
> time and due place, and bring the greater tribute
> of waters for their crooked and contrary courses.
> And so it is with the main river . . . .[36]

In this one image Edwards weaves together the various issues
involved in God's providence, and illustrates what he means
by beauty as "complexity" by way of example.[37]

For Edwards the greatest beauties are the most hidden
and the most hidden beauties are the most complex.[38] The
dendritic pattern of the water bodies converging with one
another, visually depicted, is highly complex. The total

pattern requires great distance in order to be seen by one
spectator as it actually exists. To map out the pattern
without an aerial view (a luxury Edwards obviously did not
have available) requires the corporate efforts of many
explorers and cartographers. Any part of the pattern,
viewed apart from its total context, is subject to distortion, misjudgment, and misevaluation with reference to the
total picture. Its true pattern remains hidden. So it is
with God's providence.

The complexity of the pattern of divine providence
raises the theological issues of difference and commonality,
integration, and progress. That the dispensations of providence differ from human being to human being and age to age
is portrayed by the difference in sizes of water bodies
(brook, stream, branch, and river) and the different loca-
tions of the heads of these bodies in relation to their
mouths. Yet, in spite of the relative differences, brook,
stream, branch, and river have in common that they are
made up of water and that they tend to one end. This end,
itself a body of water, is also the source:

> I need not run the parallel between this and the
> course of God's providence through all ages from
> the beginning to the end of the world, when all
> things shall have their final issue in God, the
> infinite, inextinguishable fountain whence   all
> things come at first as all the rivers come from
> the sea and whither all shall come at last. For of
> Him and to Him are all things, and He is the Alpha
> and the Omega, the beginning and the end. God hath
> provided a water course for the overflowing of the
> waters, and He turns the rivers of water wither-
> soever it pleaseth Him.[39]

This image of the convergence of water bodies to one end is
Edwards' concrete rendering of the remanation of the glory
of God to which he refers in the *Dissertation Concerning the
End for Which God Created the World*.

The last sentence of the passage just cited raises the

issue of the role played by that which appears to be
contrary to the good or the final end. Is contrariness part
of the hidden beauty of the divine providence, and if it is,
how is it integrated into the overall pattern? From the
passage on convergence cited earlier it is clear that the
movement of water that appears aimless or even contrary in
relation to larger bodies of water contributes to the
complexity of the pattern or the divine destiny. The meanderings of brook, branch, and stream are a gain rather than
a loss for "they nevertheless fail not of emptying themselves into the main river in proper time and due place, and
bring the greater tribute of waters for their crooked and
contrary courses." In addition to the meanderings of bodies
of water Edwards has a special place for obstacles:

> If a spectator were to judge by the appearance of
> things before his eyes, he would think the river
> could not reach the ocean. There appears such in-
> numerable multitude of obstacles in the way, many
> hills and high mountains, which a person that
> views at a distance sees no way between; he don't
> discover those ways through the hidden forests, and
> the openings between the mountains are not to be
> seen till we come to them, the winding passages
> through mountainous country are not to be discov-
> ered but by tracing the course of the waters
> themselves, but yet amidst all these obstacles
> those rivers find their way, and fail not at last
> of an arrival at the ocean at last, though
> they pass through so many vast regions, that seem
> to be full of obstacles for so long a course
> together. And it is observable that those very
> hills and mountains that appear like the most
> unsurmountable obstacles, instead of obstructing
> the course of these rivers, do afford the
> greatest supplies and additions. Those rivers
> will at last come to the ocean, and it is
> impossible to hinder. It is in vain for men to
> turn back the stream or put a stay to it. Whatever
> obstacles are in the way, the waters will either
> bear them away before them or will find a passage
> around them, under them, or above them.[40]

Whereas distance is required to see the pattern in its

entirety, closeness is necessary to seeing the true purpose of the obstacles. Edwards' focus is primarily on the role of obstacles in relation to the overall pattern or plan. His point is that only by tracing the course of the rivers can we discriminate what is truly an obstacle and, further, that all obstacles will be surmounted. Contrariness and obstacle are part of the divine pattern or process.

From the passages it is clear that the plan is a gradual process characterized by progress toward its end. The progress has its fits and starts and wanderings off what appears to be the proper course, but this is part of the complexity of the plan itself. Edwards concludes his image with special reference to the eschatological character of the antitype, providence:

> By what has been spoken of, it is particularly livelily represented and shown after what manner all the dispensations of providence, from the beginning of the world till the coming of Christ, all pointed to Christ, all had respect to his coming and working our redemption and setting up his kingdom in the world, and all finally issued in this great event. From time to time, in the different successive ages of the world, there began new dispensations of providence, tending to make way and forward this great event, as there are head[s] of new branches all along as we come nearer and nearer to the mouth of the main river . . . . The course of divine providence seems to be represented by a river in Gen. 41. 1,3, and Ezek. 1.1. It was over a river that Ezekiel saw the wheels of providence.[41]

In his commentaries on Revelation, his "Notes on the Bible," and his images drawn from nature Edwards devotes considerable attention to the significance of the wheel as a type of divine providence.[42] Edwards associates wheels with the spherical shape of heavenly bodies and their circular motion in relation to one another, the circularity of the season, political revolutions, and the machine, particularly the clock and the watch. In developing the wheel as a type of God's providence he returns again and again to Ezekiel's vision of wheels and wheels within wheels. The issues with which he is concerned, whether he is commenting on scripture or developing a type, are the same or similar to those that concern him in his development of the river as a type for the providence of God. His main point is that all circular movement that appears to be merely repetitious is the synchronization of the cycles, circles, and spheres of creation as they progress toward their destiny.

What distinguishes the wheel as type from the river as type is that Edwards' images of the wheel give us some indication of Edwards' view of the role of human technology and give some indication of Edwards' perception of the concrete role played by time in relation to God's providence.

Edwards was fascinated by the inventions and discoveries of human technology. In his miscellanies he says of the millennium:

> 'Tis probable that the world shall be more like
> Heaven in the millennium in this respect: that con-
> templation and spiritual employments, and those
> things that directly concern the mind and religion,
> will be more the saint's ordinary business than
> now. There will be so many contrivances and inven-
> tions to facilitate and expedite their necessary
> secular business that they shall have more time for
> more noble exercise, and that they will have better
> contrivances for assisting one another through the
> whole earth by more expedite, easy and safe com-
> munication between distant regions than now. The
> mariner's compass is a thing discovered by God to
> that end. And how exceedingly has that one thing
> enlarged and facilitated communication. And who
> can doubt but that yet God will make it more per-
> fect, so that there need not be such a tedious
> voyage in order to hear from the other hemisphere?
> And so the country about the poles need no longer
> be hid to us, but the whole earth may be as one
> community, one body in Christ.[43]

For Edwards technological advance was a sign of God's provi-

dence, and technology would advance further as the universe
progressed toward the millennium. The constitution of
nature and the disposition of providence set the standard
for technology:

> It is because the providence of God is like a
> wheel, or a machine composed of wheels, having
> wheels in the midst of wheels, that it is so
> ordered by the constitution of nature and the
> dispositions of God's providence, that almost all
> the curious machines that men contrive, to do
> notable things or produce any remarkable effect,
> are by wheels, a compage of wheels, revolving
> round and round, going and returning, representing
> the manner of the progress of things in divine
> providence.[44]

Technology is not only dependent upon the laws of nature
(which for Edwards are never separable from divine
providence), but is an extension of nature as well. It is
natural and provident for us to make machines, and the
machines themselves imitate nature and represent providence.
In this context machines have positive value. Furthermore,
there is a criterion for technological advance implicit in
this image. The constitution of nature and the dispositions
of providence set the standard for machines rather than the
other way around. The language of control, mastery, manipulation, and subjugation of nature that pervades much of the
philosophical, theological, and scientific writing since
Edwards' times is missing in Edwards' own thought.

The turning of the wheels represents "the manner of the
progress in divine providence." The wheels of the machine
parallel the "revolutions of the spheres of the heavens."[45]
Because the revolutions of the spheres of the heavens govern
the changing seasons, they are a representation of the
"changes of time by the revolutions of the wheels of
providence."[46] In his exposition of Ezekiel's vision of
wheels within wheels, Edwards elaborates at length on the

full significance of the revolution of the spheres. The
whole universe is a series of wheels within wheels that is
itself revolving.[47] In its revolutions within revolutions
it is a type of God's providence both in the natural order
in terms of changing seasons and in the moral order in terms
of changing ages. The whole system revolves as a wheel on
its way to a particular destination:

> Things in their series and course in provi-
> dence do, as it were, return to the same point or
> place whence they began, as in the turning of a
> wheel, but yet not so but that a further end is
> obtained that was at first, or the same end is
> obtained in a much further degree. So that in
> general there is a progress towards a certain fixed
> issue of things, and every revolution brings nearer
> to that issue, as it is in the motion of a wheel
> upon the earth or in the motion of a wheel on its
> axis, for if not so its motion would be in vain.[48]

Time for Edwards is the spiral-like motion of the revolutions of the spheres as they progress toward their ultimate
destination. Progress is essential to Edwards' concept of
providence, and time, as the measure of generation *and*
corruption, is essential to Edwards' concept of progress.
When the destination is reached, time itself will come to an
end although it is not clear that motion will.

Divine providence, a process of continual creation out
of nothing, is aimed or directed toward an end. It is the
process of new creation whose final end is the accomplishment of the new heaven and new earth. In the last analysis, for Edwards providence is redemption on a macrocosmic
scale.

On a somewhat more microcosmic scale Edwards contrasts
the heavens and the earth in many of his types in order to
orient human beings as to where to look for fit representations of their possible destinies:

> The purity, beauty, sublimity, and glory of
> the visible heavens as one views it in a calm and

temperate air, when one is made more sensible of
the height of them and of the beauty of their
colour, when there are here and there interposed
little clouds, livelily denotes the exaltedness and
purity of the blessedness of the heavenly inhabi-
tants. How different is the idea from that which
we have in the consideration of the dark and dire
caverns and abyss down in the depths of the earth!
This teaches us the vast difference between the
state of the departed saints and damned souls; it
shows the ineffable glory of the happiness of the
one and the unspeakable dolefulness and terrours of
the state of the other.[49]

If Edwards intended a strict vertical hierarchy of value
in this contrast between the heights of the heavens and the
depths of the earth, then many of his images that are drawn
from the earth itself that shadow forth redemption would
make no sense. While it is the case that the depths of the
earth are on occasion associated with damnation, Edwards'
point is to demonstrate limits and contrast them rather than
to denigrate the earth itself. The alternatives of salvation and damnation set the limits of human possibility.
The distance between the highest heights and the deepest
depths is a measure of the difference in the states of the
two souls, or the two possible destinations.

Edwards' use of contrast takes on a horizontal component
in addition to a vertical one in a later entry in which he
states, "As the later ages have discovered the greatness of
the heavenly bodies and their height, and the smallness of
the earth in comparison to the heavens to be vastly beyond
what it used to be, so are eternal and heavenly things
beyond what the church of God formerly imagined them to
be."[50] Here the contrast is not only between the greatness
and heights of the heavenly bodies and the smallness of the
earth, but in the scientific and spiritual discoveries of
previous ages with those of Edwards' own age. Edwards'
contrasts serve both to set the limits of the horizon of

discovery and to suggest that the limits are subject to increasing expansion. His focus on the smallness of the earth in comparison to the rest of the universe has by implication a de-anthropocentrizing effect. His contrast of the discoveries of previous ages with those of his own, coupled with the implicit suggestion that progress in discovery will continue, has a liberating effect. The human position is both humbled and exalted.

The set of contrasts in the two images taken together suggest that for Edwards the limits of human destiny are fixed. The alternatives are either salvation or damnation. Nevertheless, within these boundaries human discovery of the full significance of the alternatives is subject to expansion. Progress through the ages extends to the spiritual order as well as the secular order. For Edwards human beings are people whose feet are on the earth, whose posture is erect, and whose faces are turned toward the heavens in order that they might know their true destination.[51] His use of contrast in the images orients human beings as to their limitations and possibilities.

Particular Images of Redemption

As we have already seen, redemption for Edwards extends to non-human nature as well as human nature. In Edwards' apocalyptic vision all creation participates in the process of redemption or new creation and is itself thereby redeemed. As the type for the wheel of God's providence progressing toward the ultimate divine destination, nature historicized is the macrocosmic vehicle for redemption. Particular images drawn from nature to portray redemption can be distinguished as images that characterize divine being itself and images that characterize the redemptive forces at work in the human/divine relationship. The images

that characterize divine being are the subject of the
present examination; the images that characterize the
redemptive forces at work in human/divine relationships are
the subject of the concluding chapter.

The images that communicate the redemptive character of
God have as their antitypes Christ, the Holy Spirit, and
scripture. Sun, silkworm, and the balm of Gilead are types
of Christ.[52] Water, breath, and color, particularly the
rainbow, are types of the Holy Spirit.[53] The crowing cock
and nursing milk are types of scripture.[54] What these types
share in addition to their role as representations of the
redemptive character of God is that all of them are either
non-human or not restricted exclusively to the human arena.

Edwards' use of his scriptural interpretation to confirm
nature's status as type is most evident in his development
of the types drawn from nature to represent Christ, the Holy
Spirit, and scripture itself. Scripture confirms that the
sun that rises daily after every evening sunset is a type of
Christ's resurrection and ascension.[55] Scripture confirms
that the rainbow especially represents the "beauties and
graces" of the Holy Spirit.[56] Scripture confirms on the
basis of Peter's betrayal of Christ and his subsequent
leadership of the early church that the "awakening and
crowing of the cock to wake men out of sleep and to introduce the day seems to signifie the introducing the glorious
day of the church by ministers preaching the Gospel."[57]

The types of Christ, the Holy Spirit, and scripture that
are drawn from nature lend vividness to Edwards' christology, his concept of grace, and his understanding of the role
played by scripture as revelation. In his images of the sun
Edwards focuses primarily upon the resurrection and the full
divinity of Christ. The silkworm emphasizes the full humanity of Christ and Christ's atonement. The balm of Gilead

stresses Christ's self-sacrifice as the healing of our
wounded souls. Water, breath, and color, of which the rainbow is a special instance, represent the communication of
the common and special grace of the Holy Spirit. Crowing
cock and nursing milk typify respectively the awakening and
nurturing aspects of God's scriptural word.

What is more significant concerning these particular
types is what they have to say about nature's involvement or
participation in redemption. From rising sun to nursing
milk each of these types provide the regenerate with instances in ordinary experience that continue to redeem
throughout daily life. For those whose senses are attuned
to nature's spiritual significance the trustworthiness and
beauty of light, breath, color, fluid, and sound establishes
intimate contact with divine being. As Edwards put it, each
ray or color "play(s) a distinct tune to the soul."[58]

These particular images from nature for redemption keep
the regenerate in daily contact with divine being and assure
that redemption is an ongoing process.

Sun, silkworm, balm, water, breath, rainbow, crowing
cock, and nursing milk lend an added concreteness to
Edwards' apocalyptic vision of the active labor of the
creature as it awaits deliverance. The images from nature
that make vivid the ongoing process of redemption in the
daily lives of individual redeemed sinners continue their
operations throughout the ages. The sun continues to shine
on sinners, regenerate and unregenerate alike, until the end
of time and the regenerate, those whose senses are attuned,
will view the sun as a type of their redemption and a synec-
doche for an overall divine pattern.

New Creation

Redemption, for Edwards, is new creation, and new

creation is the focus of Edwards' apocalypticism. Edwards'
types drawn from nature that have to do with his eschatological vision are of two kinds. There are those for which
the antitype is explicitly an eschatological event, of which
some examples are, the day of judgment, the millennium and
the end of the world.[59] There are also types for which the
antitypes are more vague, for example, "heavenly inhabi-
tants" or the "more glorious times of the church."[60] The
interpretation of these types is subject to how aware one is
of Edwards' apocalyptic vision and how seriously one takes
it. One example will suffice:

> A corn of wheat is sown, then arises and
> flourishes considerably, but before it rises to its
> height, before the perfect plant arises or the
> proper and perfect fruit produced, a long winter
> comes upon it and stunds it, and then, when those
> many days of severe cold and frost are past, when
> spring comes on, it revives and flourishes far
> beyond what it did before and comes to its height a
> perfect plant. Then comes the harvest. So it is
> with Christ: he was slain and arose, and his
> church flourished glorious in the days of the
> apostles and afterward then succeeded those many
> days of affliction, persecution, and darkness and
> deadness. But we know spring is coming.[61]

This type has significance for Edwards' christology, the
life of the believer, and the life of the church apart from
consideration of his apocalyptic vision. Nevertheless,
given his apocalyptic vision, his choice of a natural phenomenon that served as a parable for the coming kingdom in
the gospels, particularly Mark, lends the type an eschatological tone. "But we know spring is coming," read with
Edwards' apocalyptic vision in the back of the mind, serves
to justify and reinforce an apocalyptic interpretation of
the image. There are many, many types like this one that
have eschatological and millennial overtones if they are
interpreted in light of Edwards' eschatology.

Edwards' concept of redemption as new creation plays a major role in his apocalyptic vision. In one type in particular Edwards spells out in detail the process of human redemption or new creation and renders explicit its eschatological significance. Edwards begins type 166 by saying, "There are two quite different things intended by the God of nature and disposer of all things to be signified by the GRAFTING of trees."[62] The first thing grafting signifies is the ingrafting of the soul of the believer to Christ. Christ is the stock, and the soul is the branch taken from Adam's stock. The work of the law and repentance serve to cut the believer's soul from Adam's stock, and the believer is brought to a vital union with Christ, the new stock. Since in the actual grafting process in the natural order the stock conforms to the branch and comes to bear its fruit, Edwards concludes this section of the type by saying, ". . . this is not all that is intended to be signified by ingrafting."[63]

He then proceeds to develop at length ingrafting as the type of redemption whereby the branch typifies Christ and the stock typifies human nature, the Church, the believer, and the human race. In his development of this section of the image he makes a note to himself to see miscellany 991. This section and miscellany 991 give an account of ingrafting and pruning as types of redemption with an eschatological destiny.[64]

The branch as a type of Christ represents first of all the incarnation of Christ, whereby Christ takes on full human nature in addition to his divine nature:

> Christ was, as it were, cut off from his natural stock in his humiliation; he emptied himself, he was in some sense cut off from the glory he had with the Father before the world was during his humbled state. And he took the human nature that was comparatively a mean, worthless, barren

stock.   This   human   nature   was   not   changed   by
Christ's taking it upon him, though it be dignified
and   its   fruit   exceedingly   changed;   even   as   the
stock is not changed by the scyon's being grafted
upon it, it remains human nature still, and will
forever.   Christ is true man still as well as God,
and   so   it   will   remain   to   all   eternity,   but   this
nature is infinitely dignified and its fruit infinitely changed for the better, by virtue of the
scyion that is implanted into it.   The nature of
neither   stock   nor   scyon   is   changed,   but   both
remain the same they were before, though both are
united in one tree and live by one life, so neither
the human nature [nor the divine] are changed one
into   the   other,   though   both   are   united   in   one
person.⁶⁵

This passage is a concise rendering of the classic formula
of the two-natured Christ   by use   of exclusively organic
imagery.   The ingrafting of Christ's divine nature to the
stock of human nature transforms human nature, infinitely
dignifying it and changing its fruits for the better.   The
Word become flesh dignifies the flesh.   Christ will remain
fully human as well as fully divine forever; the ingrafting
process will never be reversed.

Edwards extends the image of ingrafting to include the
ingrafting of the incarnate Christ to the church by saying,
"Another thing intended is Christ's being ingrafted into the
church of Christ, which was by his uniting himself with
believers in his incarnation, whereby he became a member of
the church, a branch of the church, a Son of this mother and
a brother of believers, agreeable to the church's wish."⁶⁶
The incarnation which dignifies human nature and transforms
its fruits makes the same transformation available to the
believer by the ingrafting of the fully divine and fully
human Christ to the church.

This ingrafting process began with Abraham, for Christ
is   the   seed   of   Abraham.   The   effect   this   ingrafting
accomplishes is the alteration of the fruits of human nature

rather than the changing of human nature into something
totally other:

> The stock remains the same, but the fruit is
> altered. So, by Christ being ingrafted, the
> faculties of the soul remain the same; there is the
> same human nature still, but there is new fruit of
> grace, holy exercises and practice, and true
> blessedness. The stock is the same, but the sap,
> by the union to the cyon, is changed and made
> better; so the soul, by a vital union with
> Christ, and by the faculties' being as it
> were swallowed up in Christ, are altered, sancti-
> fied, and sweetened.[67]

By the ingrafting of Christ's divine nature to human nature
and by the ingrafting of the incarnate Christ to the church,
human beings receive full human nature. Those human beings
to whom Christ is most likely to become ingrafted are those
of "sowr stock" for "Christ has more glory in saving the
sinful and miserable, for the sick need a phisician, and
Christ came not to call the righteous but sinners to
repentance."[68] Redemption is the ingrafting of Christ, the
branch, to the sour stock of sinful humanity. The results
are new creation, that is, human nature's "new fruit."

What is the position of the believer in this ingrafting
process? Edwards continued:

> Christ is ingrafted into every believer; every
> believer is ingrafted in Christ, and Christ is
> ingrafted into every believer. For the believer is
> not only in Christ, but Christ in him. Christ is
> born in the soul of the believer and brought forth
> there, and every believer is a mother of Christ.
> Grace in the soul is the infant Christ there, a
> tender twig ingrafted from an heavenly stock in the
> soul by which it bears all its fruit. The nature
> is sanctified, the sap sweetened, and the tree made
> fruitfull.[69]

Christ is ingrafted to every believer, and every believer is
ingrafted to Christ. Here Edwards is working with interaction between the two significances of the ingrafting process. The incarnation of Christ reflects a cutting-away of

Christ from the solely divine stock. The believer is cut off from the fruits of his or her own righteousness. In both cases something is destroyed and something remains. Christ remains fully divine but is not solely divine. The believer's human nature remains human but is no longer solely sinful human nature. In both cases new fruits grow. For Christ the new fruit is a fully human nature that is perfected. For the believer, "old branches and fruit are all cut off, new branches and fruit entirely new succeed: this fitly represents the change of dispositions, affections, and practices."[70]

Edwards introduces the image of human reproduction to augment and reinforce the image of grafting. The new fruit of the stock is like new fruit of the womb. The believer, male or female, is a mother of Christ. Regardless of gender, individual human souls are infused with grace by the Spirit in a manner comparable to conception, pregnancy, and delivery.

The process of ingrafting a superior branch to an inferior stock parallels the process of human reproduction. The implication is that conception marks the infusion of something superior, namely the Spirit, into something inferior, namely human nature conditioned by sin. It is also clear from the passage cited that males and females are equally subject as manifestations of fallen human nature to the infusion.

Conception as we understand it today requires the active participation of both ovum and sperm. The human body that conceives and bears new life contributes its own life to the fetus. Neither at conception nor during pregnancy is this contribution necessarily inferior either to what is infused at conception nor to the new life generated by conception. During pregnancy the fetus is utterly dependent on the mother not only for its life, but for the quality of that life. The mother's body infuses life-giving nutriment to the fetus rather than the reverse. Although Edwards states explicitly that the inferiority of human nature conditioned by sin is shared by males and females alike (the saint is the mother of Christ regardless of the saint's gender), his use of human reproduction to present his anti-Pelagian view of grace raises the issue of the application of typology on the basis of gender-specified roles.

Is Edwards assuming that fathers are solely the carriers of new life at the moment of conception? The answer depends at least in part on whether Edwards consistently uses exclusively male imagery for the deity in relation to human being, portrayed in exclusively female imagery. He does not. His concept of being in general as comprehensive and inclusive and the fecund quality he attributes to divine creativity call into question any interpretation based on stereotypes of the human/divine relationship along gender lines.

Edwards obviously did not have a twentieth-century biology of human reproduction available when observing nature and recording his types. Whatever his assumptions were, he does not appear ever to have consciously intended in his writings to devalue females in relation to males. His image of the believer as the mother of Christ tells us something highly valuable concerning the nature of divine intervention. Divine intervention as the infusion of grace stands in the most intimate relation possible to the believer. Grace works from within; it is new life itself. It is gradual in its regeneration, fecund, and nurturing.

Furthermore grace requires the care and nurture of the believer as well as the believer's active labor and delivery. The image of the believer as the mother of Christ

recalls Edwards' interpretation of Romans 8:22, the groaning
creation. In both cases new creation works organically from
within the present system to transform it. In both cases
the bearer of new creation labors actively to deliver a new
creation that liberates the bearer from bondage.

In image 166 Edwards drops the reproductive imagery and
continues his explication of the spiritual significance of
the ingrafting process. He shifts his focus for the infusion of grace through ingrafting to the pruning away of old
branches. God is the husbandman who gradually prunes away
old, corrupt branches so that "the tree becomes wholly a new
tree."[71] This is true both for the life of the individual
believer and for the corporate life of humankind.

Ingrafting and pruning work together to bring about new
creation:

> So it is Christ the heavenly branch is ingrafted
> into the bad tree of the race of mankind, and all
> other branches perish but only this ingrafted
> branch and the branches that grow from it. All
> perish in hell, and by degrees there is a visible
> destruction of them in this world, till at length
> only this cyon and the branches that grow from it
> shall remain, and all things shall be made new.
> There was, soon after this cyon was ingrafted, a
> great destruction of the nation of unbelieving
> Jews, and after that a great destruction of the
> heathen in the Roman Empire in Constantine's time,
> when the branch was grown much bigger. And
> hereafter will there be a vastly greater destruc-
> tion of the wicked all over the world, and this
> ingrafted branch shall spread and fill the earth.
> And after this, at the end, every branch and twig
> that don't proceed from this cyon shall be per-
> fectly destroyed and the whole tree shall be made
> new. God shall say, Behold, I make all things
> new, and there shall be a new heaven and a new
> earth.[72]

Edwards' concept of redemption as new creation and his apocalyptic vision are inseparable. The redemption of a single
sinner on this earth is part of the larger process of the

redemption of all human nature, if not all human beings.
The continual process of ingrafting and pruning, marked by
the imagery of reproduction, is a social as well as an individual process that has a specific end. For Edwards there
will come a time when this process will be accomplished.
That the process requires pruning as well as ingrafting is
supported by Edwards' interpretation of scripture. In
miscellany 991 Edwards elaborated further on the pruning
part of the process:

> Thus we see how God from age to age lops off other
> branches that put forth from the tree beside the
> elect line, and that have not in them the holy seed
> to be the substance and preservation of them, and
> only those branches are left wherein is this holy
> seed. And it is the holy seed, which is God's
> part, the first fruits to God and the Lamb, that
> upholds the world, and keeps it in being. When
> once all this fruit is brought forth, and ripened,
> the world will come to an end.[73]

God's lopping off of branches extends from the damnation
of individual sinners to social bodies of sinners. The criterion for pruning is the absence of ingrafting. Edwards
refers to the elect as a remnant left after every
pruning.[74] After every pruning a remnant is left that
flourishes because it now has room to grow. The final
flourishing of the remnant occurs after the final pruning,
the last cataclysm. After the final cataclysm the remnant
or the elect inherit the kingdom of Christ on earth. This
final millennium is the time when "all this fruit is brought
forth, and ripened." Once the flourishing is accomplished
the world will come to an end. The final millennium serves
as the time when flourishing can occur without hindrance
and, therefore, reach its initially intended fulfillment.

Why then end the world? As we have seen from the apocalyptic writing, the millennium is the time when the primitive intended goodness of the initial creation is restored.

History itself is not transcended during the millennium; hence, all that is, continues to come into being. The difference between the millennium and what has gone before seems to be that whatever comes into being during the millennium will do so as it was initially intended before the human fall into sin. The end of the world in contrast to the millennium is the end of history itself. The day of judgment that marks the end of the millennium is the final settling of accounts. Once creation is restored to its initially intended goodness, and accounts have been settled, time itself must come to an end in order for the initially intended goodness to be surpassed.

The initial creation of the world is only the beginning of a long involved process of creation that progresses gradually to a point of perfection that is not subject to time. Edwards characterizes this process of continual, redeeming creativity primarily in terms of an organic infusion of grace in which the creature, human and non-human, participates. Nature tells us that what does not get infused ultimately gets shed; what does get infused takes on a regenerate nature itself. Because whatever is, is what it is as a direct operation of the divine will, the divine pattern is divine destiny itself, striving toward completion.

The shedding of that which resists completion or perfection as Edwards portrays it in organic terms has evolutionary overtones. Resistance to being is overcome by being's resistance to annihilation.

For Edwards the social order is an extension of the natural order. Natural phenomena, particularly the human body, provide human beings as a society with images of the processes and consequences of human interaction. Human technology and the arts are extensions of nature, and as we have seen, nature as a source for images of divine things in

some respects supplies the standard as well as the images
for human progress, spiritual and material. Edwards'
organic vision of the apocalypse is consistent with his use
of natural imagery to shadow forth creation, providence, and
redemption in the here and now.

What, then, is the significance of divine pruning, and
what role does it play? Edwards' concept of election is as
beset with difficulties as are his biological assumptions
concerning human reproduction and his association of
blackness and darkness with wickedness. His apocalyptic
writings are filled with anti-Catholic, anti-Jewish,
anti-Islamic, anti-pagan polemic.[75] It is clear from these
writings that he identifies Roman Catholics, Jews, Muslims,
and pagans with the reprobate, those whom God "lops off"
from age to age. It is also clear from his sermons and
his writings on religious experience that in his mind many
who called themselves saints in the context of Reformed
doctrine were as subject to lopping off as any Roman
Catholic, Jew, Muslim, or pagan.[76]

The issue of God's pruning or election reflects a tension inherent in Christianity and its Hebraic roots. It is
an issue that Edwards inherited from the Reformed tradition
and consciously affirmed. For Edwards, election is determined by divine consent; that is to say, those in whom love
to being in general is not operative are simply not among
the elect. Because consent in Edwards' theology is tied to
the incarnation and atonement of Christ, there is no access
to human consent to being in general for Edwards except
Christ. By definition, anyone in whom the Spirit of Christ
does not dwell, whether that person calls himself or herself
Christian or any other name, is reprobate.

Nevertheless, as we have seen, the interaction between
Christ and the Holy Spirit is what makes human love to being

in general possible in Edwards' thought. God's pruning as
dissent to dissenting being is a logical consequence of consent to being in general. While one might disagree
completely with Edwards' identification of the reprobate
with particular groups who did not espouse his religious
views, Edwards' concern with election and damnation has
implications for social justice beyond conflicts over
creedal affirmations.

Edwards' distinction between the damned and the saved
reflects in part his attempt to discriminate what is unacceptable in human behavior or "fruits" from what is
redeemable. To discriminate between what is unacceptable
and what is redeemable is crucial to any concept of social
justice. For modern examples, human behavior that issues in
genocide, racial discrimination, the torture of political
prisoners, acid rain, rape, incest, or enforced steriliza-
tion of the human reproductive organs is unacceptable. Such
behavior exhibits dissent to being in general; it has
elicited a wide range of responses from many for whom universal love is the governing principle in their lives. In
less recent history, Bonnhoeffer's participation in the
unsuccessful attempt to kill Hitler is an example of a
response to dissent that is notable for its violence in the
name of justice.[77]

The point is that to misunderstand universal love,
either in Edwards' terms or in our own times, as undiscrimi-
nating acceptance of human behavior is equally as dangerous
as mistakenly identifying what is unacceptable. Edwards'
insight that consent to being in general is the criterion
for discriminating justice from injustice is profoundly
accurate; his conviction that accepting Christ as the only
way to actualize consent in human life led him to identify
inaccurately the character of injustice.

The violence of God's "lopping" activity is, nevertheless, in tension with Edwards' concept of divine consent.
His types on sin, the devil, and divine wrath depend basically on the assumption that evil ultimately destroys
itself. His types on providence and the beauty of redemption depend on the assumption that love transforms sin by
the power of its attraction. Both sets of types share the
premise that the process by which good overcomes evil
depends on the internal character of good and the internal
character of evil.

Divine pruning, as well as many of Edwards' notes on the
book of Revelation, presupposes an extreme recalcitrance on
the part of that which resists love's power of attraction
and a correlative response of overt destructiveness on the
part of divine being. Does the unacceptability of injustice
warrant destroying the unjust? Edwards' image of divine
pruning communicates at the very least that resistance to
annihilation includes actively opposing any force that
opposes the highest good of being in general.

Type 166, taken in conjunction with miscellany 991,
raises several issues: the relationship of justice and mercy
as characteristic of divine love; the human condition
characterized by sin, redemption, and election; and
theodicy. Edwards' position in the writings of this kind
appears to conflict with many of the other types. Proper
interpretation at this point depends upon recognizing the
role played by complexity in Edwards's conception of
excellency. Complexity provides the key to adumbrating the
tensions within Edwards' thought, regardless of whether it
resolves satisfactorily the substantive issues he is
addressing.

Complexity refers to the conjunction of what appear to
be at least distinct, and at times even conflicting, quali-

ties, characteristics, or attributes. Edwards' conversion rested on his apprehension of the conjunction of divine majesty and grace that yielded the absolute sovereignty of God. His writings represent a *tour de force* characterized by his application of his conception of complexity.

Being is complex; it requires plurality, differentiation. One alone is not excellent, hence, the trinity and its overflow *ad extra* as divine creativity. Divine creativity is complex. Organism, mechanism, and personalism conjoin to generate, sustain, and redeem all that is. Indeed, creation and redemption as new creation represent yet another conjunction that accounts for both commonality and difference in Edwards' vision. Finally, all distinctions with reference to divine being converge in consent, the harmony of beauty and morality perceivable by the truly virtuous conformed to the image of Christ.

It should, therefore, come as no surprise that divine excellency communicates itself through a complex rhythm of resistances in the mundane order. That the saint encounters divine consent as a conjunction of forces that simultaneously attract and assault is consistent, however enigmatic, with the rest of Edwards' thought. Divine pruning is correlative with divine infusion of grace; justice is conjoined with mercy.

It is likely impossible for one of a different persuasion, Christian or otherwise, to comprehend a vision of reality in which hell plays so essential a role. Eternal spiritual death portrayed as positive, violent torment of individual human beings "forever" defies reason, if not imagination. The strength of Edwards' defense of such a vision lies in his perception of the inconsistency and inadequacy of alternative positions to his own explication of scripture and doctrine.[78]

Yet, this much can be said: For Edwards, justice and mercy, conjoined as love and communicated as truth, are hardly sentimental. Love that is true is fierce in its beauty; it does not placate and falsely comfort the beholder, lover or beloved. Sin is everywhere present in the human order with a violence that enrages one, if she or he is conscious of its magnitude. A sentimental deity would be the worst affront to human dignity and liberty contrived by human imagination. A god whose glory does not include the vindication of human abuse and suffering is no god at all. In short, Edwards' god loves with a love that burns with a lifegiving light and heat. It consumes with torment all who resist its attraction just as it vivifies the attracted. This love is its own standard by which to discriminate the attracted from the resistant.

CHAPTER SEVEN

THE LIFE OF THE SAINT

Being pruned as the alternative to regeneration makes the indwelling of special grace all the more urgent for the individual human being. The prospect of being pruned thus becomes a means of heightening a conviction of sin. While a conviction of sin does not generate conversion and sanctification, it goes a long way in preparing the human soul for reception of special grace, and conversion itself marks only the beginning of the process of sanctification. The types just examined provide us with Edwards' vision of the drama of redemption on a cosmic scale; the types to which we now turn focus on the life of the individual saint in relation to the communion of saints.

Spiritual transformation is marked by the infusion of the Holy Spirit into the human heart. This operation marks the beginning of an ongoing process that must be supported, sustained, and cultivated by a community whose members are undergoing the same process. This process is not without its struggles and setbacks. Edwards' "Personal Narrative" and his types for the life of the individual saint and the communion of saints give ample evidence of the difficulties involved in sanctification. Consistent with his other types, these types reflect various rhythms of resistance both to annihilation and to being itself.

Sanctification, nevertheless, is divine being's communication of its own good to the human creature. This communication, though gradual, ultimately overcomes resistance to being in the saint's life. The types for sanctification

stress the nurturing and healing qualities of divine being
and the intimacy of positive human/divine relationships.

Edwards' types drawn from nature present the Holy
Spirit's work of saving grace as a process of organic
growth.   In one characteristic type for human redemption
Edwards focuses on human natural dependence and need:

> As all the good happiness of mankind comes by
> redemption and salvation, all his light arises out
> of darkness, all his happiness out of misery, all
> his wealth out of the most extreme poverty and his
> life out of death, agreeable to those circumstances
> of mankind and the great design and methods of
> God's grace towards him through the saviour, it is
> ordered that so many of our outward mercies and
> good things are given in a way of deliverance, pro-
> tection, or remedy from some calamity we have been
> the subjects of or exposed to . . . . But here it
> is observable that though these mercies are thus
> given as a protection or remedy from evils and
> calamities we are subject to or exposed to, yet
> they are many of them something beyond a meer
> remedy. Thus we have food not only to keep us from
> famishing and remove the pain of hunger, but to
> entertain and delight us; so we have not only
> clothes to cover our nakedness, but to adorn us,
> and so of other things. As God in the redemption
> of Christ does not only provide for salvation from
> misery, but provides for us positive blessedness
> and glory.[1]

The human body typifies the human soul. Material
poverty and bodily vulnerability bear witness to the misery
and impoverishment characteristic of the human soul. Human
neediness and dependence are given in both cases. Bodily
dependence on food, drink, protection, breath, light, sleep,
and health bespeaks the soul's dependence on redemption.
Sustenance in either case is a gift of God. The periodic
movement from bodily deprivation, whether exemplified by
hunger, thirst, the need for sleep, or disease, to the
refreshment of bodily needs and restoration of the body
bears witness to the soul's transformation from misery to

salvation.   Both bodily and spiritual needs are met on a
more than minimal basis.   The creator and redeemer of human
existence intends human being to take delight in the
fulfillment of its physical and spiritual needs.   In the
case of the human soul redemption includes not only salvation from misery but a "positive blessedness and glory."

Edwards devotes the majority of his types drawn from
nature to the transformation of the individual saint or the
life of the church as a whole.   He most frequently typifies
redemption, the transformation that not only saves us from
misery "but provides for us positive blessedness and glory,"
as organic processes that involve, most often, the human
body and, second in frequency, non-human organisms or processes having to do with agriculture and metallurgy.   Of
these types dealing with human religious transformation
twenty-seven focus directly on the human body: the senses,
bodily movement and gesture, and bodily processes.[2]
Thirteen of these twenty-seven types plus one from the non-
human animal order deal implicitly or explicitly with bodily
processes based on gender distinction that serve as paradigms for human/divine relationships.[3]

The Individual Saint

For Edwards the human heart is of special theological
significance:

> In the conception of an animal and formation of the
> embrio, the first thing appearing is the punctum
> saliens or the heart, which beats as soon as it
> exists.   And from thence the other parts gradually
> appear, as though they all gradually proceeded and
> branched forth from that beating point.   This is a
> lively image of the manner of the formation of the
> new creature.   The first thing is a new heart, a
> new sense and inclination that is a principle of
> new life, a principle that, however small, is
> active and has vigour and power, and as it more
> beats and struggles, thirsts after holiness, aims

at and tends to everything that belongs to the new
creature, and has within it the foundation and
source of the whole. It aims at perfection, and
from thence are the issues of life. From thence
the various things that belong to the new creature
all proceed and branch forth and gradually appear,
and that more and more. And this principle, from
its first existence, never ceases to exert itself,
until the new creature be compleat and comes to its
proper perfection.[4]

In miscellany 782, Edwards describes sensible knowledge of
the spiritual excellency of divine things as a sense of the
human heart, a condition for which is the indwelling of special grace. From this type we see that for Edwards the formation and development of the embryo communicates vividly
the process of spiritual regeneration as he describes it in
more technical language elsewhere.[5] This type not only
gives us a vivid image of the process of religious transformation for the individual human being but allows us to
understand better what it means for a believer to become a
"mother of Christ" and what the relationship is between the
individual saint and Edwards' cosmic vision of redemption as
new creation.

Spiritual regeneration of the individual human creature
begins as human physical life, indeed much non-human animal
life, begins with conception. As in the formation of the
embryo the heart is the first organ formed, so in spiritual
regeneration the "first thing is a new heart, a new sense
and inclination that is a principle of new life."[6] Just as
physical life is a process of development dependent upon the
heart as its foundation and source, so spiritual regeneration is developmental and dependent upon a new governing
principle for its wholeness. In both cases the life processes are gradual and aimed at perfection of the creature.

We have already seen in miscellany 782 and in Edwards'
account of his own experience that the new sense and incli-

nation that governs the regenerate life is divine love
itself permeating the human will and thereby altering the
interpretation of sensory data by the human senses. This
infusion takes time in order to reach perfection and is
beset with serious difficulties along the way. Edwards himself makes clear that the saint is a saint because there is
reason to believe that the process is taking place, not
because the saint is somehow morally superior in the
beginning. In the *Treatise Concerning Religious
Affections* Edwards states:

> There is indeed something very mysterious in
> it, that so much good, and so much bad, should be
> mixed together in the church of God: as 'tis a
> mysterious thing, and what has puzzled and amazed
> many a good Christian, that there should be that
> which is so divine and precious, as the saving
> grace of God, and the new and divine nature,
> dwelling in the same heart, with so much corrup-
> tion, hypocrisy and iniquity, in a particular
> saint. Yet neither of these, is much more
> mysterious than real. And neither of 'em is a new
> or rare thing.[7]

In his types drawn from nature, Edwards typifies this
admixture of good and bad by choosing various bodily organs
and processes to represent either regeneration or
"corruption, hypocrisy and iniquity." For example, the
respiratory process typifies the inbreathing of the Holy
Spirit. Bowels, dung, the corruption of corpses, and the
fact that we are born naked, covered in blood, and crying
all typify our common sinful condition. The lancing of
wounds represents the pain involved in the overcoming of
sin. Human tears of sorrow are a type for "the godly sorrow
flowing from the spiritual sight or knowledge."[8]

The gradual regeneration of the saint is marked by an
active resistance to annihilation of the new sense and
inclination that governs the saint's life just as the heart
of the embryo struggles and beats to keep the embryo alive
and continuing to develop. The development of the rose from

thorny branch to blossom, the burning flame, grinding corn
and baking it into bread, refining ore, tilling the soil,
sowing and cultivating seeds, and the transformation of
caterpillar to butterfly all typify one aspect or another of
the saint's struggle through daily existence toward
perfection.[9] For Edwards the new sense of the heart serves
throughout these struggles to awaken the saint to beauty and
to allow the saint to be transformed rather than devastated
by the suffering of pain and affliction. As the new sense
becomes stronger through exercise, every moment of
existence, whether painful or joyful, becomes sacred, and
each physical phenomenon becomes increasingly invested with
sacramental significance.

Edwards' point in referring to saving faith as a new
sense of the heart is that the saint lives out the gradual
spiritual transformation. The saint experiences both ordinary and extraordinary events differently because of a
change in inclination, disposition, or will. What the saint
literally sees, hears, smells, tastes, and touches takes on
heightened significance when sensed from the perspective of
growing and abiding love.

For Edwards the human will is always inclined toward or
away from its objects.[10] The objects of the understanding
alone may be neutral in valence and thereby yield speculative knowledge, but the will operating in conjunction with
the understanding grasps its object with either pleasure or
displeasure. The will *senses*, to use Edwards' word, its
object because it feels the value of its object in a way
analogous to touching the shape of an object. Sensible
knowledge requires that the senses be so intimately connected to the disposition in conjunction with the faculty of
understanding that sight, smell, taste, sound, and touch are
always valuing operations. There is no possibility for
neutral experience. Said another way, on Edwards' terms,
though one may experience indifference, one never

experiences indifferently. Difference in disposition
accounts for differences in how the several human beings
experience the same event or differences in how the same
human being experiences the same event more than once, for
example, illness. The will qualifies what the senses perceive as processed by the understanding.

The saint differs from other human beings because divine
love has become to some degree or other the governing principle of the will. Once consent to being in general has
taken hold of the human will, the saint perceives or senses
the events of reality in the context of consent. While
Edwards includes conscious deliberation, reflection, and
interpretation as operations that are part of the process of
transformation, his choice of the word *sense* indicates
that such forms of articulation are only part of a single
process that includes intuition and contemplation as well.
Consent to being in general, as it works toward perfection,
unites every human faculty with all human bodily functions
into a dynamic whole.

This process, therefore, includes for Edwards the restoration of the senses. In "The Mind," he wrote:

> Our senses when sound and in ordinary cir-
> cumstances are not properly fallible in anything
> --that is, if we mean our experience by our senses.
> If we mean anything else, neither fallibility nor
> certainty in any way belongs to the senses. Nor
> are our senses certain in anything at all any other
> way than by constant experience by our senses --
> that is, when our senses make such or such repre-
> sentations we constantly experience that things are
> in themselves thus or thus.[11]

Edwards goes on to add that trial and error play a large
part in how we learn both to train and to trust our senses.

The infusion of divine love generates a dynamic process
that over time transforms the saint into a new creature.
The saint experiences indwelling love or consent to some

degree or other. This love shapes the perception of the
objects, both physical and spiritual, of the saint's will;
the saint experiences these objects in ways different from
how they were experienced prior to regeneration. Through
experience characterized by trial and error, love dwelling
in the saint's will and the objects of the saint's will
(namely, the spiritual excellency of divine things) interact
to confirm one another. Love grows and overtakes the entire
being of the saint. The saint makes real in her or his own
life the excellency in which the saint participates and
thereby enlarges the divine life itself.

The human body and other natural phenomena support this
transformation by communicating concretely the excellency
of divine things in the saint's daily existence. Divine
love dwelling in the saint's heart is a condition for
intuiting, contemplating, and interpreting natural events
appropriately, and under this condition, the events present
the saint with a sensible knowledge of the transformation he
or she is undergoing.

This transformation is at work not only in the life of
the individual saint but in the collective life of the
people of God and the cosmos itself as well. The aim that
unites individual, community, and cosmos is perfection.
Because the individual, the community of saints, and the
cosmos are included in the divine life, the process is a
process of extending divine perfection.

We have seen in the discussion of type 166 that Edwards
describes human religious transformation as a process of
ingrafting Christ's perfected human nature, individual and
communal. The individual saint and the communion of saints
become the mother of Christ. Edwards uses conception and
pregnancy as types for how the Spirit of God comes to dwell
in the human soul in order to transform it. Regardless of

whether Edwards' biological assumptions agree with modern
biological research, the point he is trying to make becomes
clearer when placed in conjunction with his type on the conception and formation of the embryo.

In type 166 the saint with the aid of the spirit of God
conceives, bears, and gives birth to Christ. The redemption
of individual human creatures recapitulates to a large
extent the incarnation of Christ himself.   There are two
major differences between Christ's incarnation and human
redemption, however. Whereas Christ incarnate is both fully
divine and fully human, the redemption of human being is a
process aimed at achieving full perfected humanity for the
individual, not the divinization of the human.   In addition,
Christ's incarnation produces a separate, human being in
history identified as Jesus of Nazareth, whereas the Christ
brought to birth in the life of the saint is the saint himself or herself conformed to the image of Christ.

The new creature in both the type on ingrafting and the
type on the formation of the embryo is the saint.
Biological birth processes typify spiritual rebirth but only
up to a point in Edwards' thought. Life issuing from biological generation is not related to its bearer in precisely
the same way as life that issues from spiritual regeneration. Spiritual regeneration is the rebirth of the same
human being newly identified in terms of its governing principles, whereas biological generation for human beings gives
issue to an altogether new embodied being that, as such, has
never before existed.

Biological generation typifies spiritual regeneration
for Edwards because both processes issue forth new life,
however much new life in one instance differs in kind
from new life in the other instance. Both processes share
a lack of direct human control. Just as there are no bio-

logical guarantees that conception will take place or that
pregnancy will go full term to a healthy and successful
delivery, so there are no human guarantees concerning
spiritual regeneration. Just as there is an intimate biological relationship between the bearer and the fetus
itself, so there is an intimate spiritual relationship
between the saint within whose life divine love is conceived
and born and divine life itself.

In his notes on "The Mind" Edwards constructs an experiment in thought. What if, he hypothesizes, God annihilated
him and created another being with an identical
consciousness in terms of its ideas and the memory of its
ideas? Or what if God should create another being in the
same manner co-existing with Edwards? Could anyone say in
either case that the newly created beings were the same as
or identical with Jonathan Edwards himself? Edwards
responds by granting that the creator could both annihilate
and create according to such specifications; however, the
beings with consciousness identical to Edwards' in terms of
the ideas present to them and the memory of those ideas
would not be the same. He concludes by asking rhetorically,
"Will anyone say that [the new creation], in such a case, is
the same person with me when I know nothing of his suffering
and am never the better for his joys?"[12]

Edwards' point is that it is the human will qualifying
the senses, a condition for which is embodiment, in other
words, experience, that yields human identity. Although the
governing principle of the will changes with the indwelling
of divine love and although this principle transforms over
time the will itself, it is not the case that the faculty of
will is changed into something other than itself. Edwards
states in type 166 concerning ingrafting:

> Something is destroyed, and that which is new put
> into the room of it, and something remains. The

> old branches and fruit are all cut off and perish,
> new branches and fruit entirely new succeed: this
> fitly represents the change of dispositions, affec-
> tions, and practices. But the old stock and root
> remains: this fitly represents the same faculties'
> remaining, the same human nature, that is, as it
> were, the substance or substratum of these proper-
> ties, both old and new, and on which both old and
> new fruits do grow.[13]

Sanctification or spiritual regeneration gives an individual
human being new life that Edwards typifies as rebirth.
Nevertheless, sainthood for Edwards is the restoration of
what occurred before sanctification and the perfection of
what continues to occur during sanctification. Restoration
and gradual perfection are what distinguish the new creature
from the old. There is no radical disjunction in terms of
personal identity between the two.

In his use of biological generation as a type for human
spiritual regeneration Edwards is making a very subtle but
important point concerning human/divine relationships. He
is attempting to describe the human side of such relationships as one in which the human being becomes a
conscious, willing participant in the divine life while
maintaining that being's differentiation as human.
Regeneration effects a re-centering of personal worth and
identity in that divine being consents to the saint in a
manner that the saint experiences positively. Regeneration
simultaneously effects a re-centering of personal value.
The divine love in her or his own life further contributes
to the divine life itself. Divine love grows or increases
on the basis of human differentiation or subjectivity rather
than by means of the loss of human identity.

This process of ever-widening love that begins for human
beings with the transformation of the inner life elucidates
Edwards' view of perfection as the aim of each saint, the
communion of saints, and the cosmos itself. In his notes on

"The Mind" Edwards wrote:

> Seeing God has so plainly revealed Himself to
> us, and other minds are made in his image and are
> emanations from him, we may judge what is the
> excellence of other minds by what is His, which we
> have shown is love. His infinite beauty is his
> infinite mutual love of Himself. Now God is the
> prime and original being, the first and the last
> and the pattern of all and has the sum of all per-
> fection. We may therefore, doubtless, conclude
> that all that is the perfection of spirits may be
> resolved into that which is God's perfection, which
> is love.[14]

The sense of the excellency of divine things that sensible
knowledge yields according to Edwards has consent to being
in general as its first condition and yields more consent to
being in general as its consequence. Perfection, which is
love, operates in Edwards' thought as a condition for
achieving a goal, the process by which the goal is achieved,
and the goal itself.

Edwards is saying in effect that perfect love exists.
Perfect love serves as the motive for creation, and it is
further exemplified in specifically human terms in Christ's
incarnation. In both cases matter or body functions as part
of a process to communicate the existence of perfection or
love. Nevertheless, perfect love is not fully realized
throughout reality due to human sin. For Edwards this lack
of realization is not a reflection on the quality of the
love itself; rather, it appears to be a quantitative
distinction. Edwards' apocalypticism serves as his attempt,
based on his interpretation of scripture, to describe his
conviction that there would come a "time" when all that is
would be derived from and differentiated solely in terms of
love. This is his philosophy of history, so to speak. Love
itself would achieve that goal. It, like the laws of physics or the laws of biological generation, relates dynamically the particular parts in all their differentiation to

the whole. The life of the saint, the communal life of all
saints, and the cosmos in its entirety bear, in one way or
another, the process of perfection to fruition.

The Communion of Saints

The life of the saint is, therefore, in many ways an
individual instance of the life of the church as a whole,
and the life of the church recapitulates the life of the
cosmos. Edwards uses many of the same types for the church
that he uses for the individual saint.[15] What distinguishes
the types on corporate life from the types on individual
life has to do with Edwards' representation of diversity and
inter-relatedness among saints and his more frequent use of
gender differences to indicate the relationship between God
and the church.

Edwards' major types for representing diversity and
interrelatedness among saints are the rainbow and the
body.[16] The different colors of the rainbow typify both the
different beauties or attributes of God such as justice,
truth, goodness, mercy, and patience and "the virtues and
graces in the saints that are the various exercises and
fruits of the spirit in their hearts."[17] Edwards appro-
priates Paul's reference to the church as the mystical body
of Christ as a type for the organic unity achieved by a
variety of different graces or virtues that manifest themselves differently among the saints.[18] Both the rainbow and
the human body communicate that the saints differ from one
another yet share a common bond. Divine love binds them not
only to God, but by definition of consent to being in
general, to one another.

The major difference between Edwards' types regarding
the relationship between the communion of saints and God, on
the one hand, and all the rest of his types drawn from

nature, on the other hand, is the frequent dependency of
these types on gender distinctions. The church is the bride
of Christ, the mother of Christ, and by the power of the
Spirit, the children of Christ.[19] With the exceptions of
type 166 where Edwards refers to the individual saint as
being, like the church, the mother of Christ and type 104
where Edwards refers obliquely to the penis' needing a
bridle as typifying the need for restraint, Edwards' types
drawn from the body are not defined according to gender
unless they refer to the church as a whole.[20]

   Edwards cites Ephesians 5 and the Song of Solomon as his
grounds for choosing marriage to typify the relationship between Christ and Church. Christ is, of course, the bridegroom and the church, the bride. One might expect that,
given the references to Ephesians 5, Edwards would address
the church's role as obedient and receptive in relation to
Christ. Instead, Edwards ignores obedience and receptivity
altogether and stresses the intimacy of the union of bridegroom and bride:

   For we are members of his body, of his flesh, and
   of his bones. For this cause shall a man leave his
   father and mother and shall be joined unto his
   wife, and the two shall be flesh. This is a great
   mystery, but I speak concerning Christ and the
   church. By this passage of Scripture, it is evident that God hath ordered the state and constitution of the world of mankind as He has to that end
   that spiritual things might be represented by them.
   For here the Apostle tells us that it is so ordered
   of God that a man should leave his father and his
   mother and cleave to his wife for this cause, viz.,
   because Christ is so closely united to the church
   (for it is much the most natural so to understand
   it). And then, in the next words says, This is a
   great mystery, but I speak concerning Christ and
   the church, a great mystery, i.e., a mysterious
   typical representation which refers ultimately to
   the union between Christ and the church. God had
   respect to Adam and Eve as a type of Christ and the
   church when he took Eve out of Adam and gave that

institution mentioned in Genesis.[21]

In this type Edwards uses marriage not only to represent the union of Christ with the church, but also as an instance that legitimates typological interpretation in general. While it is clear from Edwards' christology and his radical anti-Pelagianism that human being is absolutely dependent upon the divine will, this particular type, like the rest of his types on marriage, does not stress the dependence of the bride upon the bridegroom.

His types on marriage characteristically stress the intimacy of human/divine relationships. Edwards seems here to be referring specifically to sexual intimacy since for him sexual intimacy is what distinguished marriage relationships from other legitimate relationships in his society. Such an interpretation suggests that Edwards is using marriage to point out that divine love includes an erotic dimension. He may well have had what we call erotic love in mind in part when he distinguished complacence or delight from benevolence as a mode of consent. This possibility finds further confirmation in his sermon on Christ's excellency and his miscellany on Psalm 96:13. In any case, Edwards' emphasis on intimacy in his use of marriage to typify human/divine relationships implies that for him divine love and human participation in that love include the tonalities of passion, fervency, and desire that we frequently restrict stereotypically to relationships between human beings.

Edwards had alternative ways of interpreting marriage available to him in Ephesians itself. He could have used marriage to typify human obedience to God or human receptivity to God. He chose intimacy instead. His focus on the intimacy of union not only serves to expand divine love and the variety of positive human responses to God normally subsumed under the word "love," but by implication, validates the expression of human sexuality between human beings as well, although Edwards himself would have restricted that validity to heterosexual marriage.

Just as marriage typifies the intimacy of human/divine relationships that makes the church the bride of Christ, so labor and delivery typifies the intimate activity within the church and the individual that makes both the mother of Christ. We have examined at great length Edwards' use of labor and delivery to typify the groaning of creation on the one hand, and spiritual regeneration in the life of the individual saint, on the other hand. The church's labor and delivery shares much in common with that of the individual saint and that of non-human creation in relation to God in that all three require grace: common grace in respect to non-human nature and special grace in respect to human indi-viduals and groups. The church's role differs slightly, however, in its relationship to the individual saints that comprise its body.

For Edwards the church has an identity distinct from the particularity of any given members. It functions as the mother of Christ to make Christ the brother of each member. The church as the mother of Christ is, therefore, the mother of each saint. In Edwards' mind, the church as mother is a dynamic spiritual as well as physical collectivity that is distinctly and exclusively female. For example, Edwards wrote, "Women travail and suffer great pains in bringing children forth, which is to represent the great preparations and sufferings of the Church in bringing forth Christ and in increasing the number of his children, and a type of those spiritual pains that are in the soul when bringing forth Christ."[22] The church labors to give birth to Christ by giving birth to more and more saints, who are themselves individually giving birth to Christ.

This collective labor and delivery, while it involves
the struggles that we have encountered in various other
types, is for Edwards predominantly a nurturing process. It
is the church's role as nurturer that qualifies it as pre-
eminently female:

> MILK represents the word of God from the breasts of
> the church, that is not only represented as a woman
> but of old was typified by heifers, the goats, etc.
> Milk by its whiteness represents the purity of the
> word of God; it fitly represents the word because
> of its sweetness and nourishing nature, and being
> for the saints in their present state, wherein they
> are children. That is, as it were, the natural
> food of a new creature or of the creature newly
> come into the world; by its whiteness and purity it
> represents holiness, that is the natural food and
> delight of the new spiritual nature, for it is
> this is the direct object of a spiritual relish and
> appetite.[23]

What is striking about his image is that mother's milk is
generated by and part of a mother's body. Furthermore,
nursing, in order to continue, requires an infant; otherwise, the milk will dry up. The image suggests further that
the milk or the word of God shares an internal organic unity
with the church. The church as the transmitter of holiness
is not simply a conduit for something external to itself but
is the generatrix of the holiness that nurtures the saint.
In other words, the church is the bearer of both holiness
and the saint. The saint, or spiritual offspring, is herself or himself a necessary part of this process. Without
the nursing saint, the milk, the word of God, and holiness
dry up. Both offspring and milk, nurtured and that which
nurtures , require one another. The implication is that the
trinity, which Edwards envisioned as a divine family or
society that invites the saint to join it, requires the
church as the Spirit's embodiment. Edwards' view of perfec-

tion as an ongoing process supports this interpretation.
Though the trinity is perfect in itself, its perfection is
extended throughout reality by means of an infusion of grace
that requires the existence of the church and, therefore,
the co-participation of the individual saint. Thus, the
church is a manifestation of the Holy Spirit. This is also
what Edwards had in mind when he wrote that the end for
which God created the world was, among other things, to provide the church as a companion or spouse to Christ.

Motherhood extends to the deity itself in Edwards'
types. For all that God is father and son, God is also
mother. Not only is the saint the mother of Christ; Christ
by the Holy Spirit is mother to the saint:

> There are many things between the young birds
> in a nest and a dam resembling what is between
> Christ and his saints. The bird shelters them; so
> Christ shelters his saints as a bird does her young
> under her wings. They are brought forth by the
> dam; so the saints are Christ's children. They are
> hatched by the brooding of the dam; so the soul is
> brought forth by the warmth and heat and brooding
> of Christ, by the heavenly dove, the Holy Spirit.
> They dwell in a nest of the dam's providing, on
> high out of the reach of harm, in some place of
> safety; so are the saints in the church. They are
> feeble and helpless, can neither fly nor go, which
> represents the infant state of the saints in this
> world. The manner of the dam's feeding the young,
> giving every one his portion, represents the manner
> of Christ's feeding his saints. When the dam
> visits the nest, all open their mouths wide
> together with a cry, and that is all that they can
> do; so should the saints do, especially at times
> when Christ makes special visits to his church by
> his spirit. They don't open their mouths in vain.
> So God says, Open thy mouth wide, and I will fill
> it. The birds grow by this nourishment till they
> fly away into heaven to sing in the firmament; so
> the saints are nourished up to glory.[24]

The dam or mother bird in relation to her baby birds typifies the relation of Christ through the Holy Spirit to the

fledgling saints. Edwards attributes the nurturing functions of sheltering, bringing forth, hatching, nesting, and
feeding to the Spirit of Christ. The Spirit broods over the
soul of each saint. Edwards emphasizes again that the context for divine nurturing is human neediness. The saint is
spiritually weak and hungry and cries out to the Spirit for
succor. In short, this type stresses the receptivity and
neediness of the saint in relation to divine mothering
rather than fathering or husbanding.

There are no types drawn from nature that deal explicitly with fathering. What this absence signifies is dif-
ficult to assess. Certainly Edwards understood the trinity
in terms of its traditional personifications as father, son,
and Holy Spirit. One can speculate that perhaps he apprehended that the the Holy Spirit represented a female principle internal to the godhead.

Edwards' types drawn from nature regarding the life of
the church indicate, in any case, his awareness and use of
gender distinctions to communicate the intimate, life-
giving, and nurturing dynamics of consent. These dynamics,
though distinguished according to gender, ultimately
transcend the boundaries of humanity and divinity. The
saint struggles to bring to birth and to nurture the new
spiritual life within. Divine love conceives, struggles to
bring to birth and to nurture the saint and thereby adds new
life to itself. Edwards' observations concerning the human
body, human intercourse, the process of gestation and child-
birth, and mothering (both human and non-human) interact
with his interpretation of scripture. This interaction
allowed him to develop a theology based on love that in turn
placed positive value on the types themselves that were
love's vehicles of communication.

Reliable, Firm, Real, and Enduring

Edwards' types drawn from nature communicate the ongoing process of the perfection of reality. This process is a rhythm of resistances. The types on sin communicate in vivid detail human being's resistance to authentic being. This resistance stems from excessive and misdirected appetites. Individual human beings exhibit this resistance by addictions that victimize the addicted. While this resistance requires individual agency, it transcends human individuality. The human addiction to power for its own sake victimizes other human beings and the rest of the created order. Sin is social as well as individual. Most especially as a social phenomenon does sin elicit the wrath of God.

Nature, more importantly, communicates consent as resistance to spiritual annihilation. The types on providence, redemption, and new creation proclaim divine triumph over sin. Nature tells the saint that resistance to being is in the process of being overcome. Divine being is overcoming sin and evil by integrating whatever force resists being, transforming that force, giving birth to new goodness, and opposing evil. One way or another divine being will ultimately perfect what it brings into existence. Typology, as Edwards developed and applied it, connects cosmology and epistemology in his thought.

Nature, like scripture, communicates through the type that the glory of God is the origin, pattern, and end of all being. The processes at work in the natural order communicate concretely the divine destiny. The content of the communication is that divine being is itself a process by which a plurality of existence, dynamically related as an organic whole, comes into perfect existence. Present existence foreshadows a realm governed exclusively by uni-

versal love. The kingdom of God on earth and the communion
of saints, bodily resurrected and dwelling eternally in the
new heaven and earth, are the fulfillment of the divine
destiny.

Nature also communicates how divine being creates and
perfects what it creates. The process by which divine being
communicates itself is typified by conception, gestation,
labor, delivery, and lactation. Fecundity is the theme that
relates the life of the individual saint to the communion of
saints and the communion of saints to the cosmos. Intimate
love relates the saint, the communion of saints, and the
cosmos to divine being itself. Nature tells us that the
exertion of divine will or love in accordance with divine
understanding or wisdom that generates and perfects its
objects is fecund and nurturing rather than indifferent.

Nature communicates to the regenerate through the type
the divine pattern or process, the human role in that process, and the consequences of being at enmity with the process. Thus, the role of human nature as divine
communication has implications for nature itself. Except
for human nature conditioned by sin, Edwards has little to
say of nature as separate from God. Though body or matter
is the image or shadow of being rather than being itself, it
is the direct operation of the divine will as guided by
divine wisdom and cannot be disassociated from being.
Nature, as the provider of types, thus participates in human
redemption. It is a vehicle of new creation aimed toward
fulfillment of the divine destiny.

Nature is also the object of redemption or new creation.
The non-human creature labors for the redemption of human
being as a means to its own deliverance. The incarnation of
Christ marks the beginning of redemption for the non-human
creature as well as the human creature in Edwards' thought.

The kingdom of God on earth includes the restoration of
creation to its primitive goodness. The new heaven and
earth are in some sense a "place" where the saints will
dwell, upon which the saints will stand, and to whose skies
they will turn their faces. Whatever else Edwards may have
meant as he struggled to interpret the groaning of creation
in Romans and the new heaven and earth of Revelation, the
implication is that non-human nature, like the human body,
will be resurrected in some sense. What precisely this
could mean is hard to tell. Nevertheless, his interpretation affirms matter and body, plurality and diversity. Non-
human nature's participation in its own redemption, its
restoration to its primitive goodness during the millennium,
and its role in the "place" for the communion of saints to
enjoy God give nature positive value apart from strictly
human consideration. One inference is that nature is the
body of God.

An examination of nature's role in Edwards' thought
reveals a coherence to the totality of his works that might
not otherwise appear. Nature as divine communication provides a unifying theme throughout his writings. Edwards'
philosophical theology, his doctrinal theology, his sermons,
and his scriptural commentary, particularly his apocalyptic
writings, are consistent with one another once it is
understood that, for Edwards, divine being communicates its
destiny through nature.

An examination of the role played by nature in Edwards'
thought requires much more than an analysis of his types
drawn from nature. Interpreting the types has required
nothing less than a comprehension of Edwards' theocentric
vision in its entirety and nature's involvement throughout
that vision. Nevertheless, the types make their own contribution to that vision. This contribution lies chiefly in
lending concreteness to Edwards' technical vocabulary and

theological doctrine. The types are concrete instances of how, what, and why divine being communicates.

For example, divine being is the origin, pattern, and end of all existence. In addition divine being includes or comprehends what it brings into existence. In the *Dissertation concerning the End for Which God Created the World* Edwards describes this creative process as a communication of being and uses the fountain as an image to emphasize the dynamic, organic aspect of divine creativity. The analysis of the image of the fountain demonstrates that the image conveys connotations of fecundity.

The analysis of Edwards' apocalyptic writings serves as additional confirmation. We found that God's initial creation of the world typifies the pattern by which divine being accomplishes its end or destiny, namely the restoration and redemption of all existence. Initial creation is the type for which the perfection of existence or new creation is the antitype. In these writings, particularly the *Humble Attempt*, Edwards becomes more explicit concerning the fecund quality of divine being. All creation as the realm of common grace labors to give birth to the new heaven and earth that begin with the kingdom of God on earth in the final millennium.

An analysis of the types demonstrates that Edwards consciously understood fecundity to be characteristic of divine being's continual, redeeming creativity. Divine fecundity characterizes the infusion of special grace in the life of the individual saint, the bonding of the individual saint with the communion of saints, and the life of the cosmos as it participates in the divine destiny. As the recurring characteristic of individual, social, and cosmic life, divine fecundity relates each instance of life to the other; it provides organic unity and wholeness. Without an

analysis of the types fecundity as characteristic of divine
being remains for the most part implicit and connotative in
Edwards' thought.

The relationship of the types to Edwards' conception of
consent is another example of the significance of the types
for the rest of his thought. Consent to being in general is
the chief motive, means, and end for all existence. In its
first instance consent to being in general is benevolence or
good will toward all being. One being's benevolence toward
all being further attracts other being to it; complacence or
delight is that quality of love elicited in response to consent on the part of the beloved. Consent as it includes
both benevolence to being in general and delight in particular being's benevolence is the condition for conscious
human participation in divine consent. Gravity as the type
for which divine consent is the antitype indicates the power
and inclusiveness of divine benevolence. The brood dam as
the type for which Christ's care for the saint is the antitype makes it clear that the saint is an object as well as a
subject of divine consent. The types on the church as the
bride of Christ are concrete instances of the intimacy
involved in divine complacence. The sheer force of the
attractiveness of divine love, its magnitude and comprehen-
siveness, and most especially, its qualities of nurture and
intimacy remain largely implicit without the types to accom-
pany Edwards' more formal writings on consent.

In addition, these types lend specificity to human participation in divine love. To participate in divine love
is, in its first instance, to resist the narrowness of one's
private affections. The gravity of divine love requires
that human benevolence be directed toward universal
existence. While human benevolence toward being in general
requires, among other things, putting aside one's own self-

interest, human participation in divine consent provides the opportunity to discover true, positive human worth. The types that stress nurturing and intimacy in the human/divine relationship make it clear that the human lover is also beloved. The types emphasize that complacence as the secondary ground and object of true virtue validates individual human being and human love for particular beings.

The significance of the types for understanding Edwards' eschatology provides us with one last example of the types' contribution to understanding his thought in general. The types on sin, divine wrath, and the final judgment raise the issue of the implications of Edwards' thought for social justice. The types on the revolutions of heavenly bodies, the periodicity of the seasons, and the convergence of water bodies indicate that Edwards understood that nature related science, the arts, politics, and history to each other as integral parts of the divine destiny itself.

That Edwards' language is religious and philosophical does not mean that he was apolitical or politically naive. His types drawn from nature on sin and divine wrath exhibit his awareness of human civil and ecclesiastical power and its abuse. These types make clear that he viewed human sin as a social condition with social consequences, as well as an individual, psychological condition. Analysis of these types allows one to consider the eschatological types, his apocalyptic writings, and his philosophical writings on injustice and dissent to being as his attempts in part to address the issue of social justice in a theocentric context. The issue of divine being's overt opposition to dissenting being, raised by the pruning imagery in the type on ingrafting and continued as a theme throughout his commentary on Revelation lends concreteness to the meaning and significance of both *consent* and *dissent*.

The types on providence that emphasize the labor of all creation toward the kingdom of God on earth further indicate that Edwards' conception of the kingdom was material, social, and political as well as spiritual. The kingdom of God on earth was for Edwards to be a time and space in which human endeavors would be unified and greatly advanced and the distribution of power would be just. In the *Humble Attempt* Edwards extends the concepts of harmony and justice to characterize the relationship between the human creature and the non-human creature as well. The kingdom of God is a time and space in which human society will live at peace with itself and in harmonious relationship with its natural environment. All creation labors toward this end.

The theme of nature as eschatologically conditioned, divine communication provides unity to the diversity of Edwards' philosophical theology and his doctrinal theology. The omnipresence of natural imagery in Edwards' sermons and doctrinal theology, his philosophical concern with the origin and status of material bodies and their role in his epistemology, the role played by nature in the salvation of sinners, nature's status as type, nature's participation in the divine destiny, the types drawn from nature, and the importance of natural phenomena to Edwards' own religious transformation indicate the high value Edwards placed on sensible and sentient reality.

Nature's worth, like the worth of the human soul, is derived from the love of God. Edwards' references to human dominion in the natural order are relatively few in number. In the various passages in which he refers to human dominion, *dominion* refers descriptively to human intelligence and does not carry connotations of antagonistic mastery and manipulation. Edwards' emphasis on the absolute sovereignty of God and total human dependence in many of his

writings highly relativizes human dominion in nature, and
the types show that human dominion does not remove human
being from nature.

Edwards strongly affirms sensible reality and the human
senses in the context of divine love. The presence of universal love in the human heart allows the human senses to
apprehend the presence of universal love operating
throughout sensible reality and, thus, to take delight and
rejoice in divine beauty or excellency. This delight, or as
Edwards would say, "the love of complacence," directed
toward divine being, renders universal existence and its
shadows in the material order truly beautiful. This dimension of divine consent, actualized in the human heart, renders every bush a burning bush, every rainbow a sign of the
covenant, and every human being a potential incarnation of
the Holy Spirit. The human perception of complacence, as
the secondary ground and object of true virtue, is the human
creature's happiness.

Delight in divine being allowed Edwards to sing out in
praise in the midst of thunder and lightning. Such delight
would be inaccessible to human being apart from the created
order. The positive value of nature is derived in that it
manifests divine love rather than generating it. Nevertheless, as a manifestation or communication of divine love,
nature is a condition for human happiness. Nature as divine
communication is of inestimable worth.

A study of nature's role in Edwards' works not only
allows greater access to the content of his thought, but a
richer picture of his person. The primary context out of
which Edwards writes is his experience of delight in divine
being. The dominating tone of his writings is joy. One of
his major aims is to foster and cultivate the conditions
that allow human beings to participate in divine life, in

other words, to be truly happy. The context of his
experience of delight, the dominating tone of his joy, and
his aim to extend human happiness must be kept in mind
when reading his works if we are truly to apprehend their
content.

ENDNOTES

INTRODUCTION

1. H. Richard Niebuhr, Coale Lectures, (*MSS*, Andover Library, Cambridge, MA.).

2. *Ibid*.

3. *The Compact Edition of the Oxford English Dictionary*, (New York: 1971). See also, Gordon D. Kaufman, "A Problem for Theology: The Concept of Nature," *Harvard Theological Review* 65, (1972), pp. 337-366.

4. I have deliberately avoided applying recent literary fads such as structuralism and deconstructionism and have instead attempted to use Edwards' own method of interpretation, namely, typological exegesis. My "method," such as it is, reflects in addition the influence of New Criticism, the first premise of which is to take the text on its own terms, not Levi-Strauss' or Derrida's.

Chapter One

1. Patricia J. Tracey, *Jonathan Edwards, Pastor: Religion and Society in Eighteenth-Century Northampton*, (New York: 1979), pp. 60-62.

2. Ola Winslow, *Jonathan Edwards*, (New York: 1940), pp. 77-79.

3. Richard L. Bushman, "Jonathan Edwards as Great Man: Identity, Conversion, and Leadership in the Great Awakening," *Soundings* LII (1969).

4. Conrad Cherry, *Nature and Religious Imagination from Edwards to Bushnell*, (Philadelphia: 1980), p. 16.

5. Patricia Tracey in *Jonathan Edwards, Pastor* sees the "Personal Narrative" as a "smoothed-out" version of Edwards' diary entries actually covering the period of his conversion. She argues that Edwards minimizes the painful character of his religious struggles (pp.60-62). I disagree. That Edwards does not specify the form his sin takes and that he may well be writing in 1739 with a confidence gained in retrospect, together, may indicate his view that sin takes on its fullest significance in light of redemption.

6. Jonathan Edwards, *The Great Awakening*, ed., C. G. Goen, vol. 4, *The Works of Jonathan Edwards*, 6 vols. (New York: 1844), p. 12.

7. Jonathan Edwards, *The Works of President Edwards*, ed., Samuel Austin, reprint of Worcester edition, 4 vols., (New York: 1844), p.12. (Hereafter cited as "Personal Narrative.")

8. *Ibid.*, p. 14.

9. *Ibid.*, p. 23.

10. *Ibid.*, p. 15.

11. *Ibid.*

12. *Ibid.*

13. *Ibid.*, p. 16.

14. *Ibid.*

15. *Ibid.*

16. *Ibid.*

17. *Ibid.*

18. *Ibid.*

19. *Ibid.*

20. *Ibid.*, p. 15.

21. *Ibid.*, p. 20.

22. *Ibid.*, p. 23.

23. *Ibid.*, p. 17.

24. *Ibid.*

25. *Ibid.*

26. *Ibid.*

27. *Ibid.*

28. *Ibid.*

29. *Ibid.*

30. *Ibid.*, p. 19.

31. *Ibid.*, p. 23.

Chapter Two

1. Wallace E. Anderson, "Editor's Introduction" to
Jonathan Edwards, *Scientific and Philosophical Writings*,
vol. 6, *The Works of Jonathan Edwards*, 6 vols. (New
Haven: 1980) p.353. (Hereafter cited as *SW.*)

2. Jonathan Edwards, *The Philosophy of Jonathan
Edwards: from His Private Notebooks*, ed., Harvey G.
Townsend (Westport, CT.: 1972), p. 262. (Hereafter cited
as *Philosophy.*)

3. Edwards, *SW, p.* 353.

4. Jonathan Edwards, *Dissertation concerning the End
for which God Created the World*, ed.,Samuel Austin, vol. 2,
The Works of President Edwards, reprint of Worcester
edition, 4 vols., (New York: 1844), p. 220. (Hereafter
cited as *The End for Which God Created.*)

5. Jonathan Edwards, *The Nature of True Virtue*,   (Ann
Arbor: 1960), p. 14.

6. Edwards, "The Mind," in *SW,*   p. 345.

7. Edwards, "Of Being," in *SW,*   p. 202.

8. *Ibid.*, p. 203.

9. Edwards, "The Mind," in *SW,*   p.338.

10. Edwards, "Of Being," in *SW,*   p. 203.

11. *Ibid.*, p. 206.

12. Jonathan Edwards, *Treatise on Grace and Other
Posthumous Writings including Observations on the Trinity*,
ed., Paul Helm (Greenwood, S.C.: 1971), p. 78. (Hereafter
cited as *Treatise on Grace.)*

13. Edwards, "An Essay on the Trinity," in *Treatise on Grace*, p. 131.

14. Edwards, "Observations Concerning the Scripture Oeconomy of the Trinity, and Covenant of Redemption," in *Treatise on Grace*, p. 79.

15. *Ibid*.

16. *Ibid*.

17. Edwards, "An Essay on the Trinity," in *Treatise on Grace*, pp. 130-131. See also "Miscellaneous Observations on Holy Scriptures," from Edwards' interleaved Bible in which he argues on the first page to interpret Genesis 1 as evidence that the world was created for redemption. In addition see "Notes on the Scriptures," Book 2: 322, 399, and 466, *(MSS*, Yale Coll.).

18. *Ibid.*, p. 111.

19. *Ibid.*, p. 109.

20. *Ibid.*, p. 131.

21. *Ibid.*, pp. 126-127.

22. Edwards, "An Essay on the Trinity," in *Treatise on Grace*, p. 111.

23. Edwards, "Miscellanies," Book 1, 94, *(MSS*, Yale Coll.).

24. *Ibid.*, p. 117.

25. *Ibid.*, p. 123.

26. Edwards, *The End for Which God Created*, p. 255.

27. *Ibid.*, pp. 206-207.

28. *Ibid.*, p. 201.

29. *Ibid.*, p. 225.

30. *Ibid.*, p. 254.

31. *Ibid*.

32. *Ibid.*, p. 234.

33. *Ibid.*, p. 244; see also, *idem*, "Notes on the Bible," 389.

34. Edwards, *The End for Which God Created*, p. 244; see also, p. 209.

35. *Ibid.*, p. 215.

36. *Ibid.*, p. 220. Edwards directly connects divine creativity with fecundity in his interpretation of Genesis 1:2. In his "Notes on the Scriptures," Book 3, he connects the spirit's moving upon the face of the waters with non-Christian cosmological myths of origin in which the world is a cosmic egg hatched into existence. (See entry 427.) He further interprets the Hebrew for "moves" as the incubation of the Spirit of God. In a traditionally Christian manner he typifies the Spirit as the dove and he connects the dove brooding over creation with the dove hovering above Christ at his baptism. (See entry 448.) (*MSS*, Yale Coll.)

37. *Ibid.*, p. 257.

Chapter Three

1. Jonathan Edwards, *Miscellaneous Observations on Important Theological Subjects*, ed., Sereno E. Dwight, vol. 7, *The Works of President Edwards with a Memoir of his Life*, 10 vols., (New York, 1829-30), (Hereafter cited as *Observations on Theological Subjects* .)

2. *Ibid.*, pp. 273-274.

3. *Ibid.*, pp. 277-278.

4. *Ibid.*, p. 278.

5. *Ibid.*, p. 282.

6. Jonathan Edwards, *Original Sin*, ed. Clyde A. Holbrook, vol. 3, *The Works of Jonathan Edwards*, 6 vols. (New Haven: 1970), pp.380-388.

7. *Ibid.*, pp. 269-270.

8. *Ibid.*, p. 289.

9. *Ibid.*, p. 277.

10. *Ibid.*

11. Edwards, "The Mind," in *SW*, p. 365.

12. Jonathan Edwards, *Images or Shadows of Divine Things*, with an introduction by Perry Miller, (New Haven: 1948), 79, p. 79. (Hereafter cited as *Images or Shadows.)*

13. Edwards, "Miscellanies," Book 1,z (*MSS*, Yale Coll.).

14. Edwards, "The Mind," in *SW* , p. 335.

15. *Ibid.*, p. 336.

16. Norman Fiering, *Jonathan Edwards' Moral Thought and Its British Context*, (Chapel Hill 1981), p.350. (Hereafter cited as Fiering with page numbers.)

17. For a discussion of the role played by beauty in Edwards' thought, see Roland Delattre's *Beauty and Sensibility in the Thought of Jonathan Edwards* (New Haven 1968). For discussions of *excellency*, see respectively Wallace Anderson's introduction to *SW*, pp. 80-82, 90-94 and Richard R. Niebuhr's *Streams of Grace: Studies of Jonathan Edwards, Samuel Taylor Coleridge, and William James*, (Kyoto 1983) pp. 12-38.

18. Edwards, *The Nature of True Virtue,* p. 2.

19. *Ibid.*, p. 3.

20. *Ibid.*, p. 5.

21. *Ibid.*, p. 8.

22. *Ibid.*

23. *Ibid.*, p. 9.

24. *Ibid.*

25. *Ibid.*, p. 14.

26. *Ibid.*, p. 10.

27. In his otherwise thorough discussion of Edwards' constructive ethics, Fiering fails to give sufficient atten-

tion to the role of complacence or delight in relation to
benevolence and its implications for particular love, especially with reference to God.

28. *Ibid.*, p. 11.

29. *Ibid.*, p. 12.

30. *Ibid.*, p. 11.

31. *Ibid.*, p. 14.

32. *Ibid.*, p. 15.

33. *Ibid.*, p. 24.

34. *Ibid.*, pp. 17-18.

35. *Ibid.*, p. 11.

36. *Ibid.*, pp. 27-28, 32.

37. *Ibid.*, p. 28.

38. *Ibid.*, pp. 85-91.

39. *Ibid.*, pp. 91-97.

40. *Ibid.*, p. 87.

41. *Ibid.*, pp. 98-99.

42. In miscellany 530 (*MSS*, Yale Coll.) Edwards
discusses different modes of self-love. He argues that
self-love, defined as a love for one's own pleasure and happiness is *not* appropriately set in opposition to love for
God because true happiness lies in love for God. He
further distinguishes "compounded" from "simple" self-love.
Simple self-love is narcissistic and exclusionary and,
therefore, a form of dissent. For further analysis see
Fiering, pp.157-158. I am grateful to Thomas Schafer for
giving me access to his transcripts of the miscellanies he
is presently editing.

43. For an extensive analysis of the role of pity in
Edwards' thought, see Fiering, pp. 214, 237, 258-259,
359-60.

44. Edwards, *Philosophy*, p. 241.

Chapter Four

1. I am indebted to Nancy Jay for the phrase, "every bush is a burning bush . . . ." This phrase was part of her response to a presentation I gave on Edwards' view of nature to the Research/Resource Associates in Women's Studies in Religion at Harvard Divinity School on March 17, 1981. I find her insight to be profoundly accurate and have simply extended it.

2. Conrad Cherry, *The Theology of Jonathan Edwards,* (New York: 1966).

3. Edwards, "Things to be Considered and Written fully about," in *SW,* LS47, pp. 241-242.

4. Edwards, *The End for Which God Created,* p. 209.

5. *Ibid.,* pp. 209-211, 217. See also, "Miscellanies," Book 1, 87, 97, and 106, (*MSS,* Yale Coll.).

6. Edwards, "The Mind," in *SW* 16, p. 345.

7. *Ibid.,* 13, p. 344.

8. Anderson, "Editor's Introduction," in *SW,* pp. 53-68.

9. Edwards, "Of Atoms," in *SW,* pp. 214-215.

10. See, for examples, Edwards, "The Mind," in *SW,* 66, p.383; idem, *Philosophy,* 383, p. 81; *idem,* "An Essay on the Trinity," in *Treatise on Grace,* p. 99.

11. Edwards, "The Mind," in *SW,* 45.8, pp. 363-364.

12. Edwards, "An Essay on the Trinity," in *Treatise on Grace,* p. 111.

13. Jonathan Edwards, *Religious Affections,* ed. John E. Smith, vol. 2, *The Works of President Edwards,* 6 vols. (New Haven, 1959), pp. 96-98 and *passim.*

14. *Ibid.,* p. 98.

15. Edwards, *Philosophy,* 383, p. 81.

16. Edwards, *Original Sin,* pp. 274, 278.

17. Edwards, "Observations Concerning the Scripture Oeconomy of the Trinity, and Covenant of Redemption," in *Treatise on Grace*, pp. 77-94, pp. 89-90.

18. Edwards, "Being of God," in *Philosophy* 749, p. 84.

19. Edwards, "The Mind," in *SW*, 45.5, p. 363.

20. Edwards, "The Beauty of the World," in *SW*, p. 305.

21. Edwards, *The Nature of True Virtue*, pp. 27-28. (I am also indebted to Robin Lovin for pointing this out in an oral presentation he gave in an Edwards Seminar at Harvard University in the Fall, 1975.)

22. *Ibid.*, p. 32.

23. *Ibid.*, pp. 30-31.

24. *Ibid.*, pp. 40-41.

25. Edwards, *Philosophy*, 201, pp. 246-247.

26. Edwards, "An Essay on the Trinity," in *Treatise on Grace*, p. 125.

27. Regarding his records of spiritual transformation see, for example, Jonathan Edwards, *The Great Awakening*, ed. C. G. Goen, vol. 4, *The Works of Jonathan Edwards*, 6 vols. (New Haven: 1972), particularly "Faithful Narrative," pp. 331-347. Regarding his sermons see, for example, Jonathan Edwards, *Selected Writings of Jonathan Edwards*, ed. Harold P. Simonson (New York: 1970), particularly "A Divine and Supernatural Light," pp. 65-88. Among his other writings see, for example, Jonathan Edwards, *The Great Awakening*, "The Distinguishing Marks," pp. 213-288; *idem*, *Religious Affections; idem*, *Philosophy*, pp. 109-126.

28. See, for example, Edwards, "An Essay on the Trinity," in *Treatise on Grace*, p. 108.

29. Edwards, *Religious Affections*, p. 96.

30. *Ibid.*

31. *Ibid.*

32. Edwards, *Philosophy*, 782, pp. 115, 118.

33. *Ibid.*, p. 118.

34. *Ibid.*, p. 119.

35. *Ibid.*, p. 118.

36. *Ibid.*, 238, p. 247.

37. *Ibid.*, 782, p. 113.

38. *Ibid.*, p. 120.

39. *Ibid.*, p. 121.

40. *Ibid.*

41. *Ibid.*, p. 122.

42. *Ibid.*

43. *Ibid.*, pp. 121-123.

44. *Ibid.*, pp. 123-124.

45. *Ibid.*, p. 123.

46. *Ibid.*, p. 125; see also, miscellanies 239, 248, 297, and 489.

47. *Ibid.*, p. 123.

48. *Ibid.*

49. Edwards, "The Mind," in *SW*, 20, p. 346.

50. Edwards, *Philosophy*, 782, p. 125.

51. *Ibid.*, p. 126.

52. *Ibid.*

53. *Ibid.*, p. 127.

54. See, for example, Edwards, "Preface," to *Religious Affections*, p. 85.

55. Jonathan Edwards, *Types of the Messiah*, ed. Sereno E. Dwight, Vol. 9, *The Works of President Edwards with a Memoir of his Life*, 10 vols., (New York, 1829-30). (Hereafter cited as *Types of the Messiah.*)

56. Jonathan Edwards, *Apocalyptic Writings*, ed.,
Stephen J. Stein, vol. 5, *The Works of Jonathan Edwards*, 6
vols. (New Haven: 1977); see particularly *Humble Attempt*,
p. 345. (Hereafter all references to this volume are cited
as *AW.*)

57. Jonathan Edwards, *A History of the Work of
Redemption*, ed., Samuel Austin, Vol 1, *The Works of
President Edwards*, 4 vols., (New York: 1844), p. 399.
(Hereafter cited as *History of Redemption.*)

58. *Ibid.*, vol. 4,"The Excellency of Christ," pp. 179-201.

59. Edwards, "The Mind," in *SW*, p. 336; see also,
pp. 332-338; 14, p. 344; and 45, pp. 362-366.

60. Edwards emphasizes that Christ remains fully human
throughout eternity in several writings and throughout "The
Excellency of Christ." See, for example, "Observations concerning the Scripture Oeconomy of the Trinity, and Covenant
of Redemption," in *Treatise on Grace*, p. 90.

61. Edwards, "The Excellency of Christ," p. 186.

62. *Ibid.*, pp. 188-189.

63. *Ibid.*, p. 189.

64. *Ibid.*

65. *Ibid.*, p. 190.

66. *Ibid.*, p. 192.

67. *Ibid.*, p. 195.

68. *Ibid.*, p. 194.

69. *Ibid.*, p. 197.

70. *Ibid.*, p. 198.

71. *Ibid.*

72. *Ibid.*, p. 199.

73. *Ibid.*, p. 201.

74. *Ibid.*, pp. 194-195.

75. *Ibid.*, p. 199.

76. Edwards, "Miscellanies," Book 1, e and z, (*MSS*, Yale Coll.).

77. *Ibid.*, p. 108.

Chapter Five

1. See "Introduction."

2. Northrup Frye, *Anatomy of Criticism*, (New York: 1969), p. 119; see pp.115-128 for his complete discussion.

3. Edwards, *Types of the Messiah*, p. 9.

4. *Ibid.*, pp. 9-10.

5. *Ibid.*, p. 17. Edwards' association of type with hieroglyphic also occurs in *Images or Shadows of Divine Things*, 206.

6. Edwards, "Notes on the Bible," 33, p. 486.

7. *Ibid.*, 389, p. 405.

8. Stephen J. Stein, "Editor's Introduction," to Edwards, *AW*, p. 1.

9. Edwards, "Appendix B," in *AW*, pp. 440-443.

10. Edwards, *Types of the Messiah*, pp. 17-18.

11. *Ibid.*, p. 43.

12. *Ibid.*, p. 44.

13. *Ibid.*, p. 59.

14. *Ibid.*, p. 110.

15. Jonathan Edwards, *Images or Shadows*, 199, pp. 129-130.

16. *Ibid.*, 118, pp. 94-95.

17. *Ibid.*, 45, p. 56.

18. *Ibid.*

19. *Ibid.*, 26, p. 49.

20. Edwards, *Types of the Messiah*, p. 28.

21. See Edwards, *Images or Shadows*, 7, 26, 45, 55, 95, 199, 201; *idem*, "Notes on the Bible," 389.

22. Edwards, *Images or Shadows*, 156, p. 109.

23. *Ibid.*, 13, p. 45.

24. *Ibid.*, 57, p. 61.

25. *Ibid.*, 70, pp. 69-70.

26. See, for example, Perry Miller, *Jonathan Edwards and Errand into the Wilderness.* as cited in bibliography.

27. Edwards, *Types of the Messiah*, p. 110.

28. Edwards, *Images or Shadows*, 8, p. 44.

29. *Ibid.*, 59, p. 65.

30. *Ibid.*, 169, pp. 119-120.

31. Stephen J. Stein, "Editor's Introduction," to Edwards, *AW*, pp. 48-55.

32. *Ibid.*, p. 13.

33. *Ibid.*, p. 14, pp. 253-297.

34. Edwards, "Apocalypse Series," in *AW*, 77, p. 183.

35. Jonathan Edwards, *Freedom of the Will*, ed. Paul Ramsey, vol. 1, *The Works of Jonathan Edwards*, 6 vols. (New Haven: 1957), pp. 403-412.

36. Edwards, *AW*, s, pp. 344-347.

37. The text reads:

> [19]For the creation waits with longing for the revealing of the sons of God; [20]for the creation was subject to futility, not of its own will but by the will of him who subjected

it in hope; [21]because the creation will be set
free from its bondage to decay and obtain the
glorious liberty of the Children of God.   [22]We
know that the whole creation has been groaning
in travail until now; ....(*The Oxford
Annotated Bible with Apocrypha, RSV*)

38. *Ibid.*

39. Edwards, *Humble Attempt,* in *AW*, p. 345.

40. *Ibid.*, pp. 344-345.

41. See, for example, Edwards, *Philosophy*, 383, p. 81.

42. Edwards, *The Nature of True Virtue,* p. 5.

43. Edwards, *Humble Attempt,* in *AW*, p. 345. See also
"Miscellaneous Observations on Holy Scriptures," the
interleaved Bible, pp. 788, 789, 804, (*MSS*, Yale Coll.).

44. *Ibid.*, "Apocalypse Series," in *AW*, 77, p. 178.
See, also, Edwards, *Philosophy*, 26, 262.

45. Edwards, *Humble Attempt,* in *AW*, p. 345, and *idem*,
"Apocalypse Series," in *AW*, 77 p. 182.

46. Edwards, "Apocalypse Series," in *AW*, 77, pp. 183-184;
see, also, 16, p. 130 and 73a, p. 166.

47. Edwards, "Apocalypse Series," in *AW*, 72, p. 165; see,
also, 73a, p. 166 and *idem, Philosophy*.

48. Edwards, "Apocalypse Series," in *AW*, 41, p. 140.

49. *Ibid.*, p. 141.

50. *Ibid.*, 73a, p. 166; see, also, 62, 64.

51. *Ibid.*, 64, p. 159.

52. *Ibid.*, 40, pp. 140-141.

53. Edwards reaches this conclusion in several of his
miscellaneous notes. Stephen Stein, in the "Editor's
Introduction" to Edwards, *AW*, refers to 702, 634, and 743.
I suggest in addition 867, 990, 1038, and 1041, found in
Edwards, *Philosophy*.

54. Edwards, *Philosophy*, 1038, p. 266.

55. Edwards, "Exposition of the Apocalypse," in *AW*, p. 104.

56. Edwards, "Apocalypse Series," in *AW*, 62, p. 158.

57. *Ibid.*, 41, p. 141.

58. *Ibid.*, 59, p. 153.

59. Edwards, "The Mind," in *SW*, 45.14, p. 366.

60. Edwards, *Original Sin*, pp. 109-113.

61. Edwards, *Types of the Messiah*, p. 111.

62. Edwards, "Exposition of the Apocalypse," in *AW*, p. 104.

63. Perry Miller, "Introduction," to Edwards, *Images or Shadows*, p. 40.

64. Edwards, *Observations on Theological Subjects*, p. 240. See also "Miscellanies," Book 1: 95, 101, 103, 149, and 159, *(MSS*, Yale Coll.).

65. Edwards, *Observations on Theological Subjects*, p. 239.

66. Edwards, "Apocalypse Series," in *AW*, 48, pp. 144-145.

67. *Ibid.*, 59, pp. 150-151.

68. Edwards, *Philosophy*, 1208, especially pp. 143, 149.

69. Edwards, *Original Sin*, pp. 395-405.

70. Edwards, *Observations on Theological Subjects*, p. 234.

71. Edwards, *Philosophy*, 1, p. 196.

72. *Ibid.*, see, also, 1006, pp. 196-197.

73. Albert Schweitzer, *The Quest of the Historical Jesus: a Critical Study of Its Progress from Reimarus to Wrede*, trans. W. Montgomery, intro. James M. Robinson (New York: 1961).

Chapter Six

1. Jonathan Edwards, *(MSS*, Yale, Coll.). See also *idem*, *Images or Shadows*, p. 1. In his "Miscellaneous Observations on Holy Scriptures," written in his interleaved Bible, Edwards distinguishes between "image" and "shadow" in his exegesis of Hebrews 10:1 (288, *MSS*,. Yale Collection). A "shadow" represents divine things more faintly and, therefore, less perfectly than an image. Nevertheless, in his application of these terms to natural phenomena, he seems to use the two words interchangeably. He furthermore uses "image" more frequently than "shadow," and "type" most frequently of all.

2. Conrad Cherry, *Nature and Religous Imagination from Edwards to Bushnell*, pp. 26-44; and Mason I. Lowance, *The Language of Canaan*, chapters 8 and 10.

3. See Chapter Four.

4. Edwards, *Images or Shadows*, 167, p. 119.

5. Miller, "Introduction," to Edwards, *Images or Shadows*, p. 36. Not included in Miller's edition is Edwards' index, found in the notebook, which contains a cross reference between types and scriptural verses. Roughly a third of the types are indexed in this fashion. (*MSS*, Yale Coll.).

6. *Ibid.*, pp. 1-7.

7. Edwards, *Images or Shadows*, 117, p. 94.

8. *Ibid.*, 145, p. 102.

9. *Ibid.*, p. 51.

10. *Ibid.*, see, also, 22, pp. 47-48.

11. *Ibid.*, particularly 105, 106, 107, 139, 159, and 175.

12. *Ibid.*, 159, p. 110.

13. *Ibid.*, 158, p. 110.

14. *Ibid.*, 176, p. 122.

15. *Ibid.*, 193, p. 128.

16. *Ibid.*, 177, pp. 122-123.

17. *Ibid.*, see respectively 61, 73, 131, 148, and 211.

18. *Ibid.*, 11, 16, 43, 63, 87, 95, 181.

19. *Ibid.*, 63, pp. 66-67.

20. *Ibid.*, 181, p. 124.

21. *Ibid.*, 167, p. 119.

22. *Ibid.*, 61, pp. 66-67.

23. *Ibid.*, 16, p. 46.

24. *Ibid.*, 43, p. 54.

25. *Ibid.*, 95, p. 87.

26. *Ibid.*, 204, p. 132.

27. *Ibid.*, 160, p. 110.

28. *Ibid.*, see respectively 27, 28, 33.

29. *Ibid.*, 74, p. 71; see, also, 107, p. 9.

30. *Ibid.*, 128, p. 97.

31. *Ibid.*, 79, p. 79.

32. *Ibid.*, 196, p. 129.

33. *Ibid.*, p. 76.

34. *Ibid.*, p. 75.

35. *Ibid.*

36. *Ibid.*, p. 76.

37. Edwards, "Beauty of the World," in *SW*, p. 306.

38. *Ibid.*

39. Edwards, *Images or Shadows*, 77, pp. 76-77.

40. Edwards, *Images or Shadows*, 77, p. 76.

41. *Ibid*.

42. See, for example, Edwards, "Apocalypse Series," in *AW*, 49; *Humble Attempt*, in *AW*, II.5; "Notes on the Bible," 389, 394, and *Images or Shadows*, 89, 154, 178, 200.

43. Edwards, *Philosophy*, 26, and 262, pp. 207-208.

44. Edwards, *Images or Shadows*, 89, pp. 85-86.

45. *Ibid*., 154, p. 105.

46. *Ibid*.

47. Edwards, "Notes on the Bible," 389, and 394.

48. *Ibid*., p. 402.

49. Edwards, *Images or Shadows*, 21, p. 47.

50. *Ibid*., 126, p. 97.

51. *Ibid*., 98, p. 88.

52. *Ibid*., 35, 50, 54, 75, 76, 80, 97, 185, 198.

53. *Ibid*., 15, 17, 58, 62, 208.

54. *Ibid*., 110, 113.

55. *Ibid*., 185, p. 125.

56. *Ibid*., 58, in conjunction with miscellany 302 and 370, pp. 63-64; see, also, "An Essay on the Trinity," in *Treatise on Grace*, pp. 126-127; and "Notes on the Bible," 238.

57. Edwards, *Images or Shadows*, 110, p. 92.

58. Edwards, "Beauty of the World," in *SW*, . 306.

59. Edwards, *Images or Shadows*, respectively 180, and 136.

60. *Ibid*., 4, 41, 72, 78, 90, 91, 102, 111, 146, 147, 152.

61. *Ibid.*, 90, p. 86.

62. *Ibid.*, 166, p. 112.

63. *Ibid.*

64. *Ibid.*, pp. 117-119.

65. *Ibid.*, p. 113.

66. *Ibid.*, p. 115.

67. *Ibid.*, p. 114.

68. *Ibid.*

69. *Ibid.*, pp. 114-115.

70. *Ibid.*, p. 113.

71. *Ibid.*, p. 116.

72. *Ibid.*

73. *Ibid.*, p. 118.

74. *Ibid.*, p. 119.

75. See, for example, Edwards, "Exposition on the Apocalypse," in *AW* p. 109, and "Apocalypse Series," 73b, 77, 78, 83, also in *AW*.

76. See, for example, John E. Smith, "Preface" to Edwards, *Religious Affections*, pp. 84-89.

77. Ederhard Bethge, *Dietrich Bonnhoeffer: Man of Vision, Man of Courage*, (New York: 1970).

78. Fiering is the most recent scholar (indeed one of the few) to take seriously Edwards' view of hell in relation to his ethics. See "Hell and the Humanitarians" in *Jonathan Edwards' Moral Thought and Its British Context*.

Chapter Seven

1. Edwards, *Images or Shadows*, 188, pp. 126-127.

2. *Ibid.*, 6, 17, 24, 39, 62, 109, 115, 141, 173, 188, 190, 193, 208. (I am listing the types dependent on gender distinctions separately below.)

3. *Ibid.*, 5, 9, 10, 12, 18, 32, 56, 85, 113, 125, 129, 130, 166.

4. *Ibid.*, 190, pp. 127-128.

5. See, for example, Edwards, *Philosophy*, 782, pp. 123-126; *idem, Religious Affections*, pp. 96-97, 264, 272-273, 286, 312, 314, 456, 429.

6. *Ibid.*, 190, p. 127.

7. John E. Smith, "Preface" to Edwards, *Religious Affections*, p. 85.

8. Edwards, *Images or Shadows*, see respectively 17, 62, 141, 208; 1, 10, 109, 115, 122; 39, 173.

9. *Ibid.*, 2, 49, 52, 88, 108, 137, 144, 152, 163, 165.

10. Edwards, *Freedom of the Will*, pp. 140, 205.

11. Edwards, "The Mind," in *SW*, 53, pp. 369-370.

12. *Ibid.*, 72, p. 386.

13. *Ibid.*

14. Edwards, *SW*, 45.4, pp. 362-363.

15. Edwards, *Images or Shadows*, 11, 44, 53, 60, 78, 94, 99, 108, 114, 129, 172, 189.

16. *Ibid.*, 58, 130.

17. *Ibid.*, 58, p. 62.

18. *Ibid.*, 130, p. 97.

19. Edwards, *Images or Shadows*, see respectively 9, 12, 32, 56, 85; 18, 53, 166, 125, 129.

20. *Ibid.*, 9, 12, 32, 56, 85; Bride and Bridegroom imagery also plays an active role in the *Dissertion concerning the End for Which God Created the World*, and "An Essay on the Trinity." It is also important to point out that Edwards interpreted the creation of Eve from Adam's rib in Genesis 2 as symbolizing the equality of male and female, the creation of human sexuality (that is, Adam was androgynous prior to Eve's existence), and the founding of the church as the bride

of Christ. See "Miscellaneous Observations on Holy
Scriptures," the interleaved Bible, pp. 15, 17, and 25,
respectively (*MSS*, Yale Coll.).

    21. Edwards, *Images or Shadows*, 56, p. 60.

    22. *Ibid.*, 18, p. 46.

    23. *Ibid.*, 113, p. 93.

    24. *Ibid.*, 125, p. 96; see, also, "Notes on the Bible,"
448, pp. 156-157.

SELECTED SOURCES

Ahlstrom, Sydney E. *A Religious History of the American People*. New Haven, CT: Yale University Press, 1972.

Aldridge, Alfred Owen. *Jonathan Edwards* Great American Thinkers, Edited by Thomas S. Knight and Arthur W. Brown New York: Washington Square Press, 1964.

Aquinas, Thomas. *Introduction to Saint Thomas Aquinas*. Edited by Anton C. Pegis. Modern Library College Editions. New York: Random House, The Modern Library, 1948.

Aristotle. *The Basic Works of Aristotle*. Edited by Richard McKeon. New York: Random House, 1966.

Auerbach, Erich. *Mimesis: The Representation of Reality in Western Literature*. Translated by Willard R. Trask. Princeton: Princeton University Press, 1953.

_____. *Scenes from the Drama of European Literature: Six Essays*. Gloucester, MA: Peter Smith. 1973.

Augustine. *The City of God*. The Modern Library. Translated by Marcus Doss, George Wilson and J. J. Smith. New York: Random House, 1950.

_____. *Confessions*. Translated by R. S. Pine-Coffin. Hammondsworth, England: Penguin Books, 1975.

_____. *On Christian Doctrine*. Translated by D. W. Robertson, Jr. New York: Bobbs-Merrill, Liberal Arts Press, 1958.

Barth, Karl. *Church Dogmatics*, Vol. 3 of *The Doctrine of Creation*, Part 2. Edited by G. W. Bromsley, and T. F. Torrance. Translated by Harold Knight, G. W. Bromsley, J. K. S. Reid, and R. H. Fuller. Edinburgh: T.S.T. Clark, 1968.

_____. *The Epistle to the Romans*. Translated from the Sixth Edition by Edwyn C. Hoskyns. New York: Oxford University Press, 1972.

_____. *The Humanity of God*. Translated by Thomas Wieser and John Newton Thomas. Richmond: John Knox Press, 1960.

_____. "No!" In *Natural Theology*. Edited and introduced
     by John Baillie, translated by Peter Fraenkel.
     London: Centenary Press, 1946.

Berkeley, George. *A Treatise Concerning the Principles of
     Human Knowledge*. Open Court Classics. La Salle:
     The Open Court Publishing Co., 1963.

Boehme, Jacob. *The Way to Christ*. The Classics of Western
     Spirituality. Edited by E. R. B. Peter and
     Winfried Zeller. New York: Paulist Press, 1978.

Brunner, Emil. "Nature and Grace,"In *Natural Theology*,
     edited and introduced by John Baillie, translated
     by Peter Fraenkel. London: Centenary Press,
     1946.

Bushman, Richard L. "Jonathan Edwards and Puritan
     Consciousness." *Journal for the Scientific Study
     of Religion* V (1966).

_____. "Jonathan Edwards as Great Man: Identity,
     Conversion and Leadership in the Great Awakening."
     Soundings LII (1969).

Calvin, John. *Institutes of the Christian Religion*. 2
     vols. Translated by Ford Lewis Battles. Edited by
     John T. McNeil and Henry P. Van Dusen.
     Philadelphia: Westminster Press, 1975.

Carse, James. *Jonathan Edwards and The Visibility of God*.
     New York: Charles Scribner's Sons, 1967.

Cassirer, Ernst. *Language and Myth*. Translated by Susanne
     K. Langer. New York: Dover Publications, 1946.

_____. *The Philosophy of the Enlightenment*. Translated
     by Fritz C. A. Koelln and James P. Pettegrove.
     Princeton: Princeton University Press, 1951.

Charity, A. C. *Events and Their Afterlife: The Dialectics
     of Christian Typology in the Bible and Dante*.
     Cambridge: Cambridge University Press, 1966.

Cherry, Conrad. *Nature and Religious Imagination: From
     Edwards to Bushnell*. Philadelphia: Fortress Press,
     1980.

_____. *The Theology of Jonathan Edwards: A Reappraisal*.
     Garden City: Doubleday, Anchor Books, 1966.

Coleridge, S. T. *Biographia Literaria.*   Vol. 1 & 2.
        Edited by J. Shawcross. London: Oxford University
        Press, 1969.

Delattre, Roland Andre. *Beauty and Sensibility in the
        Thought of Jonathan Edwards: An Essay in
        Aesthetics and Theological Ethics.*   New Haven and
        London: Yale University Press, 1968.

Dwight, Sereno E. *The Life of President Edwards.*   Vol. 1 of
        *The Works of President Edwards with a Memoir of His
        Life.*   Edited by S. E. Dwight. 10 vols. New York:
        C. & G. & H. Carvill, 1829-30.

Edwards, Jonathan. *Apocalyptic Writings: Notes on the
        Apocalypse, An Humble Attempt.*   Edited by Stephen
        J. Stein. Vol. 5. of *The Works of Jonathan
        Edwards* New Haven and London: Yale University
        Press, 1977.

_____. "The Christian Pilgrim, Hebrews xi. 13, 14."
        Vol. 7 of *The Works of President Edwards with a
        Memoir of His Life.*   Edited by Sereno E. Dwight,
        10 vols. New York: C. & G. & H. Carrill, 1829-30.

_____. *Dissertation Concerning the End for Which God
        Created the World.*   Vol. 2 of *The Works of
        President Edwards.*   4 vols. Reprint of the
        Worcester edition. New York: Leavitt, 1844.

_____. "A Divine and Supernatural Light, immediately
        imparted to the Soul by the Spirit of God, shown to
        be both a Rational and Scriptural Doctrine." Vol.
        4 of *The Works of President Edwards.*   4 vols.
        Reprint of the Worcester edition. New York:
        Leavitt, 1844.

_____. "The Excellency of Christ." Vol. 4 of *The
        Works of President Edwards.*   4 vols. Reprint of
        the Worcester edition. New York: Leavitt, 1844.

_____. "The Flying Spider." Edited by E. C. Smyth,
        Andover Review XIII (1890).

_____. *Freedom of the Will.*   Edited by Paul Ramsey.
        Vol. 1 of *The Works of Jonathan Edwards,*
        New Haven and London: Yale University Press
        1973.

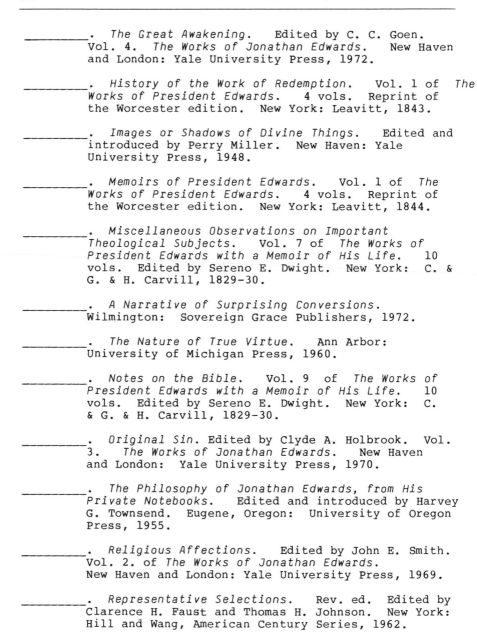_____. *The Great Awakening*.   Edited by C. C. Goen.
Vol. 4.   *The Works of Jonathan Edwards*.   New Haven
and London: Yale University Press, 1972.

_____. *History of the Work of Redemption*.   Vol. 1 of   *The
Works of President Edwards*.   4 vols.   Reprint of
the Worcester edition.   New York: Leavitt, 1843.

_____. *Images or Shadows of Divine Things*.   Edited and
introduced by Perry Miller.   New Haven: Yale
University Press, 1948.

_____. *Memoirs of President Edwards*.   Vol. 1 of   *The
Works of President Edwards*.   4 vols.   Reprint of
the Worcester edition.   New York: Leavitt, 1844.

_____. *Miscellaneous Observations on Important
Theological Subjects*.   Vol. 7 of   *The Works of
President Edwards with a Memoir of His Life*.   10
vols.   Edited by Sereno E. Dwight.   New York: C. &
G. & H. Carvill, 1829-30.

_____. *A Narrative of Surprising Conversions*.
Wilmington: Sovereign Grace Publishers, 1972.

_____. *The Nature of True Virtue*.   Ann Arbor:
University of Michigan Press, 1960.

_____. *Notes on the Bible*.   Vol. 9   of   *The Works of
President Edwards with a Memoir of His Life*.   10
vols.   Edited by Sereno E. Dwight.   New York: C.
& G. & H. Carvill, 1829-30.

_____. *Original Sin*. Edited by Clyde A. Holbrook.   Vol.
3.   *The Works of Jonathan Edwards*.   New Haven
and London: Yale University Press, 1970.

_____. *The Philosophy of Jonathan Edwards, from His
Private Notebooks*.   Edited and introduced by Harvey
G. Townsend.   Eugene, Oregon: University of Oregon
Press, 1955.

_____. *Religious Affections*.   Edited by John E. Smith.
Vol. 2. of *The Works of Jonathan Edwards*.
New Haven and London: Yale University Press, 1969.

_____. *Representative Selections*.   Rev. ed.   Edited by
Clarence H. Faust and Thomas H. Johnson.   New York:
Hill and Wang, American Century Series, 1962.

_____. "Ruth's Resolution." Vol. 4 of *The Works of President Edwards*. 4 vols. Reprint of the Worcester edition. New York: Leavitt, 1843.

_____. *Scientific and Philosophical Writings: The "Spider" Papers*, "Natural Philosophy," "The Mind." *Short Scientific and Philosophical Papers*. Edited by Wallace E. Anderson. Vol. 6. *The Works of Jonathan Edwards* New Haven and London: Yale University Press, 1980.

_____. *Selected Writings of Jonathan Edwards*. Edited by Harold P. Simonson. Milestones of Thought. New York: Frederick Ungar Publishing, 1970.

_____. "Sinners in the Hands of an Angry God." Vol 4 of *The Works of President Edwards*. 4 vols. Reprint of the Worcester edition. New York: Leavitt, 1843.

_____. *Treatise on Grace*. Edited by Paul Helm. Cambridge, England: James Clark, 1971.

_____. *Types of the Messiah*. Vol 9 of *The Works of President Edwards with a Memoir of His Life*. 10 vols. Edited by Sereno E. Dwight. New York: C. & G. & H. Carvill, 1829-30.

Einstein, Albert. *The Meaning of Relativity*. Stafford Little Lectures, 1921. 5th rev. ed. Translated by Edwin Plimpton Adams, Ernst G. Straus, and Sonja Bargmann. Princeton: Princeton University Press, 1974.

Elwood, Douglas J. *The Philosophical Theology of Jonathan Edwards*. New York: Columbia University Press, 1960.

Fiering, Norman. *Jonathan Edwards's Moral Thought and Its British Context*. Chapel Hill: University of North Carolina Press, 1981.

Frei, Hans W. *The Eclipse of Biblical Narrative: A Study in Eighteenth and Nineteenth Century Hermaneutics*. New Haven and London: Yale University Press, 1974.

Frye, Northrop. *Anatomy of Criticism: Four Essays*. New York: Atheneum, 1969.

_____. *Fearful Symmetry: A Study of William Blake*. Princeton: Princeton University Press, 1969.

Gay, Peter. *Deism: An Anthology*.   Princeton: D. Van
    Norstrand, 1968.

Hartshorne, Charles. *The Divine Relativity: A Social
    Conception of God*. New Haven and London: Yale
    University Press, 1967.

Hegel, G.W.F. *The Phenomenology of Mind*.   Translated by
    J.B. Baillie. New York and Evanston: Harper &
    Row, 1967.

Heimert, Alan. *Religion and the American Mind: from the
    Great Awakening to the Revolution*.   Cambridge:
    Harvard University Press, 1966.

Holbrook, Clyde A.   *The Ethics of Jonathan Edwards:
    Morality and Aesthetics*.   Ann Arbor: University
    of Michigan Press, 1973.

Hooykass, R. *Religion and the Rise of Modern Science*.   Grand
    Rapids: William B. Eerdmans Publishing, 1972.

Hume, David. *Dialogues Concerning Natural Religion*.   Edited
    by Norman Kemp Smith. Indianapolis: Bobbs-Merrill, 1977.

_____. *Enquiries: Concerning Human Understanding and
    Concerning the Principles of Morals*.   Edited by
    L.A. Selby-Bigge. 3rd rev. ed. Edited by P.H.
    Nidditch. Oxford: Oxford University Press,
    Clarendon Press, 1975.

_____. *The Natural History of Religion*.   Edited by H.E.
    Root. Stanford: Stanford University Press, 1972.

James, William. *Essays in Radical Empiricism and A
    Pluralistic Universe*. Edited by Ralph Barton Perry.
    New York: E.P. Dutton, 1971.

_____. *The Varieties of Religious Experience: A Study
    in Human Nature*. Gifford Lectures, Edinburgh
    1901-1902. New York: The American Library, Mentor
    Books, 1968.

Johnsen, Thomas Herbert. *The Printed Writings of Jonathan
    Edwards, 1703-1758: A Bibliography*.   Princeton:
    Princeton University Press, 1940.

Kant, Immanuel. *Anthropology From a Pragmatic Point of
    View*. Translated by Mary J. Gregor. The Hague:
    Martinus Nyhoff, 1974.

_____. *Critique of Practical Reason*. Translated by Lewis White Beck. Indianapolis and New York: Bobbs-Merrill, Liberal Arts Press, 1956.

_____. *Critique of Judgment*. Translated by James Creed Meredith. Oxford: Clarendon Press, 1928.

_____. *On History*. Edited by Lewis White Beck. Translated by Lewis White Beck, Robert E. Anchor, and Emil L. Fachenheim. Indianapolis and New York: Bobbs-Merrill, 1963.

_____. *Religion within the Limits of Reason Alone*. Translated by Theodore M. Greene and Hoyt H. Hudson. New York: Harper & Row, Torchbooks, 1960.

_____. *Universal Natural History and Theory of the Heavens*. Translated by W. Hastie. Ann Arbor: University of Michigan Press, Ann Arbor Paperbacks, 1969.

Kaufman, Gordon D. *An Essay on Theological Method*. AAR Studies in Religion, no. 11. Edited by Stephen D. Crites. Missoula: Scholars Press, 1975.

_____. "A Problem for Theology: the Concept of Nature." *Harvard Theological Review*, 65 (1972).

Kaufmann, Walter, ed. *Hegel: Texts and Commentary*. Translated by Walter Kaufmann. Garden City: Doubleday, Anchor Books, 1966.

Krikorian, Y.H., ed. *Naturalism and the Human Spirit*. New York: Columbia University Press, 1944.

Langer, Susanne K. *Philosophy in a New Key: A Study in the Symbolism of Reason, Rite, and Art*. New York: New American Library of World Literature, Mentor Books, 1964.

Lee, San Hyun. "The Concept of Habit in the Thought of Jonathan Edwards." Ph.D. dissertation, Harvard University, Cambridge, 1972.

Leibniz. *Discourse on Metaphysics/Correspondence with Arnauld/Monadology*. Reprint edition. Translated by Dr. George P. Montgomery. LaSalle: Open Court Paperbacks, 1973.

Locke, John. *An Essay Concerning Human Understanding.*   Vols.
    1 & 2. Collated and Annotated by Alexander
    Campbell Fraser. New York: Dover Publications,
    1959.

_____. *The Reasonableness of Christianity.*   Edited by
    I. T. Ramsey. Stanford: Stanford University
    Press, 1967.

Lowance, Mason I., Jr. *The Language of Canaan.*   Cambridge
    and London: Harvard University Press, 1980.

Lovejoy, Arthur O. *The Great Chain of Being: A Study of
    the History of an Idea.*   William James Lectures,
    1933. Cambridge: Harvard University Press Paper-
    back, 1973.

Miller, Perry. *Errand into the Wilderness.*   Cambridge, MA:
    Harvard University Press, 1956.

_____. *Jonathan Edwards.*   New York: Meridian Books,
    1959.

_____. "Jonathan Edwards on the Sense of the Heart,"
    Harvard Theological Review XLI (1948).

Miller, Samuel. "Life of Jonathan Edwards," Vol. 8 of
    Spark's Library of American Biography   New
    York: Harper & Bros., 1854.

More, P.E. "Edwards," In *The Cambridge History of American
    Literature.*   New York: Putnam's, 1917, pp. 57-71.

More, Thomas. *Utopia.*   St. Thomas More Project. Edited by
    Edward Surtz, S.J. New Haven and London: Yale
    University Press, 1964.

Newton, Sir Isaac. *Principia: Mathematical Principles of
    Natural Philosophy and His System of the World.*   2
    vols. Translated by Andrew Motte. Edited by
    Florian Cajori. Berkeley, Los Angeles and London:
    University of California Press, 1974.

Niebuhr, H. Richard. *The Kingdom of God in America.*   New
    York: Harper & Row, Torchbooks, 1959.

Niebuhr, Richard R. *Resurrection and Historical Reason: A
    Study of Theological Method.*   New York: Charles
    Scribner's Sons, 1957.

_____. *Streams of Grace: Studies Of Jonathan Edwards, Samuel Taylor Coleridge and William James*. Kyoto, Japan: Doshiba University Press, 1983.

_____. "The Sovereignty of God: A Comparison of John Calvin and Jonathan Edwards with respect to their Doctrines of the Sovereignty of God and Man's Knowledge thereof." B.D. Thesis, Union Theological Seminary, New York, 1950.

Otto, Rudolf. *The Idea of the Holy*. Translated by John W. Harvey, 1923. Reprint. London: Oxford University Press Paperbacks, 1969.

Pannenberg, Wolfhart. *Theology and the Kingdom of God*. Edited by Richard John Neuhaus. Philadelphia: Westminster Press, 1969.

Parkes H.B. "New England in the 1730's." *New England Quarterly* III (1930).

Plato. *The Dialogues of Plato*. Vol. 1. & 2. 3d ed. Translated by B. Jowett. New York: Random House, 1937.

Plotinus. *Porphyry on the Life of Plotinus and the Order of His Books: Enneads*. 3 vols. Greek with translation by A. H. Armstrong. Loeb Classical Library edition. London: William Hernemann, 1966.

Richardson, Herbert Warren. "The Glory of God in the Theology of Jonathan Edwards (a study in the doctrine of the Trinity)." Ph.D. dissertation, Harvard University, Cambridge, 1963.

Ricoeur, Paul. *Interpretation Theory: Discourse and the Surplus of Meaning*. Fort Worth: Texas Christian University Press, 1976.

Robinson, Henry Wheeler. *Inspiration and Revelation and the Old Testament*. Oxford: Clarendon Press, 1946.

Rousseau, Jean-Jacques. *The Creed of a Priest of Savoy*. 2nd ed. Milestones of Thought. Translated by Arthur H. Beattie. New York: Frederick Ungar Publishing, 1978.

Royce, Josiah. *The Problem of Christianity*. 2 vols. Chicago: Henry Regnery, Gateway Edition, 1968.

Rupp, George E.   "The 'Idealism' of Jonathan Edwards."
     Harvard Theological Review   62 (1969).

Russell, D.A., trans.   *'Longinus' on Sublimity*.   Oxford:
     Clarendon Press, 1965.

Schafer, Thomas A.   "The Concept of Being in the Thought of
     Jonathan Edwards."   Ph.D. dissertation, Duke
     University, 1951.

Schleiermacher, Friedrich.   *On Religion: Speeches to Its
     Cultured Despisers*.   Translated by John Oman.   New
     York: Harper & Row, Torchbooks, 1958.

Scholem, Gershom.   *Kabbalah*.   New York: New American
     Library, Meridian Books, 1978.

Schweitzer, Albert.   *The Quest of the Historical Jesus: a
     Critical Study of Its Progress from Reimarus to
     Wrede*.   Translated by W. Montgomery.   New York:
     Macmillan Publishing, 1975.

Spinoza, Benedict de.   *Ethics*.   Hafner Library of Classics,
     Number 11.   Edited by James Gutmann.   New York:
     Hafner Publishing, 1966.

Suter, Rufus.   "The Problem of Evil in the Philosophy of
     Jonathan Edwards."   *The Monist*   XLIV (1934).

Sutton, Walter, and Foster, Richard, eds.   *Modern Criticism:
     Theory and Practice*.   New York: The Odyssey Press,
     1963.

Teilhard de Chardin, Pierre.   *Christianity and Evolution*.
     Translated by Rene Hague.   New York: Harcourt
     Brace Jovanovich, Harvest Book, 1971.

Tillich, Paul.   *Systematic Theology*.   3 vols. in 1.
     Chicago: University of Chicago Press, 1967.

Tindal, Matthew.   *Christianity as Old as Creation*.   London:
     1730.

Toulmin, Stephen.   *Foresight and Understanding: An Enquiry
     into the Aims of Science*.   New York and Evanston:
     Harper & Row, Torchbooks, 1963.

Townsend, Harvey G.   "Jonathan Edwards' Later Observations
     on Nature "   *New England Quarterly*   XIII (1940)

_____. Review of *Images or Shadows of Divine Things*.
        by Jonathan Edwards, edited by Perry Miller.
        Philosophical Review LVII (1948).

_____. Review of *Jonathan Edwards, 1703-1758*, by Ola
        Winslow. *Philosophical Review* L (1941).

_____. "The Will and the Understanding in the Philosophy
        of Jonathan Edwards." *Church History* XVII (1947).

Tracy, Patricia J. *Jonathan Edwards, Pastor: Religion and
        Society in Eighteenth Century Northampton*.
        American Century Series. New York: Hill and Wang,
        1980.

Turnbull, Ralph G. *Jonathan Edwards, The Preacher*.   Grand
        Rapids: Baker Book House, 1958.

Wainwright, William J. "Jonathan Edwards and the Language
        of God" *Journal of the American Academy of
        Religion* XLVIII (1980).

Warnock, Mary. *Imagination*.   Berkeley and Los Angeles:
        University of California Press, 1978.

Whitehead, Alfred North. *Adventures of Ideas*.   New York and
        London: Collier-Macmillan, Free Press Paperback,
        1967.

_____. *Process and Reality: An Essay in Cosmology*.
        Gifford Lectures, University of Edinburgh,
        1927-28. New York and Toronto: Collier-Macmillan,
        Free Press Paperback, 1969.

Willey, Basil. *The Eighteenth Century Background: Studies
        on the Idea of Nature in the Thought of the Period*.
        Boston: Beacon Press, 1968.

Williams, George H. "Christian Attitudes Toward Nature"
        Christian Scholar's Review II (1971).

_____. *Wilderness and Paradise in Christian Thought*.
        1954. Reprint. New York: Harper & Brothers,
        1962.

Winslow, Ola. *Jonathan Edwards, 1703-1758: a Biography*.
        New York: The Macmillan Co., 1941.

Wippel, John F. and Walter, Allen B., eds. *Medieval
        Philosophy: From St. Augustine to Nicholas of*

Cusa.   Readings in the History of Philosophy.
        New York: The Free Press, 1969.

Wordsworth, William   "Observations Prefixed to 'Lyrical
        Ballads'" In *The Great Critics: an Anthology of
        Literary Criticism*.   Edited by James Harry Smith
        and Edd Winfield Parks.   New York: W. W. Norton
        & Company, 1960.

INDEX

STUDIES IN AMERICAN RELIGION